77 Letters

OPERATION MORALE BOOSTER:
VIETNAM

Janet

Susan P. Hunter

Including letters from
Joan Hunter, Bob Johnson
and Melody Johnson

DEDICATIONS

Everything I do, I do for You.

My three children, Tia, Mark, and Lisa, sounds cliché, but you truly are my world. Thank you for always encouraging me to stay the course. . Because I can't help myself and you know everything is a song ☺... #FromThisMoment, #LiveLikeYouWereDying, #BecauseYouLovedMe: ALL... #IHopeYouDance #MyWish

For Mama, thank you for the idyllic childhood you gifted Maryellen, Mike, Bill, and me. You were so content living in Dad's larger than life shadow that I hadn't fully recognized your timeless and impactful strength until now. What you did for those soldiers was...well, quintessential you! You are among the most beautiful souls walking the planet. I am so blessed to call you "Mama!"

For Bob, you indeed are a patriot above all, exuding dedication and loyalty to God, country, and family beyond measure. America will never be able to thank you enough for all you have done to enhance this great country. Whether it be in your role as a soldier, a pioneer of racial harmony and miscegenation, or a father figure, willing to stop any young kid on the street to offer words of wisdom. Your voice has now been heard. Thank you for loving humanity so much. (smile)

For "TEAM HUNTER," I love you more than you know. Thank you for taking such good care of Mom. Thank you for being the greatest siblings to grow up with (Spaceship and cardboard forts to street hockey and shoveling the driveway 'til midnight.) Thank you for marrying amazing spouses who I love equally and who have been incredibly loving to Mom. Mel, thank you for always Facetiming me when you are with our sweet "Mama."

For Melody, my new-found "Sis." You have been the hidden nugget buried deep within this story. Your wisdom garnered from your life experiences have opened my eyes like never before. Thank you for your continual encouragement and weekly "wishes for a peaceful weekend." Love you, Sis!

***

For the Vietnam Veterans,
for the reported 58,220 KIA
and the many I have met and come to love as a result of this journey:
Bill Dansby, George Sternberg, Spider Parks, Joe Ferrante & David,
to name a few... and forever in my heart, Wayne Threlkeld.
WELCOME HOME and
THANK YOU FOR YOUR SERVICE.
#BravestGeneration

May God bless you with all that is good.

ACKNOWLEDGEMENTS

At the top of this list as well, I thank you, God. This is Your message You have entrusted me to share. I hope I did this story justice in Your eyes.

Larry Rogers, thank you for strongly encouraging me to "take a stab at it yourself." For friends and family who have offered encouragement and support throughout this journey, too many to enumerate... thank you.

To the mentors along the way, each offering me nuggets for which I will forever be appreciative: David Paul Kirkpatrick, Ken Abraham, Deb Engle, Jeff Arch, and Mike Guardia... thank you.

To the plethora of information on the internet made available for writers by generous people like Jack Canfield, Bethany Atazadah, K.M. Weiland, Sarah Turner, Alessandra Torre, Brian Allain and Steve Harrison... thank you.

To Story Summit: You have changed my life... thank you. (storysummit.us)
To Instagram accounts enhancing writers like @writershelpwriters... thank you.

To Brian Sullivan, Vietnam Veteran and one of my father's most loyal students, thank you for ensuring my accuracy with all things military. Also, thank you for sharing "Paul" stories; I cherish them all.

I'd be remiss if I didn't single out a handful of friends who have gone above and beyond with encouragement, support and connections, Nancy Lima (MA), Noelle Brindamour (MA), John Hamacher (MA), Al & Deanne DeWitt (TN), Diane Rogers (TN), Kevin & Kim Gittens (TN), Felicia Smith (NJ), Kim Pecina (NJ), Susan Hurley (NJ), Wendy Long (NJ), Ed Rochford (NJ), Alan Verbeke (NJ), Wayne Tucker (TN), Don Wright (TN), Dennis Schroader, Sr. (TN), Steve Lyter (TN), and Josh Swope (TN)... thank you.

To the wind beneath my wings: Don Cisternino, Mike & Sue Hunter, Bill & Ann Hunter, Maryellen Duchesne, Nicole Duchesne, Jeff Duchesne, David Kirkpatrick, Ed Rochford, Alan Verbeke, George Kurz, Don Wright, Wayne Tucker, John & Pam Walrond, Bruce Reid, Gary & Beth Sentieri, Greg & Tammy Cook, Kerry Gaynor, Charles & Eileen Johnson, Susan Chapski, Nancy Neary, Madeleine McAveney, Nancy Bertelle, Jim Litzinger, Dennis Schroader, and Beth Alpert. Thank you for supporting our military by helping me tell their story.

To Melissa Carr, thank you for taking the best possible care of my mama in memory care and for Facetiming me when you are with her. May God bless you with all that is good.

EPIGRAPH

"To laugh often and much; to win the respect of the intelligent people and the affection of children; to earn the appreciation of honest critics and endure the betrayal of false friends; to appreciate beauty; to find the beauty in others; to leave the world a bit better whether by a healthy child, a garden patch, or a redeemed social condition; to know that one life has breathed easier because you lived here. This is to have succeeded."

~Ralph Waldo Emerson

PREFACE

There was no denying that this story, landing in my lap when it did, had to be shared with the world. The healing potential for the Vietnam Veteran population alone was enormous and long overdue and coupled with the countless examples of pioneering for societal changes, this was a human-interest story that would resonate with most. But what put this in the epic category for me was the jaw-dropping redemption. It was all too powerful to ignore or keep to myself.

Soon after deciding to share this story in some larger scale, the New Year's bell of 2020 reverberated around the world, and COVID took over, wreaking havoc in ways most of us could never have imagined. Increasingly, as spring melded into summer, I could no longer recognize our country as the America I dearly loved. It pained me to witness the hurt throughout our nation, and I felt a sense of urgency to do something, anything, to offer salve to a nation going through the most tumultuous times in my lifetime.

In the still provided by COVID restrictions and being isolated at home, I took to my laptop and raced against time as my mother's memory care facility in Massachusetts had recently reopened to the outside world. I am hoping that good ol' fashion word of mouth will help spread this story of pure human love to curb or even uproot any fear, division, and dare I say, hatred we have seen propagating in recent months. This story is frank and organic regarding volatile subjects. Please resist the temptation to allow any one aspect of their story to deter you from embracing the beauty these two unlikely people exuded, quietly playing a role in the shaping of a more perfect union.

As a country, we are in dire need of real healing, not bandage slogans, and divisive talk. If we are genuinely "all in this together," let's agree to start healing, put down our defensive walls and move forward together to a better America. We are not a perfect nation, as we are made up of over 320 million imperfect humans, but we are a virtuous country always striving to improve; greatness is a process. Let Mama, Bob, Pok Son, and Melody remind us of the America we have been and will continue to be.

77 Letters

OPERATION MORALE BOOSTER:
VIETNAM

TABLE OF CONTENTS

FOREWORD

"We intend to convince the Communists that we cannot be defeated by force of arms or by superior power.

I have asked the Commanding General, General Westmoreland, what more he needs to meet this mounting aggression. He has told me. We will meet his needs.

I have today ordered to Vietnam the Air Mobile Division and certain other forces which will raise our fighting strength from 75,000 to 125,000 men almost immediately. Additional forces will be needed later, and they will be sent as requested."

With these words, President Lyndon B. Johnson sent American troops on their march of folly into Southeast Asia. It was a war the likes of which America had never seen. Gone were the days of linear battlefields and conventional tactics. In the jungles of South Vietnam, American troops found themselves thrust into a game of geo-political combat. It was a war with no frontlines, no rear echelons, and fought against an enemy that lingered in the shadows.

Since the Fall of Saigon, several histories have been written about the war in Southeast Asia. Many of these tomes have focused on the military and political aspects of the conflict – highlighting the terrors of combat, or assigning blame for how the war was prosecuted. Social histories of the conflict tend to focus on the rise of the counterculture and the wide-spread anti-war movements.

Little attention, however, has been paid to the families who served on the American home front. Historians have paid even less attention to these families' efforts in maintaining the morale of American GIs despite the growing backlash at home. Still, these families carried on with the same burdens, uncertainties, and longings of the heart that had befallen countless wartime families in conflicts past.

Yet, until now, these families have never been given an exclusive voice in the historiography of the Vietnam War.

Susan Hunter's book, *77 Letters*, highlights the power of human interaction, emotional support, and their collective effect on the health of the human spirit. The author's mother, Joan Hunter, spearheaded "Operation Morale Booster," an ordinary humanitarian effort to ensure that every GI received a letter during his unit's weekly mail call. Her efforts captivated the heart and soul of a career soldier, Robert E. Johnson. Over a span of seven years (1966-72), Hunter and Johnson would form an unlikely "pen pal" relationship that helped Johnson through some of his darkest days – at home and abroad. The therapeutic power of friendship can be seen in each of the letters featured within this book, all tied together by Susan Hunter's deftly-written narrative.

Today we live in a world straddled by political unrest, social distancing, and high levels of distrust in our government. A book like *77 Letters* can remind us that, even during times of social upheaval, we can still find allies through the power of kindness and empathy.

-Mike Guardia
Author, *Hal Moore: A Soldier Once...and Always*

Chapter 1

Kodachrome

I felt her slipping away. I watched her blank stare, fixated on the flickering light across the room, which was apparently hollering orders to her. "Clap your hands, knock on the window, knock harder…harder!" the demands kept coming, and she obediently followed. It was gut-wrenching to watch. Who prepares themselves for this? I mean, it is understood in the cycle of life we are to outlive our parents, and God willing that is how the story goes, but I certainly hadn't considered Mama would go like this. She was always so sharp and organized; I assumed the brain would be the last thing to go. These unwelcomed demons from within making themselves undeniably present in her thoughts and actions were stripping her of her sanity while ripping apart my heart.

"Leave me alone! Get away from me!" Mama shrilled as she grabbed her bed's remote and wielded it at the flashing light.

I couldn't watch any more. I jumped into the room, "Mama, it's ok; no one is here in the room with you."

"He is trying to kill me, Susan, just look at him!"

"No one is trying to kill you. No one is here, but you and me. It's those demons in your head again trying to upset you." Trembling, she looked up at me with eyes that toggled between sadness and fright, like a neglected dog who doesn't know any better than to blindly accept what she is being told. I grabbed her hand, and we sat down on the edge of her bed. "Let's say the prayer together, Mama… In Jesus' name, I rebuke you, Satan. I will not let you disturb my peace of mind," we chanted in rote unison. I brought her in close and held her until the quivering subsided. In an act of passionate rebellion, I silently whispered a less graceful prayer, cursing Satan up and down.

It started six years ago with increased forgetfulness and confusion. It was dismissed as healthy aging as Mama, having survived Dad's abrupt early passing more than 17 years ago, was living comfortably in her late seventies. She remained content in her home in the picturesque coastal New England town of Scituate, Massachusetts. My sister, Maryellen, offered to live with her to help her manage her daily affairs and provide oversight for her wellbeing. Everything was fine until it wasn't. Moving past the forgetfulness phase, delusions started to rear its ugly head, rocking our world. Initially, the fantasies were more on the pleasant side, starring friends and family members from her past showing up at her door despite having passed decades before. Even Bobby Mitchell, "the one who got away" she would jest, was coming for visits from time to time, sending her in a tizzy about how she looked. Albeit utterly creepy, it seemed harmless and a bit comical at the time. Maybe it was merely her soul addressing some unresolved issues manifested in these delusions. In retrospect, this was a wonderfully naïve way to think of it, perhaps my endearing delusion. Fast forward six years, looking at the shell of my sweet mother, I now view it as Satan working his way into her mind, and with an abundance of patience, turning her against those closest to her.

Changing the environment of a person who has dementia is never an optimal choice, but sometimes you have to go with the lesser of two evils. She had been living with me in Nashville for the past two months after things had gotten so toxic at her home; it was no longer a healthy environment for my sister or Mama. I hated to take her away from all that was familiar to her for close to eighty years, but after a few attempts to escape the house for a delusional date in the wee hours of single-digit winter mornings, she was no longer safe to stay in her home. Additionally, she had made her demand abundantly clear when we suggested it was no longer safe for her to remain in her home. "I want to die in my own home! Over my dead body will I go into a nursing home!" she would declare as if she had any control of her end-game. After a poignant conference call with my three siblings, we decided it best she move in with me where I had security systems already in place, and I worked out of the home so I could keep a close eye on her. We also agreed to frame the move to Nashville as just a visit, inferring a temporary stay. The very next day, we packed up some things and hopped on a flight to BNA. I certainly didn't extend an invitation to the demons to join us, but they came anyway.

2

I learned that music was a great tool to help those with dementia find calm, magically tapping into their long-term memory bank, allowing withdrawals of lyrics from decades ago. It is safe to say, Frank Sinatra and Michael Bublé were on a constant loop along with a sprinkling of Ed Sheeran and Luke Combs to appease my own need for some contemporary music. Today was not like any other day with Mama; I couldn't engage her in conversations while playing a watered-down version of Scrabble. She kept darting a look over her left shoulder and then covering her ears to block out the imaginary shouting sounds she claimed were reverberating around the house. I turned the music up a notch to drown out the "screaming" and suggested we continue the game later, opting to peruse the photo albums, which typically inspired more conversation. Like music, flipping through the photo albums was akin to unlocking the secret portal to her memory bank. One four-inch square sepia photograph sent her on a vivid stroll recalling who, what, why, when, and where, rivaling the skills of an Associated Press journalist. The description of her humble childhood abode on Waldemar Avenue was so detailed; I could feel the chipped, layered dark-walnut paint on the shingles and smell the fragrance from the hydrangeas breezing across the small fenced-in backyard.

Mama indulged in a flashback to ten years old. "I would climb the creaky stairs to our walk-in attic, turning the antique cast iron doorknob and swinging open the heavy wooden door only to be overwhelmed by the aromatic yet charming nostalgic smell of our storybook attic. This garret was the type you read about in mystery novels. I could walk upright around the entire third-floor footprint of the house. There were narrow hallways jetting out the front, with a window at the end overlooking Waldemar Avenue. I put a bench with pillows below one of the windows, along with a small, colorful area rug on the attic floor just beyond the feet of the bench, creating a favorite reading nook. I loved that nook. It's as if I can feel the heat from the natural light pouring into the attic and cascading over my books. Throughout my childhood, I would climb these stairs whenever I wanted to enter the worlds of the Barnum & Bailey Circus or the Ice Follies by meandering through my father's boxes of 8x10, black & white glossy photos, my portal to this world. Many of these photographs were signed by the circus and ice show performers, often with a personal note to 'Red', Papa's nickname derived from his outstanding hair color. As the head electrician at The Boston Garden and possessing quite a likable personality, he made fast friends with many performers and athletes who came to Boston's entertainment center. I would spend hours upon hours up there." She came to a gradual stop and relished in her glow of reminiscent joy. Mama's storytelling was exquisite and always portrayed the idyllic childhood of yesteryear.

I thoroughly enjoyed listening to her stories and often wished I had grown up in those simpler times. It never ceased to baffle me; however, she could recall every detail of each picture from sixty or seventy years ago, but minutes after closing the book, she would not remember having just looked at it. Day after day, we looked through the albums. It was like the proverbial Ground Hog Day movie, where every day was a reoccurrence of the previous day. I needed to "up my game" in engaging her long-term memory if I was going to make any headway against this disease, or so I thought.

Aha, I can read her the Operation Morale Booster letters! I thought as I bounded the hardwood stairs to my home office. Throughout our childhood, Mama would tell the four of us about her gesture of support during the Vietnam War. I was only born during the war, and my three siblings only a handful of years earlier; our knowledge of the war was slim to none. Additionally, there seemed to be an understanding to never speak of this controversial war, so much so, it was not even taught in the history classes. When she periodically mentioned these Operation Morale Booster letters, it failed to pique our interest. I could tell these letters meant a lot to her, however, because when she spoke of them, she stood a little taller, held her chin a little higher, and her eyes would sparkle a little brighter.

A few years after Dad suffered his fatal massive heart attack, shaking the very foundation of our family, I traveled north to visit Mama to help her organize her home a bit. Starting at the top and making my way down to the basement was the game plan. This attic was not anything like the attic she enjoyed throughout her childhood. It was a Cape style home characterized by the sharply slanted roofline on either side, only allowing someone of smaller stature the ability to stand, and only in the center of the attic. As I organized and purged, opening the many cardboard flaps to assess the contents fashioned quite the juxtaposition. There was something pleasant about the nostalgic feeling of diving into memories of years past despite the mess and unpleasant breathing condition it generated. I continued to abrade dust from the boxes to inspect the memories within. Making my way back to the far corner of the attic where the roofline met the floorboard, I was one box away from completing the tidying up of the attic. Tough to physically get to the last remaining box, I got down on my belly and executed an amateur army crawl, a bit ironic given what I was about to uncover. Reaching around to grab the back corner of the carton, I turned it toward me enough to seize a cut-out handle on the side. I pulled it across the floorboard as I backed out of the corner, sliding it to a place where I could get up on my knees and unpack the treasure. In a moment of contrasting emotions of delight and despair, I spotted the two manila sleeves I had heard about my whole life. Although standing up on their sides, hiding the markings on the face of the envelopes, I was sure these had to be the trove of letters Mama had spoken of so often. Carefully lifting them out at the same time and placing them on the floor by my knees, my heart sank at the top envelope's state of decay.

Barely legible in black marker it read, Operation Morale Booster; the contents within, stuck together and ravaged with evidence of being water-sodden from years past. Setting it aside with a saddened heart of one who took something for granted until it was gone, I immediately perked up with delight at the sight of the envelope underneath. My heart raced. Also inscribed "Operation Morale Booster," miraculously, except for a fifty-year-old coffee mug ring stain on the outside corner of the envelope, it was in pristine condition. I grabbed both envelopes and headed to the stairway. Descending the tottering telescoping stairs, I felt like I had discovered a hidden treasure. "Mama, Mama, you will never guess what I found up in the attic!" I scurried down the stairs to the kitchen.

"You're right, I have no idea," she chimed with a bit of curiosity about my excitement.

"Your Operation Morale Booster envelopes!"

"Oh my, I haven't seen these in years... I'd say as far back as twenty-five years ago. I am a little surprised we still have them."

"Well, one of them is in rough shape," I reported as I handed over the two manila sleeves. Mama looked at both of them but focused on the decaying envelope, attempting to catch the remnants of paper fluttering to the floor in the transfer. Brushing up and discarding the mess, she handed back the intact envelope and asked me to put it somewhere safe. I offered to take it back with me, assuring her that I would provide safekeeping for them in my fireproof safe.

"Someday, we will read through them," I assured her.

"Sounds good to me."

Little did I know at that time what a treasure this would turn out to be. Truly life-changing.

Chapter 2

If Not Me

We are the product of our experiences in that each encounter, each person we meet, and each conversation we engage in, have a significance that shapes every day thereafter, whether we realize it or not. I had tucked those letters away in safe keeping through four major moves, not knowing why I was giving them such reverence, but for the promise I made Mama years ago. But here we were, that day had come, fifteen years later. Retrieving them from my file cabinet, I placed the envelope on the kitchen table and announced a new activity for us to partake in to pass the time and perhaps engage her long-term memory. "Ok, Mama, ready to embark on Operation Morale Booster?" I chortled.

"Operation Morale Booster? That was what I named my writing campaign to the soldiers during the Vietnam War," Mama exclaimed as if this was a serendipitous moment.

"I know Mama. I found your letters and thought we could read through them together like we always said we would."

"Oh, Susan! Where did you find these? They must be fifty years old," with a hint of disbelief in her tone.

"I've had them for many years, Mama, at least fifteen. We have always talked about reading through them, so let's do it today." We fanned all the letters across the table. Separating them by soldier, we created twenty-one piles, some of just a few notes, others with a dozen, and then there was one pile that was spilling over itself with seventy-seven letters. These were from Robert Johnson, who mom endearingly referred to as "Bob" in the stories she shared with us over the years. All of the soldiers' letters were handwritten and were stapled to the airmail envelopes they arrived in. In many cases, Mama had the wherewithal to attach her carbon copy typed response to the soldiers' letters, providing a full dialogue.

Mama was quiet in reflection as we touched and sorted each of the letters. I was curious about what she was thinking, but before I even had the chance to ask, she started audibly recalling.

"It was a blistering cold January night, we bustled around the kitchen preparing the table for dinner. The popular TV show, Gomer Pyle, played in the background on the black and white RCA. You weren't born yet, but Maryellen, Michael, and Billy, obediently set the table before running to the large picture window in the living room to see who would be the first to see Dad pull in the driveway after a long day at work. Almost immediately, the three of them spotted the 1964 Ford sedan's headlights turning onto the street. In unison, they screamed, 'Mommy, he's home! He's home!' I had the timing down to near perfection. The kids ran to the doorway, greeting him with hugs and kisses while I finished placing the hot casserole dishes on the trivets adorning the table. In walked your dad, Paul Hunter, a tall, dark and handsome father of three, a high school teacher and coach, and a well-respected man in town. As he hung up his coat and made his way to the kitchen, the kids scurried around him and wiggled their way into their chairs. Succumbing to their pleas, the TV remained on during dinner to watch the remaining ten minutes of their favorite show. Meatloaf, mashed potatoes, and carrots filled the plates and their bellies that night. Dinner conversations ranged from the kids' elementary classroom discoveries to age-old playground antics. After Gomer Pyle, the local news came on with a Special Report from the front lines of Vietnam. No viewer discretion was advised, so Dad and I gave each other a subtle nod deeming it suitable for family viewing while we finished dinner." Mama paused to reflect a little longer before resuming her story.

"Yeah, it was a Special Report featuring 'A Day in the Life of the 1st Cavalry.' Dad and the kids continued their conversations of school while I couldn't help but be drawn into the report reel. Images of soldiers, not much older than Dad's students, going about their duties in a land foreign to them in every aspect. Seeing through the brave smiles worn for the cameraman to please the moms and dads at home, I was able to detect fear and loneliness. Dad noticed my preoccupation and tried several times to bring me back into the lighter conversations of the day, to no avail. I was glued to these young soldiers, ground infantry commonly referred to as GIs. I was mesmerized, I failed to notice Dad excuse the kids from the table to get ready for bed. He grabbed my hand, hoping to grab my attention. In a delayed reaction, I reluctantly turned from the TV to respond to his loving touch. Before he could utter a word, I slowly shook my head and repeated, 'We have to do something, we just have to do something.' Dad brought me in close for a hug and held me tight. No further words were spoken, but undoubtedly, we both counted our blessings that Michael and Billy were far too young, and Dad, now too old, to be drafted."

"So, this is why you started Operation Morale Booster?" as I placed my hand on top of hers. She nodded. Mama, visibly deep in thought, I remained quiet and let the silence speak a thousand words.

Mama continued, "We deterged the kitchen in reverent silence while the news report continued. A particular moment of footage stopped me in my tracks; it was mail call. It was of a soldier with a large sack hanging low from across his shoulder, walking through basecamp, handing out letters from home. If watching the anticipation in the eyes of the young conscripts wasn't heart-wrenching enough, witnessing their disappointment as they were passed-by surely was. This image remained on replay for the duration of my night, stealing a night's sleep but giving me an added purpose to my life that following morning." She paused again for what seemed to be an unusually long time and then let out a sigh and a smile that beamed across her face. In a soft and melodic voice, "Bob... yeah, it was Bob. He was my purpose."

Mama's recall was unparalleled. She continued to detail the journey with such clarity as if I was living it in real-time. She explained that with hardly any sleep under her belt, she jumped out of bed before the family woke that next morning, rearing to embark on a mission of her own. Despite being a Saturday, her one day to sleep in, she grabbed a coffee and positioned herself seated at attention, eyes fixated on her 1964 IBM typewriter. She hand-fed a piece of paper through the roller and began her "Symphony of Keycaps." The typewriter keys' implacable rhythm culminated with a crescendo at the completion of each letter as she theatrically pulled the sheet of paper from the platen.

January 1966

Commanding Officer
1st Cavalry Division (Airmobile)
An Khe, Vietnam

Dear Sir:

I wonder if you wouldn't mind delivering these letters to some of the men who don't receive much mail from home. I can imagine all of the boys in Vietnam love to receive mail at Mail Call, but perhaps you know of a few who don't receive any.

My primary purpose in writing is to see that each soldier receives mail from "home" during his time serving there. The boys really need to know that the people at home really care about them.

Thank you for your help.
Joan Hunter

***

January, 1966

Dear GI in Vietnam,

This will be a short letter as it is tough to write to someone, I know nothing about. I have asked your commanding officer to deliver this letter to a GI who did not receive mail today. If you care to start a correspondence, I would be most happy to write to you whenever I have a free minute.

I would like to give you a "pen picture" of myself so that you know a little about me. To begin with... I am a thirty-year-old married housewife. My husband, Paul, is a teacher-coach at Boston College High School, Boston, Massachusetts. We have three small children, Maryellen- 6, Michael- 5, and Billy- 4. As you can see, I don't really have too much time to spare, but I will try my best. We live in

Scituate, Massachusetts, a pretty seacoast town about 26 miles south of Boston.

We, at home, are seeing on the nightly news how horrible the war is, and how you men are not only fighting a dirty war but also, how you are always trying to help the poor people of that strife-torn country. We know you are doing a good job, and we ALL are very proud of you. Please don't think I am a "kook"... I am so proud of you, and I know how much receiving mail from the States must mean to you. If you have any buddies who would also like mail, send me their names. I wish each man over there could get at least one letter every mail call. I am on a mission of my own, you see... Operation Morale Booster!

Best of luck, soldier, and I hope to hear from you.

God bless you,
Joan Hunter

***

She reviewed her typing with a scrutinizing eye and offered a nod of approval with each letter, placing it on the growing stack to the left of her typewriter. Folding the pile of letters, sealing the envelopes, and affixing the stamps, she smiled and let out an audible, "Done!" Bundling herself up in a navy, wool swing coat with a white faux fur collar, she marched out of her white Cape Cod-style house and down her quaint street to the General Store at the corner of Fay and Hatherly Roads. Waving "good morning" to all the curious moms peering out from behind their closed windows on this frigid winter morning, Mama navigated through the snow-covered sidewalk, carefully avoiding the slushy areas. She bounded up the stairs of the General Store and flung open the heavy wooden door with the strength that even surprised herself. Mr. Fallon, the jovial owner of the store, startled by the dramatic entrance, turned quickly toward the slamming door but immediately relaxed when he saw it was just sweet Mama, appearing to be on a mission of sorts.

"Good morning, Mrs. Hunter, what are you up to today?"

Mama's smile radiated as she declared, "I am headed to the front lines of Vietnam!"

"Is that so?" Mr. Fallon inquired with a grin and a wink.

"Well, my letters are anyway." Mama slightly backpedaled, then lifted her head high and announced, "Today marks the beginning of Operation Morale Booster, and this is my first batch of letters heading to Vietnam. I am on a mission to ensure every GI receives mail at every mail call. This is my gesture of support for the soldiers who are fighting in this war." She laid the handful of letters on the counter for Mr. Fallon, the small town's auxiliary postmaster, to sort into the appropriate airmail slot. "Maybe YOU might want to write a letter or two to a soldier, Mr. Fallon?" she proposed.

"Nah, I don't believe we have any business even being over there. This is Vietnam's civil war to fight."

Mama's eyes widened, and her eyebrows lifted to the middle of her forehead as she looked at him pleadingly. "Mr. Fallon, writing to the soldiers..." she gathered her composure, "My Operation Morale Booster is not about a 'yay' or 'nay' for the war. It is about supporting all these young boys who were drafted and sent a world away from their homes, family, friends, and way of life. They are out there somewhere, sleeping in the jungles and fighting all sorts of insects, leeches, obstacles, and enemies. It's about supporting each other. We are all Americans!"

Mr. Fallon shook his head in a slight nod. "I admit," he said, "I've never thought of it like that." He looked into Mama's hopeful eyes and made a commitment. "I'm not much of a letter writer, you see, but I'll tell you what... for every soldier that returns your letter, I will let you pick out one piece of candy to mail back to him."

Mama reached across the counter, offered her hand, and simply stated, "Deal!" Beaming with pride, she turned to the door, flipped up the collar of her coat to protect herself from the harsh New England wind, and made an equally dramatic exit. This sweet, wholesome young mother of three had no idea what she had just gotten herself into.

Chapter 3

Spirit in the Sky

While on the other side of the world...

"Ok, men, bring it in close... this may be the last time I get to talk to you as a whole unit, and I don't intend to take much of your time." Captain Sternberg paused as his troops shuffled closer to hear his voice. They didn't want to miss a word of his instructions.

Sternberg continued, "You know we have a big operation coming up, and we have a helluva lot of work to do to prepare. As it looks now, we will be jumping on the morning of the 26th. Now, you all know what happened to Charlie Company at Ia Drang Valley last November. For those who don't, let me put this to you bluntly." Captain Sternberg looked down at the ground, grimaced as though he had been punched in the gut. "We lost 93% of our men," he said hoarsely. The company commander indulged in a dramatic pause, shook his head slightly, and gulped hard. He rose up to the full measure of his stature and roared, "I DON'T INTEND TO HAVE THAT HAPPEN AGAIN. THIS TIME WE GET OUR REVENGE!"

Captain Sternberg detailed the preparatory work in the coming days and then concluded with an energized force, "Men, we are about to engage in Operation Masher." He dismissed the troops with the familiar close, "That's all I have, Gary Owen." The official nickname for the 7th Cavalry, Gary Owen, originating from Colonel Custer's 7th Cavalry days of the 1800s. Gary Owen was an old Irish drinking song and a favorite of Custer's, so it became the regiment's official march tune. The nickname had been passed down from one generation to the next of the mighty 7th Cavalry, and it still served as their fight song. The mention of Gary Owen fired up the company, and all boots immediately hit the ground with a sense of mission and excitement. New soldiers enlisted with the hopes of seeing combat, and their hearts were now beating faster at the prospect of the upcoming battle. This was what they had trained for.

On the evening of January 25th, platoon leader, "Big Mike," nicknamed for his big heart rather than his five-foot-six stature, called the non-commissioned officers (NCOs) to gather in the platoon command post to receive final operation orders. "Tomorrow morning at 0330 is H-Hour for the battalion," Big Mike announced. "Hard Core (B Company) and Brave Boy (A Company) are moving out tonight to sleep on the airfield. They are first to lift off; we are last. Hard Core and Brave Boy will secure the landing zone (LZ) designated as 'Dog.' Our battalion will have the 93rd ARVN (Army of the Republic of Vietnam) battalion as a back-up force." Big Mike looked around at the NCOs to make sure everyone understood. Several of the noncoms nodded in his direction.

"Alright," Big Mike continued, "On the 27th, the brigade will try to link us with the marines on the northeast coast. Highway 1 will be our right flank boundary. That is just about all I have for now. Are there any questions?" Not a word was spoken from any of the soldiers. "One more thing," Big Mike added with a droll hint of a smile. "Here is twenty dollars for each squad to buy some cold ones for your men. Have a good time tonight. I don't want nobody lying around the tent writing farewell letters home and feeling sorry for themselves." He saluted the men and exited the post.

That night the men did their best to hide their mixed emotions about downing a handful of "cold ones" as the commander put it. They weren't celebrating a victory or succumbing to the inference of the last hurrah before meeting their Maker. A young soldier, standing about five feet eight inches and not looking a day over sixteen, sat off to the side from the rest of the soldiers. He wasn't partaking in the beer, nor was he writing letters to home. He simply sat quietly, staring down onto the dirt at his feet. A seasoned soldier, heading to his bedroll to retire for the night, noticed the young soldier sitting alone. He stopped abruptly, diverted his course, and stepped over to where the youngster was seated. "Mind if I sit down?" he asked, already flopping down beside the kid.

The rookie, not lifting his head, shrugged his shoulders to say, *Would it make a difference if I did?* No way was he going to say that, though. Instead, he gave a reluctant wave of his hand.

The older soldier leaned over toward the kid. "Hey there, soldier, my name is Corporal Johnson... actually, it's Bob Johnson, but they call me Johnson here, what's yours?"

The young soldier, head hanging low, replied, "Hey, I'm Tim."

"Where ya from, Tim?"

"Missouri."

"Missouri? I'll be damned, I've never met anyone from Missouri!" Bob slapped his knee. "Do you have family there?"

"Yeah, my parents, my little sister, and my high school sweetheart, who I married just before being drafted. We are expecting a baby in six months."

Recognizing the sensitivity of his last statement compared to the uncertainty of what tomorrow may bring, Bob chose the lighter of the two topics for conversation. "Congratulations, Missouri! That is fantastic! Do you know if it is a boy or a girl?"

"No, I don't, but I hope it is a boy. I want to name him after my pop."

"Well then, I am sure you will have yourself a boy, and he will grow up to be courageous and loyal like you."

The kid turned his head up toward the corporal and said, "I hope you're right." For the first time, he noticed that the soldier talking to him in the dark was a Black man with an inviting, warm smile. The young soldier's eyes remained laser-focused on him for an awkward amount of time.

Bob laughed, "First time seeing a Black man, son?"

"As a matter of fact, yes, sir, it is."

"Well, just know, we bleed the same blood, and our hearts beat to the same rhythm. The color of our skin don't make a man, and it certainly don't make a soldier. We are one here. I will watch your back, son." The two continued to chat idly, sharing stories, and even indulging in some laughter.

The night was an anomaly of sorts. The anxiety from the uncertainty of what the next day might reveal seemed to stagnate time. Despite the calm from the warm zephyr on their skin, the skies turned dark and eerily quiet as they did in Vietnam, and the soldiers felt the day ebbing away while rattling their souls. They couldn't help but wonder if their last hours of life as they knew it was coming to an end. The night fell hard, and those among them who fell asleep as teenage boys would inevitably wake in the morning as men.

Before the sun peeked above the horizon, the soldiers loaded on the trucks and headed to An Khe airfield. Each platoon made their way onto helicopters and off to Phu Cat, code-named LZ Dog, short for Landing Zone Dog. Hard Core and Brave Boy were the first to board the choppers while the C-130 cargo carrier also lifted off to commence Operation Masher.

Everything was running smoothly, like a well-oiled machine, until a C-123 loaded with about forty-five young soldiers, within seconds of lift-off, sputtered, lurched, and plunged to the ground about fifty meters from the airfield down into a French minefield. The loud explosion upon impact pierced the heart of every soldier who witnessed it. In a moment of wide-eyed disbelief, the soldiers' jaws dropped, yet not a word was spoken. Reacting on instincts, a handful of soldiers waiting in line for their turn to board, dropped their sacks and rushed to the wreckage in hopes of pulling out survivors. They assertively reached through burning shards of material, searching, hoping, praying to find some of their buddies alive.

None were.

The rescuers returned to the airfield, reporting that there were no survivors from the C-123's apparent technical malfunction. They dolefully resumed their places in line, awaiting their pick-up by the next helicopter.

Standing nearby, Bob anxiously scanned the remaining troops, his eyes searching for "Missouri." He spotted him in the second group of soldiers waiting to board the helicopter. Bob hollered over to the kid above all the noise from the choppers and the commotion surrounding the crash. "Hey, Missouri!" The youngster turned back toward him, revealing the fright in his eyes. Bob made eye contact with the rookie soldier and held a long, firm salute. Missouri kept eye contact, conjured his composure, and offered back an attempt at an equally firm salute.

The unit arrived at LZ Dog, still in a state of shock and with pits in their stomachs, having watched the bizarre fate of their comrades play out in front of them. Few of the young men in uniform were older than twenty-one, and many were deployed before the ink was dried on their high school diplomas, but together they now stood as brothers in arms. They knew what they were sent there to do; they were our nation's bravest young men.

Amazingly, Hard Core and Brave Boy secured LZ Dog without firing a shot, believed to be an area in the absence of enemy presence. Therefore, the area was established as the battalion and brigade's forward support, as well as the basecamp for US Special Forces, Rangers, Paratroopers, and Green Berets.

To the east was the picturesque coastline of the South China Sea and to the west, rose the majestic mountains that ran alongside the An Loa Valley. Connecting the two was a peaceful valley filled with coconut trees and gently swaying fields of elephant grass, all of which provided a breathtaking variation of terrain. Nearby villages left evidence of French influence as the brightly colored buildings stood in sharp contrast to the local Vietnamese' mud huts. The landscape, too beautiful to envision a war ravaging through its countryside, would inevitably become a bloodied battlefield.

Several days before the planned attack, US aircraft had dropped thousands of leaflets into the villages, announcing the arrival of US Forces and promising safe evacuation from the war zone, as well as food and medical attention to any peacefully surrendering villager. Many locals took advantage of this, and humbly approached the US soldiers, seeking and receiving refuge. Even a handful of Viet Cong soldiers who feared their fate in the face of the mighty US Forces surfaced from hiding and willingly surrendered. The US Soldiers continued making their way through the villages and toward Bong Son Province, the Viet Cong's strongpoint. Not a shot was fired, not a drop of blood was shed thus far, but that was about to change.

The first contact with the People's Army of Vietnam (PAVN) came later that day when Hardcore drew relentless fire upon entering a village populated mostly with mud huts, often referred to as "hooches," indicative of an older Vietnam community. The attack was so severe against the US troops, the allied forces of the Army of the Republic of Vietnam (ARVN), the Vietnamese Air Force Skyraiders, felt compelled to swoop overhead and shower a motherlode of napalm over the village. Seared into the soldiers' minds were images of falling canisters, end over end, of napalm plummeting to the ground, setting the hamlet ablaze. This jellied substance caused widespread excruciating deaths from burns and asphyxiation. The burning flames enshrouded the village, and the stench of the human destruction quickly became unbearable.

The ground forces tactically scanned the village for movement and spotted three men peering out an open window of a mud hut that had miraculously been shielded from the spray of napalm. The US soldiers strategically converged around the occupied shelter,

17

forcefully but peacefully extricating three suspected Viet Cong guerrilla fighters. The men were brought out into the open street for interrogation.

At first sight, one detained was believed to be a North Vietnamese Regular Army Officer, evidenced by his close haircut and clean shave. The US soldiers quickly assumed they were dealing with a well-trained army soldier instead of a VC. This was far more disconcerting. The captives collectively refused to talk, refused to admit they were enemy fighters, and declined to reveal the suspected officer's identity.

Bob stepped forward and sternly grabbed one of the apprehended and forcibly led him behind the hut. He aimed his gun overhead and shot off a round. He left the trembling captive with another guard and returned to the street to grab the second detainee. This was an effective scare tactic, and as hoped, the internee started talking, identifying the suspected officer as a PAVN Battalion Commander.

The enemy commander didn't deny it, so Bob immediately handed the officer over to the security platoon responsible for handling prisoners of war. The other two detainees were reunited and also taken to the security platoon for further questioning. Their allegiance to the PAVN commander with whom they were hunkered down during the attack was still in question, so they remained designated as a threat.

Later that night, the company regrouped at the landing zone, waiting to be extracted back to LZ Dog, a stealth enemy sniper navigated the patrolled area. The sharpshooter utilized familiarity with the terrain and penetrated the secured perimeter. Creeping up behind a coconut tree and within a stone's throw distance, the marksman took aim and made an unapologetic statement to the United States' mighty forces. One-shot straight through the heart of a US soldier marked the first fatality for Operation Masher. Chaos ensued.

Muffled by the commotion among the Americans rising from the assassination of their comrade, the sniper escaped as deftly as he arrived. This was the bloody bookend of a day that started off with the shocking crash of the US aircraft, killing forty-five soldiers. Although the still of the night allowed for a momentary calm from fighting, it failed to provide Bob and his men any comfort from the finality of their first combat fatality, and so it was, the men slept with one eye open.

Chapter 4

Run Through the Jungle

T he next day proved equally eventful. The early morning sounds of US Aerial Rocket Artillery hovering overhead provided security and offered visual assistance to the 7th Cavalry below. As they navigated the six-foot-high elephant grass looking for evidence of the PAVN, the allies stepped forward strategically and ever so slowly. Just as an OH-13 observation helicopter performed an operational flyby, concealed enemy soldiers below suddenly opened up on the aerial target, revealing their location in the tall grass just ahead of approaching US soldiers. The enemy's fifty caliber machine guns, fixated on the chopper above, would have taken out the entire platoon in a spray of rounds had their position not been exposed moments earlier. The US platoon took full advantage of this and went on the offensive, firing indiscriminately into the elephant grass in the direction of the revealed PAVN soldiers.

In an awful twist of fate, this same chopper that essentially saved the platoon from being slaughtered was now the target of tracers ripping through the sky from enemy soldiers below. Within seconds the helicopter was hit, causing it to fiercely spiral to the ground. Immediately, Bob relayed the sergeant's trenchant orders to secure the downed chopper. Galvanizing his squad, he hollered, "Let's go! Let's go! No one gets there before we do!"

A race ensued as opposing forces each had a vested interest in reaching the chopper first. The troops blazed through the entangling grass, keeping a watchful eye on the ascending smoke from the downed helicopter. Bob and his platoon arrived at the upside-down wreckage first, one of the men pinned underneath. Six men, teeming with adrenaline and brute force, elevated the front of the helicopter as several other soldiers dragged the unconscious soldier out from under the doomed aircraft. Immediately gesturing to the medic to take over, Bob was stunned by the frightened look on the young medic's face. Apparently, he was in a state of fear paralysis. Bob barked, seeing the blood pouring from the unconscious soldier's head, "Don't just stand there, dammit, do something!"

"I can't!" the inexperienced medic cried.

Squinting his eyes in disbelief at what he just heard, Bob immediately jumped into action, pulling from basic first aid training given to all enlisted soldiers. He washed the wound with water from his canteen and applied a head dressing to stop the profuse bleeding. Other soldiers simultaneously initiated a multifaceted recovery operation, securing the downed chopper's area and guiding in a medivac to evacuate the wounded. Bob stabilized the unconscious soldier and quickly carried him over to the chopper and into the care of the senior aid serviceman. Soon after he turned to return to the downed chopper, he heard a reverberating holler from the examining medic, "Chalk up one KIA!"

Bob's heart sank, and he offered a personal moment of silence . . . killed in action as a result of saving our lives.

Later that night, back at basecamp, he learned that the soldier had died from internal suffocation and that he could have been saved with a simple procedure of slitting open the throat and inserting a tube into the soldier's windpipe allowing air to pass through freely. Bob approached the young platoon medic. "Why didn't you perform that simple procedure?" he demanded.

"I was too afraid to do it," the medic responded with his head held low.

Afraid to do it? Afraid of what? That he might die? Well, he did, Bob thought. He paused and then placed his hand on the medic's shoulder and leaned in close. "Fear and mistakes are expected and acceptable over here, son," he said quietly but firmly, "but indecisiveness or inaction is not."

Bob retreated to his bedroll and gazed into the night sky, reflecting on this fateful day. This war is not for the weak of heart, stomach, or grit, he thought. These boys, many of whom are in their teens, will mature quickly or die.

While reflecting in the still of the night, Bob was summoned by the platoon leader to be briefed on the next day's operation. Reports from a reconnaissance of no enemy sightings gave the platoon a false sense of security that securing tomorrow's landing zone (code-named Bird) was going to be easy.

January 28, 1966, 0530 hours, the troops packed up their bedrolls, fortified themselves with their breakfast C-rations, and prepared for their jump with echoes of the artillery prep-firing LZ Bird off in the distance. At 0730, troops boarded the choppers, heading off on their three-minute ride to what would soon be referred to as hell on Earth. LZ Bird was literally a cemetery, covered by more than 2000 gravestones protruding from the crystal white sandscape. "A little uncanny to be engaging in battle in a cemetery," one of the soldiers joked. Bob nodded, recognizing that humor was a great psychological technique to release the gravity of what lies ahead, saving many soldiers from going crazy during wartime.

As the 1st, 2nd, and 3rd platoons arrived at their strategic locations surrounding LZ Bird, the day took a turn for the worst. The 3rd platoon received a series of individual shots from random points of origin that quickly escalated to all-out automatic weapon fire. Simultaneously, the 2nd platoon came under heavy fire from strategically placed machineguns, and the two US platoons were caught in the murderous cross-fire of a well-executed Viet Cong ambush. Their ambush was masterfully timed to where US troops had disembarked from their several choppers and were dispersing into positions while the helicopters were far enough along on their return flight to no longer be of assistance to the troops below. This was a ground battle of opposing infantrymen cloaked with the crackling of carbines polluting the air, camouflaging the directions from which they came.

In what later seemed like divine intervention, the 1st platoon was erroneously dropped two hundred meters outside the eastern side of the LZ, which allowed them to regroup and set up a defensive action plan against the ambush. These US soldiers swiftly closed in on the enemy fire. Visible rifles peeking out the windows of a nearby hut divulged the enemy's position.

Bob saw it and crawled on his belly inch by inch until he reached close proximity to the hut's window. He pulled the pin and tossed a "Willie Peter" grenade into the window. This white phosphorus smoke grenade was an incendiary grenade that rarely allowed for survivors. When the smoke cleared, Bob ran to check the hut. He stopped in his tracks when he saw an elderly woman cradling two children lying in the far corner, dead; collateral damage of war.

He shook his head violently, having deep heartstrings for kids ... even PAVN and Viet Cong kids. *Kids have no place in a war, and it is an ultimate sin that they are caught in the cross-fires,* he thought. He was momentarily shaken but then was instantaneously brought back to reality when he heard his platoon leader, Big Mike, yelling commands, "Let's get a move on, men. We need to reinforce 3rd's position." The younger GIs were looking for direction from their sergeant in response to Big Mike's orders, but none was given. Again, Big Mike hollered, "Let's get a move on, 3rd needs us. Do you hear me, Sergeant? Move your men NOW!"

Big Mike repeatedly called for the sergeant to get the squad moving toward the 3rd platoon's position to strengthen their forces. Bob observed that the sergeant was paralyzed by fear keeping cover behind a large gravestone, so he leaped up from behind his own gravestone shelter and yelled to the squad, "You heard him, let's go fortify the 3rd!" He raced toward the 3rd platoon, glancing back over his shoulder, disappointed to see that only two men followed. They weren't more than fifty meters into their dash when an enemy machinegun opened up on them.

Bob shouted back to the two men, "Keep moving! A moving target is harder to hit!" Traversing the cemetery, taking full advantage of the gravestones' protection, the three brave and obedient soldiers made their way toward the 3rd platoon's position.

Miraculously, the bullets hit everything but them. Breathless, with sweat streaking their dirt-covered faces, the three reached the five young soldiers who had been separated from the 3rd platoon. Tucked behind a set of large gravestones, they were shuddering, worried that they didn't know where the rest of their platoon was, and were concerned their platoon leader and sergeant had already been killed. Up ahead of them were three more soldiers from another platoon pinned down by enemy fire.

Frustrated that the US machineguns couldn't provide cover because they were repeatedly jamming from white granules of sand finding its way into the guns' crevasses, Bob ordered the six soldiers to cover him using their M-16s. He signaled one of the men to follow his lead as he proceeded to jump up, swiftly zig-zagging toward the besieged US soldiers. As he approached the harboring foxhole, he recognized one of the soldiers. It was Missouri!

Within five meters of his comrades, Bob, belly to the ground, yelled over for details of the situation. "The PAVN machinegun is about two hundred meters away on the other side of the clearing," someone called out. Missouri, inexperienced in combat, peeked up from the foxhole to assess the distance for tossing a grenade. Eyes barely breaching the top of the ditch, the rookie soldier was greeted by a bullet barreling straight for him. With no time to react, Missouri reeled backward, the bullet penetrating his steel helmet and creating a reverberating sound that echoed in his ears as it hugged the wall of armor. "I'm hit, I'm hit, oh, God, I'm hit!' Missouri cried.

Bob crawled over to him to offer aid, brushing away the torrent of blood pouring down Missouri's face. Unexplainably, the bullet had pierced through the helmet on the right side and circled around on the inside of the liner, exiting the front, inflicting only a flesh wound on the kid's forehead. He assured the young soldier that he was going to be okay. "Don't know how you managed this one, Missouri, but you're gonna live to see your baby boy. Your son is going to grow up and say his dad was shot in the head and lived to talk about it." Bob smiled with just the ends of his mouth and a slight nod of the head, applied his first aid antiseptic and wrapping, and yelled for a medic.

Teeming with angered adrenaline, Bob tucked a few additional magazines into his pocket along with a grenade. No longer concerned about his own well-being, he decided to run a solo offensive and rush the PAVN position to eliminate the threat of the machine gun. He called for cover, although he knew it would only be by God's grace that he would survive this attempt. Was it a courageous act of valor or the futility of a fool? He didn't care. It had to be done.

At the first sign of the enemy pause, Bob jumped up and dashed directly toward the PAVN machine gun. He took the enemy by surprise, and with good suppressive fire from his comrades, the PAVN soldiers blindly returned fire with shots into the ground and up in the air. Bob got within sixty meters and dropped to the ground. Despite the enormous amount of adrenaline pulsating through his body, he took aim with his M-16 and efficiently took out four of the five PAVN manning the machinegun. The only remaining PAVN soldier leaped out from behind the machinegun and aggressively rushed Bob's position. Bob grabbed hold of his single remaining grenade and pulled the pin, strategically tossing it at just the right moment to collide with the approaching enemy soldier. He ducked when he saw the flash of light and heard the explosion... and then all became eerily quiet. Inching up from underneath his protective hands, he raised his head. He scanned the horizon a few times, searching for evidence of live opposition. With the confidence that all was secured, he ran back to rejoin the group.

They greeted him with combat terms of endearment: "You're crazy, but I love you, Johnson! You got those dirty SOBs!"

Lighting a cigarette, he accepted the pats on the back and left-handed compliments, savoring the minutes of calm before the inevitable storm. This moment ended abruptly when the attentive medic, Tommy, threw Bob a morphine capsule. "Keep this handy and watch over Missouri, will ya?"

Thoughts of getting out of this trench and back to the 1st platoon were now paramount in his mind. With heavy enemy fire continuing in the distance, He knew their window of opportunity to make a move was closing. A light mist was settling upon them, and the sun was sinking, adding to the obstacles of combat. About ten meters away, a comrade yelled, "Keep your eyes open, Johnson!" Two PAVNs had been spotted making their way across the clearing, heading toward the unmanned machinegun. Bob looked over at Missouri, who was tucked in the foxhole with blood saturating his head dressing. "Stay put, I will be back for you," he said. "I don't want them to put that gun back into action."

He crawled over to see for himself on his hands and knees, just hovering above the ground. Not two meters in, and in a blink of an eye, he was hit by enemy fire. The bullet's impact on the back of his shoulder flipped him on his back. In a guttural roar to the soldier ahead, "I'm hit, Goddammit, I'm hit."

Chapter 5

Have You Ever Seen the Rain

With pain searing through his shoulder, he dragged himself back to the foxhole. The heat from the bullet radiated from his back, so he reached around to feel for a bullet hole. Like a magnet to metal, his finger plugged the gushing blood from the bullet hole in the back of his shoulder just south of his neck. He reached for his first-aid packet forgetting he had used it on Missouri. Remembering the morphine capsule Tommy had tossed him; without hesitation, he injected the capsule's contents into his arm. Drawing from years of combat training, he used a towel from his pack to put pressure on the wound to curtail the bleeding and channel the morphine into the bloodstream. Having done all he could do, he sank back into the foxhole alongside Missouri, letting the morphine mask the pain to a tolerable level.

It was at this moment; Bob expressed uncharacteristic fear and sadness, truly feeling he was lying on death's doorstep next to the very kid he vowed to protect. Tears rolled down his face in defeat as he thought of his mother receiving news of his death from the Department of the Army. His whole life passed by him in an instant. One of seven children in a fatherless home, life was what they made it, and often hard. Is this how it was all going to end? He thought. Dying alone, a world away from everyone I love, in a dirty, cold trench, like those I dug with my own hands?

Before he got too deep into wallowing over his bullet wound, he heard the welcoming sound of "Huey" overhead, the choppers' nickname originating from the Iroquois Native American Indians. Just as quickly as his heart began to race with excitement, his heart sank at the sight of tracers shooting up toward the medic in the sky, projecting an audible trail of a high-pitched whistle. Huey's tail rotor was obliterated in an explosive flash of fire, casting shards of metal everywhere, littering the ground below. The chopper's main body seemed to have held its position for a moment before plummeting to the ground in a nosedive. A loud thud shook the ground upon impact, and all were assumed dead, confirmed by no return fire from the wreck. The night then lit up like the fourth of July with tracers ripping across the sky from enemy forces, aborting all other US rescue efforts.

Bob's sadness turned to anger as he repeatedly replayed the fall of the Huey in his mind. He cleared his face of any tracks of tears and glanced over at Missouri. "We need to get the hell outta here before our 'friends' come out of their ratholes and get us." He jumped up and grabbed Missouri by the arm, and led him out of the trench and through the wet terrain. Navigating the landscape with unparalleled finesse, they happened upon an extra-large foxhole. To their surprise, they reunited with their loyal medic, Tommy, sitting in the front corner with his head wrapped in soiled bandage material covering his left eye. Wounded himself and barely able to peek out the right eye, the medic continued to assist the four other wounded men in the foxhole. With the head of one severely wounded soldier propped up on his leg, the loyal combat physician was treating another comrade who had received a couple of bullets in his thigh. This sorry sight angered Bob, even more, when he recognized one of the wounded soldiers. He was a loyal and dedicated career soldier he had spent time with on a base in Germany before both volunteered for this tour in Vietnam. He channeled his anger to focus on getting everyone back to LZ Dog, forgetting about his bullet wound. "Where is the rest of the company? Anyone know?" he demanded.

The loyal medic replied, "Over there in the coconut grove about two hundred meters to our right flank. We've got a PRC (portable radio communication) with Ghost 6 trying to reach us." Ghost was the name of a nearby platoon, and the number six was code for a commander. "We can receive, but we cannot transmit." The PRC was able to receive messages from the nearby company commander but wasn't functioning to send messages back to him.

Bob noticed that the radio was missing an antenna and ordered, "Someone hand me an M-16 cleaning rod." Not sure if this was the fix, but desperate to try anything, he affixed the rod to the radio and called out, "Ghost 6, Ghost 6, this is Ghost 1,2,8, this is Ghost 1,2,8. Over." Silence. "Ghost 6, Ghost 6, this is Ghost 1,2,8, I repeat, this is Ghost 1,2,8. Over."

Still no reply.

He waited a minute or two and sent out a third call, "Ghost 6, Ghost 6, this is Ghost 1,2,8. Over."

"Ghost 1,2,8, this is Ghost 6. Over." Loud and clear, the commander's voice came through as the group collectively exhaled a loud sigh of relief; they were now able to mutually communicate. A sense of comfort and renewed hope filled the hearts of the twelve men in the foxhole.

"Ghost 6, this is Corporal Johnson. There are twelve ECHO MIKES (enlisted men). We are about two hundred meters to your left flank. We are hurt pretty bad, eight of us wounded with three on stretcher cases. Over."

"This is Ghost 6; we can't get to you at the present time. You will have to come to us somehow. Charlie got a machinegun breathing down our throats right now. Can you see them from your position? Over."

"This is 1,2,8…that's affirmative; we see it. Over."

The machinegun was firing from a trench dug out from under an elevated hut serving as a decoy. It was in such a spot that Bob had a clear view of the muzzle flashes, revealing its location with every shot. He radioed over the location, "This is Ghost 1,2,8, from your location… left five-zero, add one-five-zero (150 meters). Over."

Minutes later, a 105-round ripped across the sky falling short of its target by fifty meters.

"This is Ghost 1,2,8… correction on line… add five-zero. Over."

"This is Ghost 6, wilco, wait one. Over." The twelve men in the foxhole inched up as high as they dared, bursting with adrenaline in anticipation of Ghost 6's "will comply" response to Bob's target correction. A couple of minutes of eerie calm and then another 105-round pierced the sky and hit the target with an exceptional surgeon's precision.

"Ghost 6, this is Ghost 1,2,8…target destroyed! Over."

"This is Ghost 6, damn good job! Now, do you think you can make your way over to us? Over."

"We'll try. Over." Bob scanned the men in the foxhole to assess their condition. He made his way to Tommy and asked, "Do you think these guys can make it?"

The medic hesitated in his response. "Look, Johnson, why don't you guys go ahead and take off. I'll stay here with the wounded guys who can't make it. Maybe someone will be able to get us later."

"No! We all go, or nobody goes." The men collectively made clear their agreement, some louder than others, but all nodding affirmatively. The valiant display of esprit de corps continued as ideas of how to transport the wounded men fired around the foxhole. The men quickly dismissed the proposal of carrying the immobile men over the shoulders and running the two hundred meters to meet up with the rest of the troops, as was the idea of moving the wounded on litters. Executing either of these plans would have exposed the wounded to further bullets and would hinder the mobility of the soldiers who were still able to run. They had to be more creative than that. Despite being a time-consuming and challenging plan, the best they could come up with was dig a trench from their position to the fence, about two hundred meters away. This plan would allow the stretchers to be dragged below the earth's surface, protecting the wounded from enemy fire.

All agreed to this plan, and they immediately split the group, rotating in two-hour shifts with three men digging, three men keeping watch for PAVNs, and two men grabbing any bit of shuteye while sitting with the wounded. Bob and two others started digging the trench using their helmets, c-ration cans, and bare hands. Fortunately, the ground was mainly comprised of sand, making it was easier to move the earth to either side of the trench. In the air, the same heavy mist that posed a visibility problem earlier now added to the sand's weight and saturated their fatigues, exacerbating the chill of the damp night air. Bob and his two comrades dug for two hours and then rotated to perimeter watch. Sporadic enemy gunfire kept them alert but never amounted to a battle, and it didn't retard the digging. The night passed, ushering in the early hours of the morning. Bob's morphine and the events of the day eased him into a dead sleep despite the looming danger.

Two hours later, he woke to the sound of his men hustling to prepare their weapons for close combat. Someone whispered to him, "Beaucoup PAVNs are coming toward us!" Having just woken from a deep sleep, he glanced at his watch to mark time, which was not uncommon for soldiers to do when they believed they were about to meet their Maker. Well, this is it; at least we will go down fighting and taking some of them with us. At that moment, the loyal medic crawled over to Bob and said, "Glad to have known you, Johnson."

Bob nodded, "Yeah, sorry 'bout that, Tommy." They both smiled.

30

Off in the distant landscape of the cemetery, a large silhouette from a mass of figures emerged from the dawn's light, moving directly toward them. Grossly outnumbered, Bob and his comrades remained motionless as this dark mass approached the line of engagement. They held their position with fingertips hovering at their triggers, ready to open fire. The tension grew with each passing second as the impending bloody battle flirted with fate. At that moment, the night was so quiet one could hear the sand slide out from underneath the approaching soldiers' boots.

Bob had thoughts of how differently his life could have played-out flashing across his mind. If only he had he just been more mature to receive the love from his childhood girlfriend, Mary, which she was offering. This travel back in time seemed to last hours despite the reality of it only spanning a few seconds before what he braced to be an all-out, fight to the death engagement. Not more than a heartbeat away from a drastically different fate, a whisper came from the dark "Gary Owen."

Chapter 6

Blowin' In the Wind

The whispered brigade nickname blanketed the area and seemed to land on every drop of mist, settling deeply into each of the twelve soldiers' ears. It was their own company on a night withdrawal of the wounded and the dead. Simultaneously, the soldiers let out a collective exhale of relief and responded with the same, "Gary Owen!" One of the wounded soldiers, a sitting duck, not even able to hold a weapon, released a floodgate of tears. Bob couldn't help but think, *but for the grace of God, we did not unleash on them and take out a third of the unit in the first round.* Sending up a brief prayer of thanks, accompanied by a fist tap to the heart and then to the sky, he jumped to his feet to meet and brief the commanding officer of the night withdrawal.

He held a firm salute and snapped, "Corporal Johnson here, one of twelve, eight of us wounded, three severely." Bob relaxed his position and continued, "We took out a PAVN machinegun about two hundred meters over in that direction." He pointed off to the west. "We have had sporadic fire but nothing of substance over the last six-hours. Guessing a PAVN or two have been left behind and are just waiting us out before retreating."

After directing the CO to the wounded in the foxhole, Bob was dismissed. "Good work Corporal. Now, fall in and head back to rejoin the rest of your platoon. And take care of that shoulder of yours, Johnson," ordered the commanding officer.

The troops initiated the trek to join the company but stopped in their tracks thirty meters into their move. An illumination plane appeared overhead, dropping a parachute flare directly over them. Bellies to the ground, the men silently waited for the chaos to commence. They were sure they were about to be ambushed as a result of being exposed by the light of the flare. The soldiers laid still for more than thirty minutes without a single shot fired by enemy forces. *How can this be?* Bob thought as he glanced toward the sky. The men got up and started moving cautiously ahead, grinning in disbelief with each step. Their best guess was that the PAVN were searching for their handful of soldiers who had been left behind and were more concerned about retrieving them than they were about going on the offense.

Stepping over the enormous number of casualties from both sides of this war was damaging on the psyche. It took the company two hours to cross the battle-torn graveyard and reach the western side of LZ Bird. Bob propped himself up against a coconut tree, took out his Zippo lighter, and lit a cigarette, physically and emotionally exhausted from the last twenty-four hours. He was not a smoker, but in his mind, the nicotine helped combat the increasing pain from the bullet camping out in the shoulder. The cigarette also offered some warmth to the chilled to the bone body. He marveled at how every taste bud on his tongue seemed to savor the cigarette's flavor in such a situation despite having a distaste for tobacco under normal conditions.

He did his best to relax and take in the moment of calm. He allowed his thoughts to drift far away from Vietnam and back to his neighborhood in Philadelphia, Pennsylvania. He reminisced about his workouts in the boxing ring, the evocative smell of sweat, and the act of gearing up for a big fight and walking down streets populated with familiar homes and storefronts. His trip down memory lane was abruptly interrupted by the soldier sitting up on the other side of the same tree.

Shivering and complaining, a thick Bostonian accent grunt, "Hey Brotha, can ya help me heah, I'm wicked cold." Bob empathetically reached around to tuck the soldier's poncho around him a little tighter and brought his cigarette up to the soldier's lips to share a drag. The soldier struggled to inhale and then sputtered, "This sure is a helluva waah out heah, ain't it? I don't think I'm gonna make it home to see my motha afta all."

"Sure, you are kid, take one day at a time," Bob reassured in an exhausted monotone voice.

A few moments of silence pass, and again a wheezing voice is heard through the din of the night, "Hey Brotha, can you get unda my lina to wahhm me a bit?"

Bob cocked his head to the side in a gesture of momentary disbelief at the request. He assessed his comrade's condition and realized he was in dire shape, so he agreed. He tucked himself under the liner allowing his body heat to warm the dying soldier and then again bringing his cigarette back up to his comrade's lips. This time, the young Bostonian's head flopped to the side.

Bob shouted to the nearby medic, "We need help here...NOW!" The doctor was on the scene within seconds. "I'm sorry, sir," the doc whispered, "he's gone." In a suspension of time, just like that, he witnessed the fermata of the last breath of life seamlessly crossing over to the entrance of death. The medic immediately pronounced the soldier dead and carried him away to be prepared for his farewell trip home to his loved ones, all in a blink of an eye and seemingly far too routine. Bob just sat there in a state of shock. As eventful as the first three days had been for him, already having received a bullet wound, he wondered if he would make it out of Vietnam alive. Something has got to change, or I surely won't survive this. He took one last drag of the cigarette in hopes of numbing this perpetuating pain, snuffed the remainder of the smoke into the sand next to him, and like a velvet curtain rolling down at the end of the performance, he closed his eyes, drifting off to sleep for the duration of the afternoon and night.

Chapter 7

The Letter

A new day dawned over the coconut grove. Bob woke to the sun shining, the trees swaying, and a scattering of white puffy clouds sailing across the blue open sky. Groggy from the long hard sleep, he slowly rose to stretch every aching muscle of his five-foot, eleven-inch well defined, athletic body and dust the sand from his dark skin and bloodied fatigues. Taking a moment to inhale the morning air, the refreshed soldier glanced at the sky with a smile of gratitude. His shoulder was throbbing in pain, but he was grateful for another day. He removed his shirt and hung it on a tree limb to thoroughly dry in the warmth of the sun. Making his way over to the orderly to have his wounded shoulder examined, he passed a few battle-worn soldiers congregating off to the side hollering over, "There he is, the man of the hour."

"You greased those SOBs singlehandedly, you, crazy grunt."

"Charlie's got a mark on your head now, Brother."

Word of his heroic rush on the machinegun had circulated the camp, and the soldiers of all ranks were not shy about giving him kudos for his bravery. This recognition humbled Bob and he repeatedly reminded them that he could not have done it without the cover his men provided. "Thank you, but it was a team effort," was his canned but sincere response.

While returning from the dispensary, he was called to a meeting to hear from the Brigade Commander. The entire company congregated and were greeted with adulating words, "Men, I am proud of you. You men of Charlie Company not only defeated an enemy that outnumbered you five to one, but you took the stronghold from them. You have been baptized in blood, but you have been crowned in victory and glory. I salute you."

Shortly following the pep talk, the Huey medic evacuation choppers arrived to take Bob and the other wounded back to LZ Dog, and then continue onto the 85th Field Hospital in Qui Nhon.

Before take-off, Bob went to see if any letters from home had arrived while he was gone. His expectations were low since he was only away a few days, but since a lifetime of events occurred in those few days, he felt the need for a connection to someone who cared. He corresponded with his mother and a few relatives, but he never shared much in his letters to ease their worried minds. Nonetheless, hearing from them made all the difference, just to know he had not been forgotten.

As he crossed basecamp shirtless, donning only a shoulder bandage, he reflected on all that had happened. The helicopter crash, the stealth sniper, ducking behind gravestones in the graveyard battle, the solo rush on the machine gun, Missouri's miraculous bullet in and around the helmet, the shot to his shoulder, and the whisper of "Gary Owen." It all seemed surreal. Still, in disbelief of how he defied the odds with so many near-death experiences in the last two days, he tried to stop himself from replaying the scenes in his head of those who perished right before his eyes. He toggled between wanting to talk to someone about everything he had just experienced and wanting to protect the younger men from hearing of the horror. He chose to reflect quietly and keep to himself, refraining from engaging in any conversation.

He arrived at the mail area and was greeted by the on-duty officer who informed him there were no letters. He rolled his eyes and raised his eyebrows, divulging the disappointment his mouth refused to express. The officer lifted his hand, gesturing to a bin in the corner. "Grab a few from there," he suggested.

He looked over to this pile of letters; most addressed "To Any Soldier." Itching with curiosity and yearning for a diversion from his current thoughts, he reached into this pile and grabbed a handful of letters. He rifled through them, looking at the names and states on the return addresses. There was one from Audra in Ohio, Beth in Wisconsin, sisters, Diane, Deanne and Kim from Illinois, Teresa from Kentucky, Tammy from Florida, and a whole group from The Lonely Hearts' Club in New Jersey; all intriguing but one, in particular, caught his eye. It was from a Joan Hunter from Scituate, Massachusetts. He questioned himself as to why this name had piqued his interest, and the best he could come up with was that he immediately thought of Joan of Arc, the patron saint of military personnel. Although he was not Catholic, he was a history buff, and he was familiar with Joan of Arc's prominence and her heartstrings toward the French soldiers during the Hundred Year War. Tantalized by the powerful military connection and belief in Divine Providence, he stared at the envelope and allowed his imagination to wander; I want to know everything about Joan.

He looked up at the clerk and asked, "Have you ever heard of Scituate, Massachusetts?"

The soldier astounded Johnson with his response. "As a matter of fact, I have! My grandparents are from Boston, and they summer in Scituate, at Lighthouse Point!"

Lighthouse Point, huh, that means it's on the ocean. Bob's imagination further took flight. He lifted the envelope to his nose as if hoping to smell the sea. He tossed the other letters back into the bin, and with a farewell wave to the mail clerk, he clutched her letter to his chest and walked out of the tent. He opened the already unsealed envelope and pulled out two typed letters. The top note was addressed to the commanding officer of his unit. Attached by a single staple, was another letter, generically addressed to a "GI". The message seemed so simple, yet it already lifted his spirits and bolstered his morale.

He reread the letter several times and pondered on the magnitude of this gesture from a housewife who was raising three small children. Overcome with joy; he indulged in the thought that this woman may be the voice of many who cared but just didn't act. He felt honored to have had her letter in his hand and vowed to himself to be a worthy and respectful correspondent. He retreated to his bedroll with the letters in hand and a little pep to his step. He was amazed at the difference receiving this generic letter had already made, and he believed her mission to be sincere and authentic.

Bob tucked the envelope away in his pack, wincing in pain, a reminder of his wounded shoulder. The excitement of the letter and the thoughts of this new pen pal momentarily trumped the gravity of his condition. He gathered his pack together, retrieved his drying shirt from the tree limb, and got in line to hop on the Huey heading to the 85th Field Hospital. His recovery time at the hospital would also afford him time to respond to his new pen pal. He was curious about what motivated her to initiate Operation Morale Booster and was intrigued to know more. From her letter, she was clearly busy and apparently not lonely, having a husband and three young children in tow. She made no mention of her personal opinion of the war, and her focus was one hundred percent that of compassion and support for the soldiers. It appeared that there was nothing in this for her. She seemed content to give of herself, offer the soldiers companionship from afar, provide a respite from the war, and assure them they were cared about and never forgotten.

Bob hopped onto the Huey wearing a satisfied smile the entire flight over to the 85th. He thoroughly enjoyed the bird's eye view of the beautiful countryside. The contrast of beauty to the horrific events of the past few days was almost too surreal to accept. The erosion and intentional defoliation of the landscape caused by war could not erase its beauty. He took it all in and vowed to let it all out, by sharing the beauty of Vietnam with this new gem in his life named Joan.

Moments before landing at the 85th Field Hospital, Bob had a panic about composing his first letter to her. Nothing in her letter suggested that she was White, but for some reason, placing her in a suburb of Boston, in a coastal town, made him feel that she was. This idea didn't concern him except that she may not be interested in conversing with a man of color. He deliberated about whether he should divulge this in his first letter. He wanted to be forthright, but he also had high hopes for engendering a relationship where he could be his authentic self, sharing his creative side and deepest thoughts. This internal conflict monopolized the better part of the next twenty-four hours as he made his way through the hospital admitting process. He made a few attempts of the pen to paper, to no avail. The struggle was real, diverting his attention so much that it overshadowed the pain from the bullet wound, already proving to be a godsend. But could he, would he, divulge that he was a man of color?

Chapter 8

Massachusetts

F orty-eight hours had passed since Bob arrived at the hospital. During which time, he had ample opportunity to mull over the direction for the content of his first letter to Mama. Today was the day to take that leap and respond. He felt it was wise to write to the family and not just to her since she mentioned them in her letter. Doing this would also serve to ease any concerns my dad may have had with her conversing with soldiers in general and specifically, a Black soldier. Determined to mirror her authenticity and honesty, he was at peace, letting the chips fall where they may for when the time was organically right to divulge that he was a man of color. He believed that her heart was pure and that his skin color was not a prerequisite for being a pen pal. So, heart to mouth and pen to paper, he began his letter:

Cpl. Robert E. Johnson
RA 13638238 Co-C.
2/7th Cav. 1st Cavalry

February /66

Dear Mrs. Hunter and Family:

I sincerely hope that this letter will find you and your family in the best of health and enjoying the many splendors that life may have to offer.

Before I say anything else, I think it would be proper to introduce myself at this time. I am Corporal Robert E. Johnson. I am 24 years old (almost 25), and I am originally from Philadelphia, PA. I have been in the service for 7 years, 8 months; Vietnam 3 months.

I received your letter this morning, and I can't possibly begin to express my sincere appreciation for you writing to us. As you suspected, we do look forward to the mail call (those who do get letters). I am not writing to you just to have someone to write to, but perhaps to let you know how wonderful it is for us to see the way people at home genuinely feel about us GIs being here.

I recently received a bullet wound in my shoulder during Operation Masher, which began at the end of January. I admit I had forgotten all about the true meaning of why I was in Vietnam. I had become selfish as a result of being wounded and seeing too many of my buddies killed. I had begun to wonder if this was worth all the American blood that had been spilled and all the men who died a world away from their home. But you know something, it is people like you, who keep us reminded of the real reason we fight, and for some of us, die over here. It is for the freedom and democracy for people like the Vietnamese to live free of communist tyranny.

People like yourself are fighting this war just as much and just as hard as we are over here. Yes, you, too, are fighting, not with bullets and guns, but with pens and paper. With your moral support, we shall win this war; we shall win together as Americans.

You asked for me not to think that you are a "kook." I don't think you are at all. Perhaps by the time you finish this letter, you will feel that I am a "kook." (smile)

To describe me in a little bit more detail... well, to begin with, I am not married, nor do I have a family of my own. As I said, I have been in the Army for 7 years (almost 8). I have been to Europe twice, Japan, Korea, and now, Vietnam. I enlisted to come here while stationed in Germany. I enjoy Army life, but I am getting out when this war is over. I am hoping to go back to school with classes at the University of Maryland and also hoping to buy myself a small house on the GI Bill. Of course, these are only future dreams I hope to become a reality.

To tell you a little bit about my job here, if you are interested, I am a Paratrooper and Ranger. I am a squad leader. (Forward Reconnaissance) I have been put in for sergeant.

I would like to say more, but it seems that the words won't come, so I will close at this time. I would sincerely like to become your pen pal.

With Affection and Sincerity,
Cpl. Robert E. Johnson

P.S. Please excuse my handwriting and English. I know it must be almost unbearable to you. Being the wife of a teacher, you must also be an educated woman.

***

"This was pretty bold of him to write to you during that period of civil discord, don't you think?" I suggested.

"I guess so in hindsight, but honestly, I didn't think anything of it. I mean, I didn't mention I was White, and he didn't mention he was Black; that would have just seemed so awkward and unnecessary. We were just two people befriending each other in a time of need." Mama paused before offering resounding words summing up her philosophy on race, "Skin color has never mattered to me, and I never understood why it did to others. I look at the character of a person, the content, and not the form; always have and always will."

"Did he ever mention he was a man of color? I mean before he sent a photo of himself."

"I am sure he did at some point because we spoke about interracial relationships quite a bit, but it wasn't monumental to us, so I can't recall at what point that was."

"Did you ever tell him you were White?"

"No, I don't think I ever did. I guess I never felt the need. Or maybe I just assumed he assumed, and perhaps that was wrong of me. I don't know, Susan," as she shook her head in shallow frustration, "the whole race thing was as foreign to me then as it is now. I know we have come a long, long way, but we have yet to reach that state where all men are created equal also prosper equally, but I am not sure we ever will. The prospering part has a lot to do with the choices each person makes."

"Was there much racism in Scituate back then?"

"Well, hard to say as it was a town primarily populated by the Irish and the Italian. We had a few Black families in town and several other ethnicities, but it was heavily populated with White families. I never heard of anyone bothering any of the minority families, but then again, Dad and I were pretty strong in our beliefs. Sometimes, that alone provided a shield as no one would speak ill around us because they knew they would be confronted with opposition."

Mama continued enlightening me about the history of Scituate concerning race relations, particularly about Chief Justice William Cushing. He was a member of a prominent family that moved to Scituate back in the late 1600s. Cushing aspired to the level of Chief Justice in the United States Supreme Court and is revered for stewarding the country from the concept of slavery and moving toward the ideals our Founding Fathers mapped out for us. He worked toward and established Scituate as a role model town for embracing diversity.

"Dang, how did I not know all this?" I grabbed my phone and googled Chief Justice William Cushing.

"Mama, get this… while serving as Chief Justice of the Supreme Judicial Court of Massachusetts, Cushing decided a landmark case in 1781. An enslaved, Quock Walker, ran away from his owner and filed a suit for his freedom. Chief Justice Cushing ruled:

'… our Constitution of Government, by which the people of this Commonwealth have solemnly bound themselves, sets out with declaring that all men are created equal- and that every subject is entitled to liberty, and to have it guarded by the laws, as well as life and property- and in short is totally repugnant to the idea of being born slaves. This being the case, I think the idea of slavery is inconsistent with our own conduct and Constitution; and there can be no such thing as perpetual servitude of a rational creature, unless his liberty is forfeited by some criminal conduct or given up by personal consent or contract…' Harper, Douglass. Emancipation in Massachusetts (2003) Slavery in the North. Retrieved 2010-05-22.

"Essentially, ruling that slavery was inconsistent and incompatible with Massachusetts law and abolishing it forever. Mama! That is almost a hundred years before the Emancipation Proclamation!"

"Wow, see, you learn something new every day. That handheld computer of yours is handy to have around. Perhaps this deep-seated drive toward tolerance and understanding is why I never really felt a sense of racism in town, but there was still some lurking. Even on that sweet little street of ours. I was shocked at what one of our neighbors did to me, and you will be too."

Just the thought of anyone doing ANYTHING to Mama got my hair up on end. I had to know more.

Chapter 9

Dust in the Wind

After crafting his first response to his Operation Morale Booster pen pal, inspiration exuded him in all that he did. Bob's creative juices began to flow like a snow adorned mountain melting into a babbling brook in the first of spring. He spent much of the three weeks recovering in the 85th writing letters, drawing sketches, and creating comic strips. Although Bob felt obligated to leave the educational system in the ninth grade to become a professional boxer to help provide for the family, he was teeming with intelligence. Bob also possessed a gift of strong abilities in both writing poetry and drawing. To entertain those recovering in the hospitals as well as his compatriots at basecamp, he started a comic strip of his own, a spin-off of the popular character, Beetle Bailey. He called it Beetle Bailey Goes to Vietnam, developing this character to mimic the combat soldier's lifestyle with the mission of bringing levity to the men who were healing and serving alongside him. It was a welcomed diversion and even served as a form of therapy at times. Bob was not only dealing with the healing process and rehabilitation that accompanied a bullet wound, he was also having to come to grips with the fact that his brothers in arms were dying out in the battlefields as he slept safely in a hospital bed. As a natural-born protector of others, this pained him more than a bullet itself. This artistic ability manifested itself as a result of his willingness to express insight into both grave and trite matters.

Later that night, he started to pen a poem about the call of duty to his country and its philosophy regarding freedom. After being shaken by the horrific events that he experienced during Operation Masher, he believed this to be his inner voice reinforcing his belief system, not only regarding the duty to one's country but also to all of humanity. These tenets are what compelled him to volunteer to go to Vietnam in the first place; to fight for the freedom of democracy, even for people he did not know. Regardless of where this inspiration originated, composing this poem was already finding purpose in the healing process. Hearing Bob recite and edit the poem as he was writing it, a fellow 7th Cavalry soldier, two beds down, called over to him, "Hey Johnson, I heard you singlehandedly took down a machinegun. Did they put you in for the Silver Star?"

"Nah, I got put in for a Bronze Star with Valor." Bob piped back. "As far as I am concerned, every man in that graveyard battle should have gotten a Bronze Star with Valor, but what the hell is a medal anyway? You and I know what we have done, and besides, ya gotta pay a dime for a cup of coffee whether you got a decoration on your chest or not." They both let out a brief chuckle.

"I heard it was a helluva blood bath," his comrade piped back.

"Yeah, aren't they all, though?" Bob got back to composing his poem. Pen to paper, he inserted a line, "Here he stands without a doubt, he is determined to stomp communism out." He reread it a few times, looked up with a smile of contentment, and then closed his notebook. He tucked his notepad under his pillow and vowed to revisit this poem in the not too distant future so he could include it in his next letter to Mama.

Three weeks pass and a fully recovered Corporal Bob Johnson was sent back to An Khe for duty, excited to get back to his men and catch up on all that had transpired while he was gone. During the three weeks he recovered in the 85th, Operation Masher had continued to suffer the fatalities of too many men. Names of those who had perished were not definitive, but the numbers were. This ambivalence played heavy on his heart. Bob felt an unrealistic sense of responsibility to keep all his fellow soldiers safe; thus, he felt the pain of every fallen comrade. He imagined the parents' faces upon receiving the news of their son's death. It was often too hard to bear, even in his thoughts. His heart was too large and his thinking too deep; a skilled fighter and a killing machine, albeit, but only out of necessity to help others live freely.

Letters from Mama crossed in the mail with his over the next few weeks, quickly establishing a trusting relationship with each receiving a new note about every seven to ten days. Bob had just finished writing her a letter and was bringing it to the designated tent to mail when he saw his company unloading from trucks returning from twenty-seven days of constant combat while out on Operation

48

Masher. As expected, these young men had aged harshly. They were all battle-worn and about fifteen pounds lighter than when they departed for LZ Dog less than a month ago. Some walked back to their bunkers with glazed eyes traumatized by what they had just endured while others were hooting and hollering, jumping from the back of the truck. He noticed many new faces filing out of the truck but was thrilled to see a lot of the guys he had served alongside in the first three days of the operation, making it back in one piece. It was a bittersweet reunion for some as they were happy to see that he had fully recovered, but also a little disappointed for him; hoping that his bullet wound would have earned him a one-way ticket back to the States. Above the mini reunions' rowdiness, Bob heard a familiar voice from the rear of the truck calling him over. He looked up to see Big Mike standing there with a wide smile.

"Hey Johnson, how's that shoulder of yours?" Big Mike hollered.

Bob walked over to him as he answered, "Ok, sir, a little stiff, but it's ok."

"I want you to know that I recognized you worked hard up there. I have recommended you for the Bronze Star."

Bob humbly replied, "I know, sir, I found out about it the other day. Ya know," he continued, "a lot of good men died up there that day, sir."

"Johnson, the men who are out there doing their jobs, are the ones most likely to get the recognition," Big Mike explained.

"Perhaps so, but a lot of men died in that graveyard who never got the chance to do their job the way they would have liked to have done it," Bob proposed. At that moment, the conversation was abruptly interrupted as Big Mike was requested to report to the orderly room immediately.

Bob spent the day catching up with his comrades, hearing a plethora of stories, much like what he experienced during those three fateful days. He later retreated to his tent and got comfortable lying on his bedroll with just the light from a candle burning beside him. The emotionally drained GI pulled out the growing pile of letters to reread the ones from Mama. He could feel his body ease into a peaceful sense of calm merely reading them. Serving as a respite from the jungle's challenges and the horrors of the war, he allowed himself this momentary escape. She wrote of her idyllic town of Scituate, Massachusetts, a picturesque coastal town, complete with a working Coast Guard station and a small fishing fleet. She wrote about her daily activities as a young mother of three young children; four, five, and six years old. Her daily routine would include walking them to the school bus stop, helping them with their homework, baking chocolate chip cookies, getting them to help with chores, and taking them to the beach down the street from their home. Mama was not shy about how much she adored Dad, who was in the background of every correspondence, often referring to him to as her "rock," an excellent provider, and a great father. She painted a picture-perfect life back home, which encouraged Bob to endure the war and return home to the States to build a similar experience for himself. Mama also had a way with words. She was very frank in her content and a little bit of a spitfire in her personality. Mama was busy with the three small children and being a homemaker, but always found time to write to him. This particular night, he reread her most recent letter over and over.

April 5, 1966

Dear Bob,

We are all doing well and looking forward to Easter Sunday. The children all have Easter outfits; we will be sure to take some pictures to send you. We will go to church and then to Winthrop, (a town north of Boston) where my family lives, and spend the day there. Paul will go into the Boston Garden to see one of the Boston Celtics' playoff games with my Dad, and then we will eat our big dinner at night. I hope you have the best Easter possible. We'll be thinking of you.

Yes, Paul loves almost all sports and seems to have the natural ability to do well in anything he attempts. A couple of summers ago, he thought he'd try his hand at tennis. It came to him quite naturally and is doing well. I took tennis lessons this past winter at night school so I won't be left at home when he goes to the courts this summer. He received a scholarship in high school to go to Fordham University for football. He accepted the award and played only two years because Fordham dropped the football program. They kept him there as a baseball player and swimmer and honored the scholarship. In his senior year, he won "The Athlete of the Year." So, you were right; he does love sports. He was in the Army for a 6-month tour of duty and played for the Army volleyball team. He had a pretty easy tour of duty, huh?

You asked about my flying day, well, yes, I did enjoy it and had a great time flying all over this country. I lived in Chicago for nine months and flew to both coasts, but then I put in for a transfer and came home to Boston. Here, I lived with my family, about 2 miles from the airport. It seemed almost as soon as I met Paul; I also developed a fear of flying and quit quite abruptly. I returned to my first job at IBM Corporation and was a secretary to the typewriter department manager. I stayed there almost to the time I was to have my first child.

I don't know where to begin to tell you what life in the States is like now. All last year, the northeast part of the country had the worst drought in forty years. We had bans placed on our water, and many towns were on emergency water supplies. This spring doesn't look to be much better so far.

The styles here are probably a little different. The boys look like girls (long hair and fancy clothes) and the girls look like boys!! Everyone loves the Beatles from England and everyone plays a steel guitar!!! That is slightly exaggerated, but not much.

Many people have moved out to the suburbs, and that sometimes presents "suburbia" problems. The men have to drive an hour or so each way to work, getting them home later, and then don't have much time or energy to play with their children. Therefore, the mother has to do more of the jobs once associated with the father. In general, the men seem to be working too hard to keep up with the fast pace of the business world. It has enormous pressures, and everything revolves around making money. Our life hasn't changed much, though; teaching isn't so competitive, and Paul loves his job. He is fabulous with the kids and loves playing with them. He is a great husband and father, and I thank God for him every day.

I can't think of any other things to tell you about the States, but if you have anything particular in mind, then let me know.

Well, I have to close for now to start supper. Take care and drop me a line when you can find the time.

Sincerely,
Joan

***

Perhaps twenty times, he read her typed notes, until his eyelids succumbed to their heaviness. He fell asleep with her letter on his chest and a smile on his face, the candle still flickering in the moonlight, like the calm before the storm.

Chapter 10

Sittin' on the Dock of the Bay

Immediately the following morning "chow," consisting of eggs, bacon, and toast, Bob tucked himself back in his bunker to quickly jot down a note to Mama to inform her that he was going to be away from basecamp for a week. He shared with her that he had been granted five-days R&R (rest and relaxation) in Bangkok. R&R was the respite offered to soldiers returning from heavy combat before being sent back into the jungle to fight the sandflies, leeches, and every other insect one can imagine, not to mention the Viet Cong and the People's Army of Vietnam. In his letter, he made sure to give mention of gratitude to my sister, Maryellen, a sweet little six-year-old girl who had sent along a crayon written note and picture with Mama's most recent letter. He detailed how innocently Maryellen had colored an image of the American flag with each of the fifty stars shaped like hearts. She wrote in the note that she loved all fifty states and added, "Thank you for protecting all of them!"

Bob confided that these words, "from the mouths of babes," brought a lump to his throat. "I stared at her drawing, and for that moment, time stopped. I envisioned what it would be like to have a daughter of my own; to teach and protect." Lost in his visual, he dragged his finger across all fifty hearts and thought; *this is why we fight. We fight for the freedom of all kids.* Referencing that moment, he shared, "Innocent letters like the one from little Maryellen, inspire me to fight with even more heart and help the locals rebuild with even more compassion. This war is as much about defeating the Viet Cong and PAVN, who collectively symbolized communism, as it is about the pacification and rebuilding of the infrastructure and the trust of the South Vietnamese people." Bob brought the letter to a close with his usual, "So until, Bob"

***

"Ooooo, he signed it 'Bob' and not 'Robert,' already getting comfortable with y'all," I teased.

"Yeah, now that you mention it, I do recall he would vary his salutations, and it was interesting to match them to what state of mind he was in at the time of writing the letters. Most often with 'So Until,' and then he'd change up the names... 'Robert' was very formal and was used in brief letters or those talking about a significant matter like when he was in the hospital. He would sign it, 'Bob' and 'Bobby,' most of the time. Although his nickname in the Army was 'Johnson,' that name was reserved for his comrades.

"Your father explained it as an unwritten rule within the Army of assigning nicknames to soldiers. Most GIs never even knew the full names of the men they fought alongside. This intentional technique of keeping a personal distance from your comrades was purely for emotional survival. They achieved this by establishing a brotherhood earned by serving alongside one another in life and death scenarios while simultaneously not allowing for closeness in a personal way that could negatively impact the men when the inevitable fatality occurred."

"Got it, that makes sense. Hmmm, it'll be interesting to watch how Bob signs his letters now that you gave me the heads up." Teeming with curiosity and loving her total recall on all things Operation Morale Booster, I probed further, "So tell me more, like how you found the time to carry out this mission."

Mama explained, exuding pride from the inferred admiration I subtly extended, "I was busy at home with the three kids, but I organized the files of all the soldiers I was personally writing to and set aside a little time every day. I had a system set up just off the kitchen, in the den, where Dad had his desk. At night, when Maryellen, Michael, and Billy were in bed, Dad and I would resume our work in the den for an hour or two before catching up on the news and retiring for the night. Dad drew up lesson plans and assignments for his US History classes, while I would read and respond to my Operation Morale Booster pen pals. I always read the soldiers' letters aloud. When reading Bob's notes, Dad would stop what he was doing and turn to watch me read, not wanting to miss a word. Bob's letters, almost always addressed to both of us, would strike a delicate balance of describing recent military operations to grab Dad's attention. Then, he peppered in a more delicate

54

conversation that would go deeper to the heart of his feelings to engage my interest.

"We both enjoyed all the letters from 'my soldiers,' but we held heartstrings for Bob's. I created an index card for each soldier, where I chronicled the correspondence and made notations of any critical dates or family information that would enhance the personalization of my responses. Birthdates, hometowns, and family names were of most significance. I often asked about family members in my letters to keep the soldiers connected to their respective families by encouraging them to write about them. I also kept a running list of Commanding Officers and their addresses, which I would jot down from local newspaper articles. You wouldn't remember this, Susan, but I also pinned up a three-foot by four-foot map of the country on the den wall so I could show the four of you where all of these soldiers were from; a red dot marking the approximate position of the towns within the states. This ritual became something we all looked forward to; a silver lining in living through this war."

Mama recounted one letter she recalled Dad particularly enjoying, detailing a Long-Range Reconnaissance Patrol. "Bob explained it as a volunteer mission of thirty-three men; Rangers and Paratroopers combined and handpicked to operate solely on their own, separated from their platoon."

"That's crazy! That area is replete with tunnels and dangers of ambush."

"Yeah, they were dangerous missions these soldiers went on," Mama agreed. "They were responsible for reconnoitering information to the Battalion Headquarters concerning the movement of the Viet Cong. They also cleared landing zones for the choppers and the troopers making air assaults."

"How'd they do that?"

"They would take down trees and then set a controlled fire to the land to clear the brush. One time he even got stuck in one of these fires and suffered awful burns. Everything they did was dangerous. He told us about one mission that had him as close as two miles from the Cambodian border rescuing and securing an F100 jet fighter that had been shot down over North Vietnam. The details of his operations were jarring at times, but I could tell that he deliberately refrained from getting too graphic to protect me from the true nightmare of it all." Mama paused with a pensive look on her face. "Although he made attempts to shield us from the horrors of what he was experiencing, it was inevitable that some of it would bleed through, and it did."

I was reading through a letter and came across a telling excerpt. "Mama, he was so motivated by the idea of spreading freedom to all people and stopping anything that resembled communism. Look what he wrote here:"

"Despite the danger, I feel it is an honor to be risking my life for something precious as freedom, even if it is for the freedom of men, women, and children a world away. I feel that freedom should be a right afforded to all mankind and that I am fighting communism from creeping into America. I am fighting so the Vietnamese people would have the ability to live in a democracy, governing themselves as we do in America. Russia declared they were going to dominate us by spreading communism one country at a time, and we can't let that happen. We need to spread democracy so people can experience the joy of liberty. I am a Black man, and life always seemed harder, but with each passing year, we are gaining more success and establishing our place as a true equal, no longer oppressed nor pitied. I denounce the riots going on today. My race should never be aligned with violence. Despite our current civil unrest, I am proud of America for the progress we have made so far, and I am hopeful about where we are going to be in my lifetime. America made a bold stand to the whole world by abolishing slavery when we were the youngest of the countries. This oppressive system had been accepted for thousands of years and across the globe, yet it was America who said, 'No more!' So, to that end, I will fight for freedom."

He further explained that it wasn't until he entered the Army and traveled to foreign lands that he witnessed people who were genuinely oppressed and forced into hardships. Bob shared that the people in Vietnam didn't know any better than to "accept a leader who has the biggest bowl of rice to offer them, even if it is a communist leader like Ho Chi Minh." Despite having been recently decorated with the Bronze Star, a Purple Heart, and the Soldier Commendation Ribbon for his courageous work during Operation Masher, Bob admitted that these did not hold lasting value to him.

He compared the significance of an award to the intangible and eternal value of knowing he was fighting for humankind's freedom. Bob exuded so much love for humanity, and the beauty of God's work in nature, Mama, admitted it was hard for her to place him in the middle of this awful war. She looked up from the letter before finishing and stared at me as if she was searching for something big, she wanted to share.

"I remember a closing line of his that stopped us in our tracks." Mama recollected. "He closed with an unforgettable statement, 'Please excuse the dirty writing material and my English. It's hard to write in a foxhole.' We were stunned, visualizing this letter being written from a foxhole in a combat zone a world away in the same gory war we were watching on TV every night. I remember Dad reflecting on all Bob had detailed in his letter, commenting on his unparalleled selflessness." Mama smiled as she sat a little taller in her chair, "This was when I got the idea to invite Dad's students to participate in Operation Morale Booster. I thought it would be a win/win experience for the students to communicate directly with those on the front lines, and vice versa, for Bob and the other soldiers to feel the appreciation and sincere interest from the next set of possible conscripts."

Beaming with pride, Dad applauded the idea, and Mama immediately took to her typewriter to compose a brief explanation of Operation Morale Booster, inclusive of an invitation to participate. With characteristics quintessential of her touch, she included a comic strip clipped from a newspaper. It was a sketch depicting a young soldier carrying an overflowing sack of letters as a handful of other soldiers grabbed at the falling letters as they fluttered to the ground. The eye-catching illustration conveyed how much enjoyment the soldiers would get from the students' notes. She buttoned it up with a Bible verse from Matthew about doing to others as you would want to be done to you, and she tucked it in a manila envelope for Dad to take to school the next day.

This notion started an unquenchable fire in her belly. She began thinking about other schools she could invite to participate, further expanding her sights to include the ladies in her sodality group at church and local civic groups like the Cub Scouts of America. Mama didn't get much sleep that night as she lay in bed, eyes wide open, head-spinning, and overflowing ideas of how to enlist more support for her writing campaign. Nothing could have prepared her for how her request for participation was going to be received.

Chapter 11

Imagine

Back across the globe, it was morning for Bob, and he was on his way to Bangkok for his R&R. Soldiers, accustomed to grabbing a couple of hours sleep here and there against a tree or in a ditch, were often riddled with guilt when given the opportunity to sleep in a real bed and waking only when the body felt sufficiently rested. Bob spent the next five days, palling around with another comrade, drinking, eating, and socializing to his heart's content. After the five days of R&R, he was ready to return to duty, refreshed, and eager to "get back to work" and "get this war over with."

Almost immediately upon returning to basecamp, he received orders of a 0800 departure for the next mission. This order allowed him twelve hours to clean his fatigues, get a status update from the men as to what had transpired over the last five days, and check his mail.

To his surprise, there was another letter from Mama despite the likelihood that his most recent note had not made it to the States. Her letter took him on a more descriptive literary journey through her scenic seaside town of Scituate. She wrote:

"Today, since it is Saturday and Paul does not have to go to work, I took the car out for a drive to run some errands. As I cruised around town, I couldn't help but think of you and how I would love to show you our iconic little shore town. Established in 1636, Scituate continues to be one of the most picturesque towns in New England, with its eight miles of winding coastline inclusive of 1st, 2nd, and 3rd cliffs and marshes, marveled by artists of all ages. These artists can be seen on any given day of the year, capturing the seascape's beauty. The nostalgia of the New England style homes, storefronts, and gardens have the town teeming with charm. As I mentioned in an earlier letter, Scituate Harbor is one of the last remaining commercial fishing piers on the coast of Massachusetts and home to one of the finest Coast Guard Stations. Their presence adds to the beauty and the uniqueness of the town. It is the supermodel in the eyes of landscape photographers."

Mama continued, "As rich in beauty, Scituate is rich in history. Originally named Satuit, understood by the American Indian residents as 'Cold Brook,' it is situated equidistant from Plymouth and Boston, the far more famous colonial settlements. Plimoth Plantation is memorialized in history books claiming Christopher Columbus took his first step onto the soil of 'The New World.' Later, the Indians and Pilgrims broke bread marking the first Thanksgiving dinner. Scituate proudly boasts of Abigail and Rebecca Bates' textbook stories, scaring off the approaching British Army, believed to have been a result of their magnitude of sound, playing their fife and drum as they marched toward the lighthouse point. As Scituate historians would tout it, the girls played so loudly; the British Army assumed their surprise attack was no longer a surprise and that an entire army would be awaiting their arrival. The Brits deemed it a bust and retreated, leaving the girls to celebrate, marking their place in history."

Mama interjected that she hoped he was enjoying this virtual tour around Scituate and pointed out that she was making a concerted effort to appeal to his love for history with all these tidbits of information. Also recalling Bob's affinity for creative writing, specifically poetry, she shared, "A small cape style home at 47 Old Oaken Bucket Road, here in town, was the inspiration for 'The Old Oaken Bucket;' a poem written by Samuel Woodworth in 1817. This literary gem transcended time with its popularity expanding to include a famous song by the same name. Have you ever heard of it before?"

"Scituate, fittingly nicknamed the Irish Riviera, was home to more Irish immigrants than any other nationality, tallying at a consistent fifty percent. This migration was driven by the discovery of the Irish mossing hotbed in Scituate's coastal waters in the late 1800s. It led to the economic boom for this sweet little shore town nestled on the shoreline between Boston and Cape Cod.

"But it's not all a bed of roses here," she forewarned. "For the maritime buffs, numerous ships have fallen victim to the unforgiving forces of the infamous nor'easters laying many ships to rest along our rocky coast. The Portland Gale of 1898, and the Etrusco of 1956, were two of the more widely written about shipwrecks off the coast of Scituate.

"However, all in all, it is a terrific town to live and raise children. If and when you come to Massachusetts, and I hope you do… you can see for yourself." She closed the letter with a litany of things she needed to do, starting with preparing dinner for the family. She wished him well and thanked him again for his service. "Take care, and please know that we are remembering you and your friends in our prayers. Sincerely, Joan."

***

He folded up the letter and tucked it away in his left shirt pocket over his heart to take it along with him the next morning when he headed out for 0800 rollcall. He was sure he would want to take this literary trip again and again while out on this five-day reconnaissance patrol. He spent the next hour tending to the things he needed to do at basecamp and then laid down for the night with thoughts of Scituate racing around his head. What tomorrow will bring was always a mystery, but he knew for sure there was a family in Scituate, Massachusetts, who cared about him and his wellbeing. Now, if he could just survive the next five days while out on patrol. Unfortunately, that is always hanging in the balance in war.

Chapter 12

Some Kind of Wonderful

I t's hard to imagine how a unit could head out on what they believe to be a five-day mission, carrying supplies for five, six, or seven days, allowing for some forgiveness, but having it turn into a twelve-day patrol. Rationing their food and water for a mission that unexpectedly was extended almost three-fold, had to have been near impossible. Paling in comparison but enough to turn many-a-stomachs was their inability to shower. Multi-day patrols, coupled with the fact that when sitting still in the jungles, strictly forbidden to make a sound, you were out of luck when nature called, yet this was their reality. The lucky ones returned to their garrison, but more likely a bivouac, a temporary camp without tents or cover. The men would return thoroughly exhausted, a few pounds lighter and a mess. This existence was Bob's Army life; he chose it and never complained.

He returned to temporary basecamp greeted by a pile of letters from Dad's students and a letter from Mama. He was so moved by the number of the letters from the boys that before regrouping from the patrol and reading them all, he immediately shot out a short letter to her thanking her repeatedly. Later that same day, after an enjoyable dinner, he read through each and every message. It took him every bit of two hours to do this. He shared them with his comrades and couldn't help but feel like a celebrity having received so many letters. Perhaps, as a result, he felt compelled to write to her again later that night.

April 7/66

Hello Joan and Family:

I sincerely hope this finds the family in the best of health and enjoying the many splendors of spring. For me, I am doing just fine. I feel so good today; I mean terrific! We had been running through these jungles for the past nine days and nights without a break; eating rice and c-ration and getting 2-3 hours sleep a night, until last night. We rejoined our battalion and were placed in reserve, where we have been all day. Earlier this morning, we were allowed to go to the river to swim and wash our clothes. We all have been wearing our clothing for 12 days without a change, so you can imagine how great it felt to do both.

Then came your letters! I wasn't able to read through them all until after dinner, which was another treat, hot chow. All these good things make me think that we have a really big mission coming up. It always seems to work this way.

I must admit, I thoroughly enjoyed each letter from Paul's students. I will send over anything I deem worthy to help them understand what is actually happening over here. Knowledge is power. It seems as though Mr. Hunter keeps them up to date with the action over here. He is a man I highly admire. Judging from your letters, he is very devoted to his profession. Many of the Non-Coms (corporals and sergeants) are single because their devotion can only be to one. Paul is devoted to both his family and his profession, which is rare and quite admirable.

You know something, Joan, it is funny about this place... even though you don't know what is waiting for you on each trail or behind each tree, I think this is one of the most beautiful countries I have ever seen. When you go to the coast, you see the clear China Sea, so calm and clear; the white sandy beach touching the jungle's edge. Up in the mountains, you can look down into the jade green valleys and fertile rice paddies. I mean, it is spectacular!

Yesterday, as we flew over the jungles and mountains in the helicopter looking for Viet Cong, I felt like a giant eagle gliding over God's country. I cringe when I watch the pristine green jungle being barbarically invaded and destroyed by substantial raging fiery flames to rid the enemy of hiding areas. I think of how it is no sin to kill Viet Congs or any man, but surely it is a sin to set fire to nature. Perhaps, I feel this way because most of my life has been spent in the city. The Infantry has taught me to love the countryside. I know that even now, when I lay in my sleeping bag and look up at the sky, it looks like a big sea, with billions of little diamonds in it. It makes me feel truly free for that moment anyway. Still, I never fall into a false sense of security because I know the sky may turn into the 4th of July at any given moment with rocket artillery shells and the smell of gun smoke. Everything here seems to be so unreal. When the jungle is still and peaceful, you can't believe that there is a war going on here with men trying to kill each other. Every time I see a dead man, comrade, or enemy soldier, I say he is only asleep. It is all so unreal.

Please ask Mr. Hunter to speak to the boys and tell them that the men here are proud to know that we have a healthy reserve backing us up, though we hope to have this war over by the time they finish school. But they must finish school first. A man cannot go very far without an education today, in civilian life or the Army.

With Affection,
Bobby

***

Bob retired to his bedroll, filled with a sense of contentment. He is back from a job well done, cleaned up, organized, and proud, having rejuvenated his battalion by sharing his letters. He drifted off to sleep, thinking, *I just may be the luckiest man on Earth.*

Not more than seven days later, while sitting in the company orderly room on CQ (Charge of Quarters), a soldier, donning a canvas pouch hanging around his neck and across his chest, approached Bob. Tossing him an envelope, he announced, "Looks like another Operation Morale Booster letter, sir." Bob's eyes lit up as he excitedly grabbed the letter off the ground, marveling at the speed at which he and Mama were able to correspond across the world and during wartime. He tore open the envelope and read:

April 15, 1966

Dear Bob,

Well, now I have two letters from you to answer, so here goes! Your recent assignment sounds very interesting and also very, very dangerous. Be careful. Paul seems to know and understand what your job is there. I don't remember if I told you already or not, but he was in the Army for a short while, and he, too, loves the Infantry and thinks that it is the most crucial division. Paul was in the ROTC (Reserve Officers' Training Corps) program in college and graduated from college with the 2nd Lieutenant's rank. Post-graduation, he spent six months active duty (here in the states) and was in Inactive Reserve for about six years, going to weekly meetings and attending a two-week summer camp. He got out a year ago with the rank of Captain. Don't hold that against him, though. (smile) He, too, used to love to sleep out at night and look up at the sky and stars. He says there is nothing like it. As for me... I'd rather be inside!

I must tell you that I am happy you seem to admire Paul because he genuinely does admire you. He enjoys reading all your letters, as do I. You have a knack of expressing your thoughts and dreams, which not everyone can do. Paul tells me that you must be a courageous soldier to be a Ranger and a Paratrooper. You seem to have a great philosophy on life, and you come across in your letters as a really nice person to know. Well, enough flattery for one day!!! I don't want you to get a big head!! (smile)

Maryellen was most happy to hear you loved her note. Up 'til then, she was a little jealous about the time I spend writing to soldiers. At that age, children demand all your attention and time, and she couldn't understand why I was always writing letters to soldiers. Now, she has a different attitude and is happy to see me getting messages and answering them.

When you come back to the States, you will be quite surprised to see how much the Black community has advanced in the past few years. There have been many changes for them, and many more will come, I hope. You will see many Black folks doing the news, doing many commercials, and having significant parts in the programs on television. Our Attorney General of Massachusetts, Edward Brooke, is the highest elected official in the United States of the Black race.

He will probably run for the Senate this coming election. So, you see, Bob, things have changed some for the Black community and will continue to do so.

The way you describe Vietnam does sound like a beautiful place, and it does seem a sin to harm its natural beauty with war. I hope the war ends before too much more is damaged, and too many more lives are lost. The political troubles that we hear about are very alarming. What a crazy mixed-up world we live. You have to learn, as you have, to enjoy all the little things and do the very best you can each day and hope and pray for the future.

Well, Bob, I hope you make the rank of sergeant real soon. Let us know when you do. When you come home in November, you will be most welcome in our home. Take care, and please know that we remember you and your friends in our prayers.

Sincerely,
Joan

***

"You will be most welcome in our home," he repeated. Fixated on her parting words, even mesmerized by it. *Wow, can it be true? They have never met me, and we have only been communicating for a couple of months. I am a soldier fighting a war, and I am a Black man.* Dumbfounded, Bob reflected on all that had transpired in his heart since that fateful day, less than two months ago, when he grabbed her letter from that pile.

His mind wandered off to her comments on the amelioration of the Black race in the United States. Although he was happy to hear of such advancements, he couldn't help but think of the stark contrast racial equality held in the Army; same countrymen, set in a very different scenario. Men in the Army lived, survived, and died together. They risked their lives for each other daily without hesitation, bonded by their mission and love for the country. There was no regard or significance placed on the color of one's skin. He couldn't help but wonder if he'd be better to stay in the Army where he felt "social equality," as he liked to call it instead of leaving the Army when this war is over and returning to a country still plagued with racial discrimination. *Ah, I guess I can cross that bridge when I come to it. First, we need to end this war;* he re-centered his thoughts.

He took one last indulgent moment to reread her ending two sentences a few more times before folding up the typed letter and tucking it in his left shirt pocket. He had to put his thoughts of visiting Scituate and the Hunter family to the back of his mind while on duty but secretly hoped for time to pass without incident so he could get back to his bedroll to scribe a quick note to her later that night.

Writing by candlelight, Bob scribbled a few thoughts that had lingered in the back of his mind ever since he read her letter earlier in the day. As always, he began his letter:

"With each stroke of this pen, I hope this finds the family in the best of health and enjoying all that spring may have to offer. As for myself, I am doing just fine. You know, it seems funny how a few words can ease a troubled mind. Each time I receive a letter from you, I feel relaxed even though many times, it is only for a moment. But over here, sometimes a moment can be a lifetime. However, the time has no meaning over here, it is only night and day. For some reason, I seem to love the nighttime best."

He elaborated by sharing his thoughts on the peacefulness of the night's sky despite many soldiers' belief that the night brings death. For him, the still of the night, coupled with the stars' brilliance, lured him to daydream about desires for his future. Post-war, he envisioned going to school and getting an education in graphic arts at the University of Maryland. Upon graduation and employment, he hoped to buy himself a small home in North Carolina on the GI Bill. Once fortified with a diploma, job, and home, he would begin his search for a wife and start a family.

"I have often thought of someday getting married and having a small family, but I know that as long as I am in the Army, they would have to be second in my life. Don't get me wrong, I don' t mean that I would not strive for the best for them, because I would, but I have to place the Army and my country above all. I hope to get out of the service next year, but if the war is not any better, I probably will stay in longer to train the young men who will be rolling in as the next sea of infantry. I have seen too many young men die here as a result of insufficient training before arriving. When the time is right, and my duty is done, I will return to the States and start a family."

But until then, he explained, he was entirely devoted to the Army. "It is just safer this way." He justified. Additionally, he admitted that he feared having a woman on his mind while in combat, causing him to make a misstep in a moment of daydreaming, costing him his life or that of one of his comrades.

Marshaling his thoughts about his enemy, he offered some perspectives to be passed on to Dad's students:

"I was thrilled to know that the boys in Mr. Hunter's class are interested in Vietnam. I am sending a pamphlet on the Viet Cong soldier. It is funny that when you sit down and think about it, the Viet Cong feel that they are fighting for right, answering the call to nationalism. They have been under foreign domination for over a hundred years. First, ruled by China in the 1400s, followed by the French for the last hundred years. Even Japan crept in a military presence at the borders during the 1940s. So, you see, many Vietnamese are dedicated to Vietnam itself and not necessarily communism. Much like we are dedicated to America and our belief in democracy. The spread of communism will be the byproduct of their victory, so that's why we have declared them enemies of the United States."

***

I was so impressed by reading Bob's letters in that he felt it was important for him to share his unbiased and honest thoughts on the Viet Cong, the enemy whose tactics were of barbaric guerilla warfare. It would have been easy to believe that all the soldiers had strong detest for them, and to some degree, they had to raise arms against them. But being true to himself and his genuine love for all of humanity, he offered his point of view to be shared with the students' young minds. His dissecting the concept of right and wrong, illuminating the fact that to the Viet Cong, they believed they were justified in their beliefs and actions just as strongly as the American soldiers thought they were right to raise arms against them. I reread a line from one of his letters that I felt was a quintessential patriotic declaration that might be heard from any person who takes up arms on behalf of their country:

"May America always be true and right, but right or wrong, still my country, for I shall stand by her and guide her."

Bob finished up this letter, "It's late at night, and my candle is just about to burn out, so I must come to a quick close. Candles are worth their weight in gold over here, our only means of light at night." I laughed; he already knew Mama well enough to know, the next package he received would include a bunch of candles.

As Divine Providence continued to protect him, just as he rolled to the side to snuff out the diminishing candle, without warning the sound of a sniper shot… svifft whizzed by him, just inches from his head; this was the reality of their existence. As Bob described it in his next letter, "When you can feel the heat, and hear the snap, you know it was close." The Viet Cong were everywhere, and they were nowhere, moving about like phantoms, only attacking when undetectable, retreating when they weren't. Not an hour of life was taken for granted in the jungles of Vietnam. Those soldiers void of religion when they arrived, sought one very quickly, as there was no rhyme or reason as to who made it through each day.

Chapter 13

Feel Like I'm Fixin' to Die

Back in the States, Mama had been full throttle executing her Operation Morale Booster mission. She marched her way into the kids' school and knocked on Mr. Curtis' door, the Wampatuck Elementary School principal. "Come in," he permitted. Mama opened the door and announced her arrival with friendly fanfare. His eyes lit up only slightly less than his smile as he jumped up to greet her. Mama approached the desk and extended her hand across to offer a proper handshake, but Mr. Curtis just looked at her hand, then back up at her eyes, and then again back down at her extended hand. "A handshake?" he asked as he hesitantly reached for her hand.

"Yes, a handshake. Today, I am here on professional business." She could get away with such antics as he had been close friends with Mama for the better part of a decade, having married one of her best friends. "Jim, I think you need to be a part of my mission: Operation Morale Booster," she excitedly proposed, eyes brimming with anticipation.

"What sort of mission is this, Joan?" he probed beaming a brilliant smile that twinkled his eyes.

"It's a writing campaign to show support for our young soldiers in Vietnam. Essentially, I am wondering if you would be open to welcoming your students to write a letter or draw a picture for a soldier, so the soldiers in Vietnam know they have not been forgotten. I will collect them and send them to the battalions I am already connected with."

Clapping his hands together in one loud gesture of mutual excitement, "Okay, sounds good to me, Joan. How do you plan to execute this?"

"I'm glad you asked," holding back the happy grin, "I happened to bring along some flyers to display in the teachers' room explaining the mission and the logistics." Mama handed the principal her flyers.

He chuckled as this ambush of hers was quintessential Joan, great heart, a dash of feistiness, and a boat-load of organizational skills.

"Well, Joan, you have made it difficult to say 'no,' so let's get started with Operation Morale Booster Comes to Wampatuck!" Jim concluded with the warmest smile and a firm handshake.

In just a couple of months, she had the students corresponding with twenty-one soldiers ranging in age from eighteen to twenty-eight, and having come from twelve different states. The children wrote of their uncles serving in Vietnam and the pen-pals, being sensitive to this, always made sure to let them know their "uncle says hello." Each of the notes from the soldiers were riveting but one was beyond astounding. As I read it aloud to Mama, I got chills with each line.

An Khe
April/66

Dear Mrs. Hunter and students,

I am very sorry I couldn't answer your letter sooner, but we have been swamped going from mission to mission in the field and going through the hardships of an infantry soldier. We are dirty, filthy, and have no water to drink most of the time and are just trying to stay alive one more day. It is dreadful here, but the American people don't know it, but God knows the truth.

I was born in Havana, Cuba, but came to America to seek freedom from government tyranny. I am a regular soldier, so I volunteered to go to Vietnam. I feel it is my duty as a soldier and an American to be here fighting for what my country believes; that all men are created equal and that all mankind deserves to be free and this freedom is the only way to make the world a better world.

We will stop communism here to prove they won't take over the world, little by little, as they say, they will do.

Cuba was once a beautiful island, but the communists took it over, and now it is a place where people who were once free, are no longer free. The communist government feels their people are only bodies with no feelings and no rights because they belong to the party-state. This philosophy is why people escape Cuba by the hundreds every day, seeking a place to live free and be happy again. Additionally, it's why so many Cubans have come to America, the "land of the FREE" and "home of the BRAVE." Once they have the opportunity to live again and be happy and work for a new way of life, many of them join in the Army and volunteer for Vietnam to fight and die under the American flag because they are proud to fight for a country that embraces freedom and pursuit of happiness.

I have been in the Army for fourteen years, and I have been to many countries, and there is no place in the world like the GOOD USA, America, the Beautiful... but sadly, Americans don't realize this.

Please tell the students that we read all their letters at the Cambodia border. Although we had to bury them there, they did boost our morale. It is good to know people care for us in the States, so thank you again.

We lost a few boys at the Cambodia border, and our platoon leader and 2nd Lieutenant got hit pretty bad. We head out again on the 23rd to back to Bong Son, where we lost seventeen men last February. The majority of them were Hispanics from Texas; this is where I am from as well. They are all very young, but none of us complain. Live or die; we know we are fighting for a good cause; freedom for mankind. If I live through this war, I can go home proud because I fought for my country, America! I have three children. My baby was only a few days old when I was deployed.

Well, thank you again for your letters of support. We appreciate them more than you can imagine. Please say hello to your husband.

Sincerely,
Jorge

***

"First of all, WOW, that was some letter! But Mama, you're so cute! Listen to a part of your response."

"From your experience of watching your home of Cuba, being taken over by communists, you can appreciate the USA. Please don't be too harsh on those Americans who don't already realize how fortunate they are. It is true, we sometimes take too much for granted, and don't know the hardships others who don't have freedoms as we do. It is because we have never come that close to losing our freedom..."

***

Mama concluded, "Yes, Mr. Curtis was thrilled at the response and touted to other elementary schools in town about how the Wampatuck students were getting a lesson on patriotism that couldn't be learned by simply reading a book or singing a song. This mission had taken on a life of its own, and I couldn't have been more thrilled. It was fulfilling for all of us."

Little four-year-old Billy, was even given a roll in the Operation Morale Booster logistics. Not quite in full-time school yet, he was able to meet Mr. Baker, the kind old mailman, at the curb every day to accept the letters with a big smile and firm salute. Executing an about-face, he would march back into the house and dump all the mail onto the kitchen table. He would separate all the envelopes adorned with the red, white, and blue stripes along the perimeter and those stamped with "AIRMAIL Free Postage Vietnam." Using her ornate silver letter opener, Mama would pierce the top of the envelope and surgically tear open the top seam. Carefully removing the letter and any accompanying newspaper articles, she would read through the day's mail and set them aside to share with Dad later that night. Bob's envelope, always placed on the top of the pile.

Cpl. Robert E. Johnson
RA 13638238 Recon Plt.
Delta Company 2/7 Cav.1st Cav.
Airmobile Div. APO
San Francisco, 96490 Calif

April 23/66

Hi Joan,

I was just sitting here in my tent, relaxing. I thought that I would take this opportunity to write to you. For the past three days, my platoon has been here in a small seaport town named Qui Nhon. It is right on the coast of the South China Sea. To us, this is the same as being on vacation. I guess by now you are probably wondering why we are here.

Our trucks have been getting hi-jacked while enroute from Qui Nhon to An Khe, the town where our Division is based, about eighty miles from here. Anyway, about one of every three truckloads of supplies never get to us. So, we were pulled off the combat line to escort these trucks to Division. So far, we have not lost any vehicles or had any trouble except a little sniper fire. We have it made. We work in five groups, four hours on duty, and eight hours off. Almost every day, I have been going to the beach; it is lovely.

I hope Mr. Hunter and the boys like the pamphlet I sent to you concerning the Viet Cong Army. I read it and liked it very much. It told me a lot about the Viet Cong that I did not know or fully understand.

I am delighted that you offered to welcome me to your home as a guest. Thank you very much; however, I don't think that I will be returning to the USA in November, as I initially thought. The reason being, next month I go up for reclassification. At this time, I will be given the choice of where I want to be stationed when I get back, but I think I am going to extend my tour of duty over here for six months or until my discharge date, which is in June of next year. I have not decided what I will do yet. There is so much that I want to do, but each call for sacrifice on my part. For example, over here, I feel like someone, and I have a purpose, plus I make much more money, which I definitely will need all I can get when I do get out. In Vietnam, I make $410 a month. In the States, I only make $352 a month.

I am putting $385 a month in the bank, so you see, the remaining six more months will mean a lot. Plus, I don't think I would feel right sitting in the States where it is safe. So, it is a little bit of a problem. If I return to the states in November, I will have plenty of time to look around and decide where I want to go to school and buy my home on the GI Bill. Perhaps, I will have my mind made up by then. Whatever I do, if it is wrong, I can blame it on fate. (smile)

Well, it is about time I start cleaning my weapon and checking on my squad—some of these guys you have to act as a mother or a father. For many of them, this is like being in the middle of the ocean.

So, until the next time.
Bob

P.S. Perhaps the next time I write, I will have a picture for you. (smile)

***

For Mama, the idea of being able to put a face to the name was momentarily overwhelming. Anxious to respond, she stole a few minutes to compose a letter while Billy was busy playing with his toys.

May 6, 1966

Dear Bob,

...The other night on Channel 2, the educational channel here in Boston, we saw a documentary on the war filmed by some Canadians. It was a bit different from what we see on the nightly newsreels, more sadistic, gorier, dirtier, and a little too depressing for me to watch. I can't explain it except to say the whole thing is pretty ugly. Boy, now you also have to deal with the monsoon season; you men are slopping around in the mud. This film did an excellent job showing how entangled and muddy the jungles are that you have to make your way through.

I am finally sending you a picture I had made up this week from our Christmas slides. We look forward to receiving one of you!

As I am upstairs typing this letter, I can hear the news on the radio downstairs describing a big battle the GIs of the 1st Cavalry are winning right now, about 270 miles northeast of Saigon along the coast. As I can picture in my mind, that is about where you are, right? Between this and your escorting missions, you must be pretty busy.

I am glad you got a chance to have "a vacation" as you put it. You have an admirable way of looking at the bright side of things. Is the water warm or cold for swimming? The water here in Scituate is frigid. We like to call it refreshing. It sounds better that way.

Well, Bob, please take care of yourself, and God Bless you.

Sincerely,
Joan

***

No sooner did she get this in the mail, when another letter from Bob arrived...written on American Red Cross stationery. This letterhead immediately gave her heart cause to skip a beat.

American Red Cross Hospital

May 4/66

Hi Joan:

I sincerely hope that this letter finds you and Mr. Hunter in the best of health and enjoying all that the spring may offer. As for myself, I am doing fine, although not in the best of health. Currently, I am at Clark Airfare Base hospital in the Philippines, on my way to Japan. I came down with malaria two weeks ago, just after my last letter. For three days, I had to sit in a bed of ice to keep my fever down, which hovered between 103 and 105 degrees. I have it pretty bad and will be in Japan for approximately two months as a result. From there, I will either be sent home to the States or back to Vietnam.

I am beginning to get sick again, so I have to go. Please excuse this letter for being so short.

Always,
Robert

***

The stationery and the formal sign-off rattled Mama. Mixed emotions enveloped her heart knowing he was once again in the hospital, but simultaneously grateful that he was not in the current hotbed of fighting in Qui Nhon. In her eyes, coming down with malaria may have saved his life.

May 9, 1966

Dear Bob,

...The American Red Cross stationery was a little alarming as I figured you had been wounded again. That malaria must be an awful thing to keep you in the hospital for such a long time. Be assured that we will keep you well supplied with letters and whatever else you wish to receive if we can send it.

The past weekend we were thinking of you quite often as the news had much about a fierce battle near the coast of Qui Nhon. I figured that was the place you described with the scenic beaches, right? The news said they were killing VC by the hundreds and described our casualties as "fairly light." Just what does that mean?

Well, Bob, political troubles in Vietnam and the war, in general, have become quite emotive subjects, dividing and confusing to many people. I only wish everyone would put the guns away for a while, sit down, and straighten out our position and come up with a game plan. It seems such a sin for human lives to be lost while the world's leaders are deciding what "our policy" in Vietnam is going to be.

Please don't be in a hurry to return there when you are better from malaria. But, as you said, "fate" will decide your future. Good luck, and know our thoughts and prayers go with you, whatever you choose.

Yesterday was Mother's Day in the States. We had a delightful day with a visit from my parents. Paul's parents came down for dinner on Thursday instead because his father is a Boston City Police Officer and works on Sundays. We had a beautiful day showing the grandparents some recent home movies we took of the kids since Christmas. We have them coasting, ice skating, roller skating, and climbing on the breakwater rocks near the lighthouse here in Scituate. These movies are great treasures and are great to save and look back on when the kids grow up. It sure doesn't take very long for them to grow, and it is hard to remember when they were so small. All in all, it was a lovely day.

Well, old friend, please take care of yourself and fight that malaria as well as you fight the VC.

As always, in our thoughts and prayers,
Joan

***

Mama finished reading her letter but continued to openly reflect, "Grabbing the envelope, I inserted this letter with visible hesitance. I remember something felt different this time. Like this time, we may not hear back from him. I took a lasting look at the family picture I was including and tried to pour all the love and support I could into this jagged-edged vintage color photo. As I did, I couldn't help but wonder what he looked like. I wondered if his eyes revealed that of the brave soldier he portrayed in his letters, or those of a dutiful son, who was projecting bravery only to protect the hearts of his loved ones.

"My mind wandered to his mother. Does she even know that he has been stricken with malaria? Does she know that he has been writing to her? If something happens to him, how will we ever find out, we are not family? Before allowing my spiraling thoughts to gain momentum, I calmed myself and offered up a prayer. 'Lord, I find comfort knowing his wellbeing is in Your hands, and I only pray for Your will be done.' Sealing and stamping the envelope, I hurried down to see Mr. Fallon at the General Store to get the letter in that day's mail and then make it back in time to get the kids off the school bus."

Mama went about her usual duties over the next few days, never allowing Bob's wellbeing to stray too far from the forefront of her mind. Filling a care package with art supplies and the promised candy from Mr. Fallon lifted her spirits, and she had hoped it would do the same for him. He was the only soldier Mama was writing to who was suffering from malaria. It was ironic that of all the dangers the soldiers faced in Vietnam, an insect was the one she now feared most.

It seemed like forever since she had heard from Bob, and she feared the worst. It was May 20, his birthday, and all she could think about was if he was able to celebrate his 25th birthday or not. Mama decided to make a cake, celebrate it for him, and then send him a picture of the family. She was preoccupied with making the cake in the kitchen; she forgot to send Billy out to the curb to meet the mailman. Instead, Mr. Baker came knocking on the screen door and shouting into the house, "You've got mail from Vietnam, Mrs. Hunter." She wiped her hands upon her apron and anxiously scurried toward the door.

Chapter 14

I'd Love to Change the World

US Army Hospital Camp Zuma
Japan. APO San Francisco 96343 Calif

May 13/66!!!

Hi Joan and Paul:

I received your letter today. I was happy to hear from you. Today is Friday the 13th, and I woke up this morning with the feeling that my day was going to be all wrong, and that is precisely how it started. First, my temperature went back up to 103 degrees, which meant I was put back into the icebox. My doctor also told me that my old shoulder wound had to be re-operated due to old particles left in it. So, you see how my day started. Then at noon, I received your letter, which seemed to change everything.

As for myself, I am doing just fine, although they are having problems keeping my temperature down. Each time it goes up, they have to bed me down in ice cubes. As awful as it is, putting me in ice is the only way to control it, and believe me, it is hell (excuse the expression). My doctor told me this morning that I have to be here for at least another month. I don't think I will be able to make it that long, and I told him this. This place is driving me crazy. (smile) I can't stand confinement or to be cooped up. I know that they have to have it this way, but it is just getting to me. It has been three weeks now. They were thinking about sending me back to the States, which is still in the wind. I signed a statement last week stating that I wanted to go back to Qui Nhon, even at the point of perhaps getting a relapse, which could result in death.

Malaria is a funny kind of disease. A man can get it, and it not bother him for another ten years, and then it comes back and kills him. Some of the guys that are here have been here as long as three or four months. I wish I could find a way to surrender and just accept my present situation. The Red Cross volunteers bring us books and magazines to read, but somehow it seems as if I can't get enough to read since I hardly sleep at night and only an hour or two during the day. So, reading is the only thing I do.

I also have been keeping up with the news in Vietnam. As you said, "The war in Vietnam is very confusing." - especially when you are not there to know what is going on. Vietnam is a mental war more than a shooting one. Sure, a lot of Viet Cong are being killed and a lot more Americans than you can imagine, a whole lot more. The worst part, as for the fighting men, is that you wait, and wait, for Charlie; maybe two to three months pass by, and we may only get sniper fire here and there, then all hell breaks loose. It's not like World War II or Korea, where you knew who you were fighting, and there's the enemy's side, and there's our side. Vietnam has no physically definable enemies and no front lines. The kids, women, and men you see every day in the rice paddies and fields are those we fight at night.

As for the political aspect of the war, it sure is confusing. We are beginning to think that the efforts to stop this war have ceased somewhere along the line—duplicity at its finest. You see, Joan, this is a big deal for everyone. There are big shots on both sides getting rich off of this war. Just sit and think of how much our government is spending on shipping men and supplies over here using commercial transport. Think of all the new factories manufacturing war materials; think of how many people at home who were out of work now have jobs because of this war. Do you want to know what is most upsetting? We are getting killed by our weapons, yes, armaments made in the USA. Most of the firearms captured from the Viet Cong are weapons made by the USA, old and new.

During March and April, we were on a mission along the Cambodian border. The Viet Cong jumped us and ran across the border, knowing we were not allowed to go after them because of political reasons. They actually have areas where we are not permitted to fire our weapons. I know you have heard of all the tons of rice we captured. Have you ever wondered what we do with it? Well, I will tell you: we give it back to the Vietnamese, who are quite often Viet Cong when we should be destroying all of it.

As for it being a sin for human lives to be lost while the world's leaders decide our fate, I agree, but in their eyes, what is one life or a thousand? Power and greed seem to be a substitute for everything. You know for every enemy soldier killed over here, there are four men to replace him the next day. We have the manpower and weapons to defeat the communists if allowed, but we are forbidden. Many in our country feel this is wrong for us to be involved; this we may never really know. But right or wrong; still our country and we must stand by her until the end.

You said that the news at home reported our casualties as "light," and what does that mean? Well, to begin with, for security reasons, our casualty numbers are never given, nor are the units involved. This practice keeps the Viet Cong from getting an accurate account of our strength and damage affected. But believe me, often these numbers are incredibly high. To give you a general idea, last November, in Ia Drang, my company lost all but nine out of the two-hundred men. Months later, during Operation Masher, when I was shot on the 28th of January, we had landed on the LZ at 0800 in the morning, and an hour later, we had forty-seven men wounded, fifteen killed. That battle lasted two days; even our wounded fought to the death. We eliminated 400 VC in twenty-four hours. This operation was when I got my Bronze Star. Eleven other men and I were separated and cut off from the company for eighteen hours. I was wounded as was most of the other men, but we killed twenty-two PAVN. I had to kill five men in hand-to-hand combat. This last big battle you mentioned hearing on the radio was near the coast of Qui Nhon; the name of the area is Bong Son - this is the very same place where we did all of this fighting in Operation Masher. It took us forty-three days of constant battle. We then turned this area over to the South Vietnamese Army, and what happened…three months later, we had to go back and retake it; the futility of it all wreaking havoc on the psyche. This war is a real rat race. I will surely be glad when it is over, but I don't think I would feel right sitting somewhere safe and sound as I am now in this hospital with the war going on. I feel committed and obligated to be there on the front lines. I will be relieved to get back to work. Don't think I am mad or a sadist - I just feel this way. Each man is supposed to have a purpose in life, and I guess this is mine. It is a good thing that I am not the President because I would bomb Hanoi, Peking, Moscow, and Paris with de Gaulle in it. (smile)

Since I have been in the hospital, I have become a poet. Would you like to read what I wrote? It's not done... I have a bit in the middle I still aim to complete. Well, whether you do or not, here it goes. (smile)

Soldier standing oh so tall, waiting to answer his country's call.
He stands to serve her well, from the clouds of heaven to the gates of hell.

Wearing a green uniform, he has served America since the day he was born.
From Yorktown to the icy banks of the Delaware shores,
He fought without fear throughout the long year.

Here in Vietnam, he stands to fight on another foreign land. He serves America and NATO now, but his goal is still the same.
Here, he stands for freedom's name.

In Ia-Drang Valley and An Lo his blood ran free.
For America and Liberty.

Here he is seen in the Army green,
Some wearing the green beret~ others with silver wings on their chest.
The whole world knows that here stand's America's best.

*** "I still need to add a part in here" (smile)***

Here he stands without any doubt –
he is determined to stomp communism out.
I am that soldier standing tall, waiting to answer my country's call.

I had some postcards picked up at the hospital in Japan. It is a stunningly beautiful country but nowhere near as impressive as our country, America, the great. I thought perhaps; you would like to see what it looks like. Although you still see all the old Japanese structures around, most of the old customs are gone. It has become westernized, similar to our own country. I have not been able to see if it has changed any since the last time I was here in 1961 and '62, but I intend to do so.

From what I understand, I will be getting fourteen days' leave when I get out of the hospital, and before I go back to Vietnam. Perhaps I will be able to pick you up some kind of souvenir. I would like to show you my sincere gratitude for your friendship, so whether you intend to accept it or not, I am still going to send it to you. I also believe I will be able to send you a picture of myself soon.

In two weeks, I should be able to leave the hospital area. At present, I am not allowed out of my ward area, which is like being in a large cell. I am glad to know that I will live to see another birthday, which, for a while, looked as though I would not. (smile) I will be twenty-five on the twentieth, getting old.

As for fighting this malaria, it can beat a guy up pretty bad. I was 165 pounds when I arrived three weeks ago; now I am down to 143 pounds. I burn up for fifteen minutes, and then I freeze for fifteen minutes. I'd much rather get shot. Every morning they take blood out of me for blood tests. The quinine they give me stops me from eating. I have three to four bowel movements a day. It is beginning to slow down, but it still leaves me pretty weak. Well, friend, I have to close now and please don't worry about me.

So, until the next time,
Bobby

P.S. I apologize for my sloppy handwriting; I am writing on a notepad while sitting in my bed. I was looking through today's paper, and they had a list of the amount of US Troops killed since the war started. I don't know whether they tell you how many are killed in the news. Here are some clippings.

***

These articles, in pristine condition, were still in the envelope. Mama meticulously unfolded the newspapers, which spanned four pages. She studied each. The first headline, 82 US Troops Killed, showcased the number of US troops killed during the week of May 7th, with an additional mention of 615 WIA (Wounded in Action). According to the article, it was the second week since January 1, 1961, in which America suffered more KIA (Killed in Action) than the enemy. These latest statistics brought the total American deaths to 1,386 in the first quarter of 1966. Comparatively, the enemy KIA topped at 16,514 for the same period.

The second clipping was a gray-scaled map labeled Action in Vietnam. The territories of, Cambodia, Thailand, Red China, Laos and Hainan (southernmost island of China), North Vietnam, and the Republic of Vietnam were marked, and bold arrows indicated where the US had executed significant airstrikes. Bob added notations in blue ink where the 1st Cavalry had lost the big battle of Ia Drang in November 1965, as well as just south of there, where he had been assigned before getting malaria.

The third clipping was an article detailing the achievements of Operations Maili, Wayne, Montgomery, and Birmingham. The Flying Horsemen were noted as having captured several weapons, including an M16 rifle, which was believed to be the first M16 seized from the VC. The Third Marine Division Leathernecks, finishing a four-day sweep just southwest of Hue, executed the confiscation of 20,000 pounds of rice. At the same time, the First Infantry Division claimed 107 VC KIA, twenty-six captured and twenty-eight detained for questioning, while simultaneously seizing a total of 1,850 tons of rice.

I couldn't help but comment, "Well, after reading his letter, I don't see why they considered the capturing of rice as an achievement when it's ultimately returned to them."

"I didn't either," Mama agreed, "but I just focused on the fact that I had heard from him and that his spirits seemed a little brighter than in his previous letter. I was more confident at this point that he was going to see his 25th birthday."

May 20, 1966

Dear Bob,

Well, I thought you were going to get your first experience reading a letter from me written in script. I did write this whole letter on the front steps in my handwriting but just couldn't stand to send it, so here I am back at the typewriter. My handwriting is so poor that I am ashamed to send it to you or anyone. So, don't ever feel as though you have to apologize for your writing. It couldn't be worse than mine. OK?

******** HAPPY BIRTHDAY*********

I was glad you told me it was your birthday because I felt it was coming soon (by your first letter when you said you were "almost twenty-five") so I sent you a card in anticipation of it being so. My good friend and neighbor, Marilou, was so kind as to drive me to the harbor to get you a card and get it into the mail. I wanted to be sure you received it in time for your big day. Now, you are a quarter of a century-old!! Doesn't that make you feel ancient? I should talk, huh? I just turned thirty last January. That was rough!!

The harbor is what we call our shopping center. It is a beautiful harbor, and in the summer, it is teeming with boats. I hope you will see it someday. There are many sailboats and small motorboats, as well as plenty of large yachts. We don't own a boat as the children are so small and can't swim yet. Someday, Paul wants to get a small boat with an outboard motor so he and the boys can go fishing and explore up and down the coastline. My folks do have a beautiful forty-two-foot Chris Craft named Kitty Wake, and they come into the harbor many weekends. When they are visiting, we do go out for cruises along the shore.

You probably think they are rich, but they aren't. Both of my parents work hard and have no other significant expenses, and they both love boating. They firmly believe "you can't take it with you," so they spend their money and enjoy life to the fullest. As I may have mentioned earlier, my father is the head electrician at the Boston Garden. This venue is where the Boston Celtics and Boston Bruins play, and the circuses come to town. It is a hectic job in the winter. He has to be there for all events, but it isn't so bad in the summer, allowing him to enjoy the boat. They are great people, and I know you would like them. I have a brother, also an electrician, who is a year younger than me. He is married to a wonderful woman, and they have a one-year-old baby girl.

Today, we received your long letter and also the pretty postcards of Japan. That National Park is, indeed, beautiful. Your bout with malaria sounds just awful. I didn't realize that it can come back in later years once you overcome it. That is not too comforting, is it? I hope you can leave the hospital real soon so you can have a much-earned vacation.

You have become quite the poet, Bob. Your poem was quite good, and you show continued talent in being able to express yourself. After your time with the Army, you should consider either becoming a writer or perhaps a minister!! At any rate… keep writing your poems. They are insightful. I intend to send your poetry to the Boston Globe (newspaper) and also to the President. I don't mess around… I go to the very top.

All you had to say about the war was very interesting but bothersome at the same time. Each newscast of the war is ever puzzling, leaving us all in a state of uncertainty. Some days it seems downright futile. I don't know about the Ky guy!!! How do you like him? He seems to be causing a great deal of trouble lately. Also, I don't like the vague terms used by the news to quantify the number of casualties at the end of each week; "light" and "heavy" are impersonal and so non-definitive.

Well, old bean, I must close for now. Take care and hope you can beat that fever soon. I bet you'll hate the sight of ice cubes after this is behind you.

Take care, and God Bless you, our friend.
Paul & Joan

***

Over the next couple of weeks, Bob continued his recovery in Japan's hospital, affording him plenty of time to work on his other creative outlets such as painting, drawing, poetry, and creating more Beetle Bailey Goes to Vietnam comic strips. During this time, the two engaged in deep conversations regarding real accounts for what is happening in Vietnam, the concept of interracial marriages, and life in general.

May/66

Hi Paul and Joan,

I hope this letter finds you enjoying all the splendors life has to offer. As for me, I am doing just fine.

I am reading today's paper... well, actually, it's tomorrow's paper. We get these newspapers a day ahead of time. Isn't that something, reading about the day's news before it happens. (smile) Anyway, it made me think of some of the questions that you had asked me in your last letter. Perhaps some of these news clippings will clear up some of your questions.

(1.) Here is a clipping of the latest KIA (Killed in Action) list. Perhaps you may know some of them. They are listed once a week. This list is only a small amount of the KIAs and does not include WIA and MIA (Wounded in Action and Missing in Action).

(2.) Details where the big battle is being fought right now. This clipping confirms the fact that the VCs are using our weapons.

(3.) The M16 is the latest weapon developed by the Army. We have only had it for about a year. How the Viet Cong got them, nobody knows.

(4.) Additional challenges we have to put up within the jungles. Tigers are eating soldiers! That's the truth!

(5.) Shows you the M16 rifles. (All of the men on the left are in my squad)

All of these clippings are out of the Stars and Stripes newspaper, exclusively distributed to servicemen overseas. It tells part of the truth, but not the whole truth. (smile) I guess this is all a part of the reality of life. It is what makes the world go around.

Sometimes I wonder what people think they prove by engaging in wars and destruction. It seems that man is defeating his purpose in life, whether it be communism or democracy. I mean, each political philosophy is trying to prove by force, which is the best way of life. I feel that freedom is for man to choose his way of life as long as it does not interfere with someone else's belief.

We, as Americans, have always been taught how wrong communism is. How can we, as individuals, say that is wrong when the only thing most of us know about it is what we read of it? If we talked to people who live in communist countries to hear what they have to say, maybe we would see things differently, maybe not. Based on the conversations I have had with our allies as well as with our prisoners, communist governments say how good their way of life is, yet they put fences up to keep their people inside, like a mass prison. How good can it be then? I believe communist governments are only good for the top few, awful for the people they rule, yet they are gaining power and momentum because they promise a bouquet of roses and people want to believe them. Russia has vowed to crush us by spreading communism, one country at a time. This momentum is why we have to stop it here, away from our shores.

On the other hand, it is said that in America, we have freedom of the press and speech. Well then, how come our newspapers and broadcasts only tell part of the truth, and in many cases an angled version of the truth? So, you see what I mean; it is all a rat race.

I was reading a book last night on interracial marriages. In the book, it stated that quite a few of our states still have laws against miscegenation. This fact not only baffles me to no end, but it also angers me. I feel if a Black man falls in love and decides to marry a White woman or vice versa, then it is his or their business; after all, no one can live their life for them. Love is love, the most beautiful of all emotions. God makes it clear that we are to love one another period. There is no asterisk qualifying that love was confined to those of similar color skin. Our skin color is merely the clothing of our souls, and He clothed us all.

In Vietnam, we die together and live as one, both Black and White, as equals. Yet, I read in the papers of all the rioting and demonstrations dividing us at home. When stationed in Germany, I almost married a German girl, just to prove that a White woman and a Black man could be happy together.

After this war, there will inevitably be another one; the war to end all wars. Until then, mixed marriages should be encouraged in the States. Eventually, there will be no differences in race or color because they will be mixed up like a fruit cake. Then our racial problems will be over. Of course, I am not serious about this ending all racial problems, but it would be nice to end all of this division and hatred. I hope to live to see this become a reality. Well, it is time for the lights to go out, so I will close for now.

As Always,
Bobby

***

The back and forth continued.

Mama: "Sadly, I think that if you had married that German girl, you would not have found that you could live as well in the States as you had hoped. The Black folks are finally gaining their rightful places in this country, but I don't think the average American (both White and Black) are quite ready to accept mixed marriages. Your feelings are very idealistic. Yes, it would be great if we were all just one big happy race with no problems. I would love that, too. However, I am no pioneer like you, so although I think the final idea of all being one race is great, I hate to think of those decades which would have to pass before this was to be fully accepted and universal. My main concern would be for the children of a mixed marriage, where either race does not completely accept them. They are the ones who would suffer greatly. Once it was fully accepted by all, or at least most, yes, it would be nice."

***

Bob: "You said you hate to think of the decades that would have to pass before interracial marriages were entirely accepted and universal. What is a decade or two? Just remember, it seems like only yesterday I was going to the movies to see Flash Gordon and Buck Rogers going to the moon. People said then; it would be decades before man would venture into outer space and reach the moon. Now, what do we have? Where is your decade? Today a dream, tomorrow a reality. (smile) It was only just yesterday; you were changing your young son's diapers. Time is only a figure of speech to complicate the mind.

"My mother once said to me that 'if you make your bed hard, you will be laying in it each night.' Meaning, if I chose to marry a White girl, and my life was hard as a result, it was all my own doing, and therefore, I must deal with it every day and every night. But one cannot always control one's emotions, and love is a strong emotion."

***

Mama and I break from reading the letters to prepare for lunch. As I mix the chicken salad, I am itching to know more about how she was feeling at that time, having this awkward conversation with a man of color at that time of heightened racial divide. "I am surprised you were so frank with Bob talking about interracial relationships. Weren't you afraid of offending him?"

"No, not really. I felt secure he knew where my heart was; we essentially wanted the same outcome. How we were going to get there was the question. We all come from various backgrounds, and as a result, we have different levels of understanding, acceptance, and risk tolerance. Whether hard to say or hard to hear, all perspectives must be respectfully brought to the table if we are ever going to have an effective dialogue of how things can move forward successfully."

I loved seeing this part of Mama; full of heart but also level headed. I think she welcomed hearing this part of herself, too. I didn't want the conversation to end as it was so engaging; it kept the demons away for the time being. We enjoyed our lunch out on the screened-in porch embracing the crisp March air, and after cleaning up the kitchen, we reconvene at the table to pick up where we had left off. A surprise was in store for me immediately upon returning to the summer of 1966.

Chapter 15

American Pie

Accompanied by an 8x10 painting, perhaps a self-portrait, Bob divulged some intimate feelings, even against "America the Great." His pride for America was waning amid this morally ambiguous war.

Bob: "Perhaps, today, I am a little depressed after reading today's paper. I included three articles that made me ashamed of my race and America. I am aware of all the anti-Vietnam war demonstrations in America today and have grown accustomed to it; I have managed to overlook most of it. But what I read today was disheartening beyond measure: Vietnam War Veterans (wounded at that) were turned away from a hotel in Chicago because they are Vietnam Veterans... A grieving mother was refused a pauper's burial plot for her son killed in Vietnam... and in a third article, a Black turncoat from the Korean War, who made a broadcast over Radio Hanoi concerning the Blacks fighting in Vietnam... and the United States is accepting him back???... What is the US coming to? What are we fighting for? If situations like these are allowed to exist, then our existence in America is no better than that of the people we are fighting. I wrote a letter to the President about my concern for the direction our country is heading and the only reply I got was, 'Sorry About That,' which has become the battle cry in Vietnam."

***

I read ahead while Mama stepped away for a few minutes to grab a tissue. "Oh Mama, I love what you wrote here," I hollered down the hall.

Mama: "I detect that you are a little down in the dumps about something and a bit bitter at the whole world in general. I, too, am a pessimist at times and sometimes think we are all going straight to ---! But good ol' Paul, the eternal optimist, quickly brings my thinking back to where it should be. Bob, what can either you or I do to change the way the world and people are? Not much. There will always be war, hate, prejudice, poverty, problems, etc. All we can do is bring as much happiness and love to the people in our daily lives. Live each day as if it may be our last and always be ready to meet God. I can already see that you enjoy all the little things of life, such as the stars at night, which you so nicely describe. These are the essential things. We cannot change the world, but maybe we can change the world for one person. My mission right now is to make your world a little brighter. Anything more than that is frosting on the cake.

"A couple of weeks ago, I saw the award-winning picture, *A Patch of Blue*. It was well done; starring Sidney Portier and Elizabeth Hartman. Hartman plays the part of a White, blind girl who lives in deplorable conditions with her awful mother. A Black social worker befriends her, the first person who has ever been kind to her, and as a result, she falls in love with him. It has a rather sad ending, but there are a few laughs in it as well. Both Portier and Hartman are masterful. Hartman is nominated for an Academy Award for her portrayal of the blind girl. If you get a chance, I highly recommend it.

"Last week was a bad one for me. I had to attend the wake of a life-long family friend. She was ninety years old and a living saint. This sweet old lady lived across the street from me growing up but was confined to her bed for the past thirty-five years due to crippling arthritis. She was adored by hundreds of children who would visit her every day. As we got older, we would bring our 'special' boyfriends over to seek her approval. On our wedding days, we would bring the entire wedding party over for inspection. We affectionately called her 'Aunt Margaret.' She was an inspiration to many of us and always offered us words of wisdom. Aunt Margaret was as youthful in her mind as any of the children. We just saw her on Easter Sunday. Over forty-five children formed a line and paraded by to show off their Easter outfits. Sitting there like a queen, she would smile and hand out dimes to each child. I loved her so much, and I am saddened to see her go. However, she will be much happier now as I am sure she is in Heaven, and it was my privilege to have known her as closely as I did. She made all of us feel special. I think that is a recipe in life to follow."

***

Good ol' Mr. Baker, always smiling and making a bugling announcement of each arriving letter from Vietnam. Back and forth, the letters crossed the globe at lightning speed. The conversations grew deeper, covering topics of courage, marriage, and the morality of war. Mama could sense that his morale was slumping, so she sent art supplies to encourage his creative expressions. She sent one of his poems to the President of the United States hoping for a response that might perk his spirits, but even the mention of her sending it along to the White House completely backfired.

Chapter 16

The Willing Conscript

June/66

Dear Joan:

I received your letter today and like always, more than glad to hear from you and Mr. Hunter. However, I was a little disappointed. Don't get me wrong, I truly appreciate what you did, sending my poem to the White House, but you see, Joan, I don't feel as though I deserve any more attention than any of the other thousands of GIs serving in Vietnam. We all have the same mission and are universally fighting for the same principles.

You point out that I am a very devoted American, but perhaps if I were a communist, I would also be loyal. My dedication to the Army, may be because I am ignorant of any other way of life.

You know, Joan, they say that there is no such thing as a live hero, which I think is right. I may have been reacting to fear and fear alone. I know I am a coward deep within. In 1961, when I re-enlisted in the Army, it was motivated by fear. I was afraid of getting out of the Army because I was a Black man with little education and no skilled training, so I stayed in the service. Do you want to know why I volunteered to come to Vietnam? I was thinking like a schoolboy. I wanted to see if a war was like it is in the movies, and I wanted to come back home as a hero like they did after World War II. I wanted to show my country that I was worthy of being a respected citizen.

You wrote to the President about me getting wounded during Operation Masher. Well, that day, I broke down and cried. What I did those three days was out of fear, fear of dying before having attained worthiness during my life. I indeed ran upon a Viet Cong machine gun, but only because I was so afraid, I did not think about the danger involved; that boiling point where nothing mattered.

As for the ones who truly deserve the medals, it is people like you, Joan, for what you and your Operation Morale Booster have done for us. The mothers and fathers who have sons serving in Vietnam, (there are even some daughters serving in this war!) or who share the pain and suffering of their sons, should be recognized, not me or anyone like me because Mom and Pop are fighting the mental war. The battles we fight are nothing compared to the ones the parents have to fight. Our fights last an hour, a day or a week, but mom and pop, it is a twenty-four hour, seven days a week battle of worrying. For them, battles are lost when their sons have gone missing, are killed in action, or come home bearing the scars and wounds which remain embedded within their hearts for eternity. This is a war no one outlives.

With affection,
Bob

Chapter 17

Please Don't Let Me Be Misunderstood

"Wow, Mama, you kind of just got your hand slapped from a world away," making light of the subject.

"Yeah, I sure did. I remember that day like it was yesterday. It pained me to read of his sadness. And when he wrote, he yearned to feel 'worthy,' that hit me hard." Mama was quiet, and I could tell she was digging for something more. "I didn't mean to take him into darker places, divulging all those intimate feelings." She paused again. "Knowing how much he admired your father, I purposely included a more direct dialogue from him in my next letter to remind Bob that Dad was also thinking of him."

May 31, 1966

Dear Bob,

Did you receive the art book I sent you yet? I thought you would be able to learn more about drawing with the help of this book. Your picture shows talent; I have it hanging in my kitchen. Again, you have a flair for the artistic. I will not compliment you too much as I don't think you like to receive compliments!! Your last letter about my writing to the President sounded much like a scolding. Was it meant to be?

Since you spoke so much about fear in your last letter, Paul asked me to send a message to you about courage.

They are thoughts written by Aristotle, a great Greek philosopher who greatly influenced some of the foundations of Christian philosophy.

In one of his books, "Ethics", Aristotle tried to answer the questions: What is the good for which men seek? What makes a man happy? He examined such concepts as wealth, health, and honor, but he decided that these were not the final good as each of those were sought for the sake of something else.

Some people seek wealth, health, or honor only to find that they still are not happy. Aristotle finally concluded that happiness comes from virtuous living. Man is authentically pleased when he does good things and finds pleasure in doing them.

Next, Aristotle considered virtues such as courage, temperance, liberality, and justice. His purpose was to find how the virtuous person acts regarding each. What is a courageous person? He is one who may fear plausible catastrophes yet faces them bravely. Then, the man who faces and who fears the right things and from the right motive, in the right way and at the right time... is brave. The man, however, who exceeds in fearlessness, is rash, is a madman.

On the other hand, the coward exudes dismay as he fears everything and is a despairing person. The virtuous man seeks the mean, the sensible attitude. He does the best he can under the existing circumstances. We believe this describes you.

I hope all this will mean something to you as Paul thought it was the best way he knew to express his feelings on courage, etc. Bob, don't be that "Angry Man" in the picture you painted. I felt that it was a self-portrait, was it? Next time, send me one titled "The Happier Man," please. (smile)

How is your malaria coming along? Do you still get those very high fevers? You hadn't mentioned it in your last letter.

You asked if I thought our marriage would be as appreciated if everything had been laid out for us on a platter instead of going through the typical difficulties. Well, Bob, you are not getting too personal, but on that subject, I could go on for hours, so I will wait until November, or whenever you do come to talk about it. All I can tell you now is that we have a pleasant life together without too many of the problems that many marriages have. We do have things pretty easy, or they seem to come easy to us because we both give 100 percent to each other and our family. I thank God each day for the wonderful man He gave me, and we both try to make each other happy.

Well, ole bean... I really must close now and hope to have a letter from you soon.

With our affection,

Joan and Paul

***

"So, you hung his portrait up in our kitchen? That was pretty bold for back then." I grabbed the top of her hand in a gesture of pride, "Good for you!"

"I did, but it was the cause of a falling out I had with 'Ms. Nebnose' across the street," Mama rolling her eyes.

"What happened?"

"Well, to make a long story short, I would always see Ms. Nebnose peering out her window as I walked down the street to mail my letters. She also took observation that Mr. Baker would make the extra effort to deliver my mail to my door from time to time. I guess she felt the need to know what I was up to so, she came over to inquire, of course, strategically bringing along some banana bread. Graciously, I invited her in for some coffee to accompany the baked goods, and as expected, she accepted and immediately made herself comfortable at the kitchen table."

Mama chuckled softly and proceeded to detail the encounter. As enthralled as I was by the story, it wasn't lost on me how exemplary her recall continued to be this entire time. I couldn't have been happier. I felt like it was rallying her brain to beat the beast within. Mama adjusted herself in her chair and continued. "Well, I proceeded to tell her about the night I came up with the idea for Operation Morale Booster and how I have since grown the pen pal base to include over twenty soldiers and over seventy-five students from both BC High and Wampatuck. She was only mildly engaged as she undoubtedly had her strong opinions about our involvement in the war. I could sense this underpinning of disapproval, so I emphasized that this effort was not an overt approval for the war but rather supporting those who were there on behalf of the United States. This clarification seemed to soften her a bit. Then I saw her spot, and double-take, the painting of Bob on the wall. She was not shy about asking who the painting depicted, and why it was hanging up in the home. I was equally bold in my response." Mama smiled, "The exchange went something like this."

"Ms. Nebnose looked me in the eye and asked in the most judgmental tone, 'Is this one of the soldiers you are writing to?'

" 'Yes, as a matter of fact, it is. That is a painting I believe to be a self-portrait of Bob Johnson, a twenty-five-year-old from Philadelphia. I have been writing to him for several months now.' I got up from the table to grab the unframed portrait from the wall.

"Ms. Nebnose indignantly responded, 'Don't you think it is inappropriate to be writing to a Black man?'

"Aghast at her audacity, I paused to calm myself before answering, 'Certainly not! He is wearing the United States uniform, isn't he?' I snapped back at her. 'What difference does it make if his skin is black, white, brown, or yellow for that matter?' I gave her a scowl that was completely uncharacteristic of me.

" 'Does Paul know you are writing to a Colored man?' Ms. Nebnose unapologetically asked, further revealing the racism in her heart. 'I mean, you are touching the papers he has touched.'

" 'What? Why would you even...' dumbfounded at her gross ignorance. 'Paul supports what I am doing with every fiber of his being. In fact, of all the soldiers I write to and receive letters from, Bob is his favorite. We have even invited him to stay with us when he comes home on leave.' I fired her way, accompanied by a feisty grin.

"Well, that about set Ms. Nebnose off in a frenzy, spouting off about how irresponsible and distasteful I was behaving by befriending a Black man. I can't recall every word she yelped, but I remember her parting words as she barged out the front door. 'UGGH, don't you dare bring a Colored man into this neighborhood!'

"Before I could say another word, she was gone; left without even taking her sweater," Mama concluded the story, shaking her head in disbelief, even just hearing herself tell the story. "Hard to believe, huh?"

"Uh yeaaahh. Dang, that is one ugly heart. Good for you for standing up to her, Mama. I know you usually prefer to avoid confrontation like the plague. Did she ever come around and apologize?"

"No, no she didn't. Susan, you know, we're all products of our life's experiences. I didn't know why she was so racist, so hateful, so fearful... and it wasn't my place to judge. I thought about trying to smooth things over, but I also refused to compromise my tenets to make her feel more comfortable. I felt it was unlikely she would change her belief system at her age as she was in her fifties. I also felt solace that her beliefs were not going to be passed onto the next generation as she had never married and had no significant exposure to children, so I let it go. Although I still saw her peering out her window when I made my way down to the general store, we never spoke again."

Mama glanced down at the next letter in the pile and quickly recalled what was to come. She looked back up at me with eyes of uncertainty. "Well, if you thought that irrational experience blindsided me, wait until you read what happens next."

Chapter 18

The Times They Are a Changin'

Bob wrote in a letter, "It seems like I spend half the day wondering how two people could be as wonderful as you. In your note included with the artbook, you stated that you both understood my reasoning for loving the service and wanting to sign on for another tour. If you do, you both are smarter than Einstein! I sometimes wonder what kind of man I am myself. Sometimes I get so fed up with myself, I feel like shooting myself."

***

This declaration didn't sit well with Mama, so in the next series of correspondence, she pleaded for an opportunity to speak directly to him, asking if there was a way, he could receive a call from the States while at the hospital. She included her telephone number just in case he needed a lifeline. The phone never rang.

Weeks rolled on, and much of the exchange between Mama and Bob during the late spring months of '66 delved deeply into the miscegenation concept. His letters were not as concerning, but she made sure to send him plenty of mail from the kids since children were clearly his soft spot. On what seemed to be an ordinary day, the most extraordinary thing occurred. The phone rang, and in only four little words, this gravelly voice was etched in her brain. "Hi Joan, it's Bob." A slight pause and then again, "It's Bob Johnson." Mama's stunned face slowly morphed into a tremulous smile.

"Hi Bob, it is so good to hear from you. Where are you?"

"Still in the hospital. They are letting me make one call." There was a seemingly long pause. "You are right," Bob conceded. "You are right about our country, not being ready for interracial relationships." Another pause. "I am alone in this, and it saddens me and scares me at the same time."

"Bob, I agree with you that love should be colorblind. You are not alone in your thinking. I am just not the pioneer you are. I don't have the grit as you do. I just don't have it in me. But I am just one person." There was silence on the other end. Mama filled the silence by elaborating, "You are a history buff, look back in history… pioneers are often alone at first, often thought to be crazy, even hated. But in reality, they are exceptional, and they are strong, they are visionaries who see how great things can be. We need these people. YOU are one of those people. But soon, you won't be alone. You will join another like-minded person, and then the power of two propagates until there are four, then eight, and then sixteen, and so on and so on, until it morphs into a new norm, until the next visionary comes along. Your vision is for a better America, and America is always striving to improve. As I said in the letters, I totally believe it is the direction we must go, but I, personally, wouldn't have the heart to bring a child into this world knowing he or she is going to suffer for the betterment of mankind. I know it is a small sacrifice to make for humanity, but I personally couldn't do it."

"I understand. I just feel alone in my thinking. But I am also scared because I feel so strongly about marking my worth that I will continue in this direction despite the fact my child will suffer greatly." Bob let out a deep sigh. "This conviction torments me greatly. If I truly have heartstrings for children, why am I even considering inflicting this on a child… MY child?"

"Bob, you are a good man with a great heart. If that is the path you decide to go, go confidently, but go for the right reasons~ because you are in love… not because you want to further mankind. Real love is the answer. It is always the answer."

Mama heard a muffled voice on Bob's end, just as he abruptly ends the call. "Ok, I gotta go now. Thanks for answering. I just wanted to hear your voice. Now, I know what you sound like, Joan."

"Ok, Bob, good to hear your voice as well. Take care of yourself, ole bean, and know we are thinking of you all the time." And just like that, the sound of his voice was now a memory, gone as quickly as it came.

Later that week, two poems accompany his next letter with strict orders to refrain from sending these to the President, followed by his signature "(smile)."

"Alone Am I"

Lonely: without company, unfrequented solitary, also desolate

Can a man be surrounded by people of company,
and yet be alone?
Without love, without someone to love,
or without the love of someone.
Surely, this is truly being alone and knowing loneliness.
Desiring to be loved, wanting contentment of others, and yet
confined to a mental cell,
which there is no key to the door, no passage to freedom is truly
being alone.
During the day, I am surrounded by those who compose my time,
but the night I must bear desolation, and perhaps too,
the day is also my night.
Is there no such refuge from loneliness for me?
Was my life meant to be comprised of loneliness?

No true family have I, nor a love of my own,
true friendship I have never known.
From childhood to manhood, I have grown alone.
Around the world I have been, many cities and countries I have
seen alone.
Many people I have met, who offered friendship,
that I have learned to regret.
No man is an island, no man stands alone,
no one except I, for I am the lonely GI

***

"The Letter, The Letter"

A letter came today, from our son far away, it read…

Dear Mom and Pop:
I hope that this letter will find you both doing well. I don't have
much to say except I am doing fine and soon we will be going to

battle not far away. Don't worry about me. I will be coming home soon and no more will I roam.

The Letter, The Letter

Another letter came today, it read:

Dear Madam:
We regret to inform you, that your son is dead. He died in a battle far away. The Lord Giveth and the Lord Taketh away.

The Letter, The Letter

A letter came today, from my husband far away. It read...

To My Darling Wife:
May this letter fill your heart with joy and say hello to our darling little boy. Though I find the way hard and long, but your love keeps me going on.

The Letter, The Letter

Another letter came today, it read...
Dear Ma'am: I regret to inform you that your husband died yesterday in battle. The Lord Giveth and the Lord Taketh Away.

The Letter, The Letter

A letter came today from my sweetheart far away, it read:
With All My Love:
With each stroke of my pen, I write of my love for you to the dying end. I saw his mother today, she said, "Mary, Don is dead. He died in Vietnam. The Lord Giveth and the Lord Taketh away.

The Letter, The Letter

***

I placed his letter on the pile and sighed, "Wow, these two poems don't sound very uplifting. It breaks my heart to read these."

"Yeah, Dad and I talked about that as well. We weren't sure if these poems were a means of catharsis or reason for concern. Dad strongly felt Bob just needed to get out of the hospital and back into the fight alongside his comrades, claiming perhaps the feeling of being useless to the cause is descending him into the depression expressed in his poems." Feasible as that seemed, Mama immediately jumped into action:

Dear Bob,

Now, you have me troubled and concerned. Your last three letters seemed so angry. CHEER UP, my friend... Don't dwell on all the things you read in the paper. Don't forget, only the bad stories get into print, but there are millions of good ideas and good deeds that are never noticed by the newspapers and other media outlets. It would do your heart right to realize that we all care about this crazy world of ours, and we all do care about our soldiers in Vietnam. Try to focus on all the positive things happening.

On another note, Paul wanted me to tell you that his baseball team did well this season, came out in 2nd place in the city league, and then played in the State Tournament. This season was the first time in nine years that BC High played in the State Tournament. They lost 2-0, ending their season, but he was very proud of them.

We enjoyed your Beetle Bailey cartoons, but I must tell you that I was so excited to see your picture when I saw that you had enclosed snapshots but was equally disappointed when I turned it over, and it wasn't of you. You had promised us a picture, "real soon." How about it????

This past weekend we hosted our 5th annual cookout. I told everyone about you as our friends were interested in who the portrait painting hanging in the kitchen was. (smile)

Well, old friend, please cheer up and try to look on the brighter side of things. If you need anything, please let us know. Be well, and write again when you can.

Your friends,
Paul and Joan

***

Bob's next letter stunned the entire family.

Chapter 19
Bridge Over Troubled Water

June/66

Hi Joan and Paul,

I received your letter yesterday, and it found me doing well. I feel like I need to clarify a few things. My message about your writing to the President was not intended to be a scolding. I am just one of the thousands of men who are working just as hard as I am. I am just blessed to have pulled your letter from the pile of generic letters to answer. I still think back to that fateful day. I breathe a sigh of relief thinking about how empty my life would be right now if I hadn't chosen YOUR letter. Well, anyway, I appreciate everything you do for me and all the care you show me. Did you ever hear back from the President? "Sorry 'Bout That!"

I received some terrible news today. I once said that perhaps the fate of contracting malaria had brought me here to Japan unwittingly escaping the mortar attack that ensued hours after I left basecamp, but there's more. A buddy wrote and told me that our reconnaissance platoon jumped into a hot LZ where the VCs were waiting to execute an ambush. One helicopter was shot down. Twenty-five of the twenty-seven men left in the platoon were killed. My old company went in and recovered the bodies (Company C 2/7).

Can I confide in you? Ever since I have been in Vietnam, strange things have been happening to me that I can't explain. It first started in January… I was sent out on patrol, set to ambush any VC trying to slip into the division area. I had just dozed off to sleep when my RTO (Radio Telephone Operator) shook me and said I had screamed in my sleep. I explained that I had just had a dream of a VC trying to penetrate the perimeter, and we caught him. Later that night, we found one doing just that and we caught him. A while back, I had another dream. There were three strange images…1. A gate guard 2. A surgeon waiting at the door for me at the entrance and 3. A deformed baby laying in a bed next to me. When I got wounded during Operation Masher, I was evacuated to the 85th Field Hospital. I passed through a gate with a gate guard, the surgeon met me at the door, and the next morning I woke up with a young deformed Vietnamese boy in the bed across from me. Lastly, during my flight to Vietnam, I joked about a dream I had the night before of getting wounded by the first of the year. Then I got shot on January 28th. The doctor told me I received a miracle wound. The bullet hit my right shoulder and continued to hit my collar bone without damaging either bone. Two days later, they extracted the round and was deemed healed by the medics, so it didn't need a bandage or any medical treatment. Why these miraculous things happen to me, God only knows. Hmmm, God only knows.

As for now, I have an urge to stay in Vietnam, yet I am terrified. What is really odd though, I don't fear death. It sounds crazy, but I don't. I fear not living. As for my malaria, it is just about over. Actually, it never really is over as it can resurface at any time. One thing is for sure though, I am losing a lot of pay sitting here, so I need to get back to work. Combat, Jump, and Overseas pay: ($133/ month), are all deducted the whole time I am in the hospital recovering from malaria. They don't consider Japan overseas… 4,000 miles from the States. (smile)

Well, here I am, back to my poetry:

"The Mighty Four"

United together, both in peace and war,
fighting victoriously for freedom and liberty.
The Mighty Four: The Army, Navy, Air Force,
and the Marine Corp.
On the land, sea, and air, they are there, standing side-by-side,
serving with honor and pride.
All brave, courageous and bold.
It is yours and our freedom they hold;
The Mighty Four: The Army, Navy, Air Force,

and the Marine Corp.
On the ground, at seas of raining death on the enemy
from the sky.
They shall never let democracy and freedom die.
The Mighty Four: The Army, Navy, Air Force,
and the Marine Corp.

So, until the next time my friends,
Bobby

***

A mere three days after receiving this letter from Bob, another one arrives.

Hi Friend:

Just a note to let you know that I will be back in Vietnam when you receive this letter! My plane leaves at 1330 today (in about 45 minutes). I will write to you as soon as I can. I thought I'd send you a picture of The Happier Man. (smile) I had this taken a while ago but only just got ahold of it to send to you and the family. Have your kids ever seen a Black man before?

So Until,
Bobby

P.S. I feel like a new baby boy, just wonderful!

***

"Wow, that is a 180 from the letters just before. It looks like Dad was right; he just needed to get back into action." I observed with a happy heart. "So, tell me, what was it like for the kids to see a picture of Bob?"

Mama explained the entire day as if it was yesterday. "Billy and I met Mr. Baker at the curb. Billy was holding his dutiful salute to the sweet old mailman as he drove down the street and up along the sidewalk curb. With an artificial bugle blow, Mr. Baker announced his delivery as he always did when Billy was waiting. 'You've got mail from Vietnam, Corporal Billy!' and offered him a salute in return. Billy looked up at me with eyes of great anticipation and a smile that spanned the width of his All-American face. I let him carry in the letters from the front lines while taking the responsibility of the circulars. He ran them in to the kitchen table, as always, and eagerly waited for me to get the letter opener. There were three letters from three different soldiers, and one was from Bob. I quickly perused the letters quietly, beaming when I saw the photo. I jumped up from the kitchen table and tucked them away in the den. Billy's captivated eyes toggled between childlike anticipation to utter confusion as he followed me into the den. 'What Mommy? Why are you putting the letters away? Won't you read them to me?'

"With exaggerated animation, I reconsidered and pulled two of the three letters out, casually leaving Bob's behind, and read them aloud to satisfy his curiosity. I could not wait to show the family the contents of the letters. The photograph in particular." Mama paused to indulge in a dreamy reflection, "Finally, I could look into his eyes, even if only one dimensional, and see all the physical characteristics that up until now, I had to create in my imagination. Studying it all to determine if they matched the emotional characteristics of the man I had come to know through words on a paper and a single phone call from the other side of the globe."

"So, what were their reactions?"

"Well, five-thirty rolled around and everyone gathered at the table. I announced that I had a surprise but not until everything on their plates was eaten. To no surprise, dinner was exceptionally quiet as the focus was on eating to hurry along with the surprise. Clearing the table of all dishes, the kids and Dad returned to their seats and turned their attention to me. I pulled out the letter from Bob. As I read it aloud, Maryellen picked up on his hint at a photo and squealed with excitement. 'He sent a picture! What does he look like?'

"Michael chimed in, 'Is he in uniform? Is he holding a gun?' I toyed with their animation for just a minute, enjoying their utter excitement and sincere interest. I grabbed the snapshot to show them. The kids got higher in their chairs, leaning over the table for a

116

better look. Dad shot me an endearing look acknowledging how much this meant to me. It was a memorable moment for the family."

I took a look the photograph he enclosed to see for myself now that I had essentially known him the same way Mama did at this point having read all their letters. His photo was of a devoted soldier, void of any evidence of fear finding refuge in his eyes. The tonality of his eyes expressed a dichotomy of sorts—that of a resolute soldier and a preacher. Maybe I manifested this sense because of his letters, but I no longer possessed an ability to separate the two. His headshot revealed the intense heat of the day as the sweat reflected white off his dark brown skin. Donning his uniform, inclusive of a camouflage cover, he looked younger than I imagined based on the maturity of his letters and his worldly knowledge. His five-day old growth of a mustache was barely detected against his dark skin and his resting lips. It was such a luxury to see what he looked like; I couldn't imagine having to wait six months as she did.

Mama grabbed her response letter and started reading it aloud...

"We loved your picture, and all agree you look mighty handsome in your uniform. I showed it to the kids and I was thrilled with their reaction. They know the color of your skin is different from ours but didn't think anything of it, only commenting on how hot you appeared because the sweat on your skin really gleams. They remarked how nice you look in your 'cool uniform.' Fortunately, this is quite different from the way we were brought up, but as you say, it's all a process, and we must endure ugly times in order to get to the goal of universal acceptance. Maryellen drew you a picture but struggled a bit writing a letter to tell you about her dance recital and school.

"Well, you sound quite chipper and ready to go, go, go. I am so happy to see your spirits had picked up so much before you went back to 'work' as you say. Please keep your thoughts there and always remember that we care very much about what happens to you. And although I don't write as often as you do, we are continually thinking of you, praying for your safety, and telling all of our friends about you. (smile)

"Bob, I must run now, but I will write again soon. Thanks again for the picture! We were thrilled to hear you were boarding the plane for Vietnam. Take care, and may God continue to bless YOU!"

***

As Mama and I continued to read through the pile of letters, it was easy to see the relationship blossoming as did her outreach of Operation Morale Booster. Summer days came and went just slightly faster than the letters between these two unlikely soulmates. Her list of soldiers had grown to include over thirty she was personally writing to, keeping her quite busy. While schools were on summer break, she invited Cub Scouts and church groups to join in on the mission. She hosted parties for the ladies in the neighborhood and her church's Sodality Club to assemble care packages to send to many of the soldiers. Although always invited, Ms. Nebnose never attended. All was good leading up to the fateful August day when Mr. Baker came knocking on the screen door, not wearing his typical cheerful smile.

Chapter 20

Volunteers

Mama got lost in her own detailing of the moment, "I approached the screen door, heart sinking with each step as I made eye contact with Mr. Baker. Immediately, my eyes diverted down to the recognizable red, white, and blue striped envelope in his hand. Not a word was spoken as I slowly opened the door and reached for the envelope. My eyes, now glossed over with tears, returned to meet those of the warm-hearted mailman. 'I'm sorry, Mrs. Hunter.' Mr. Baker delivered in a somber caring voice, as he dolefully turned to make his way back to his truck. I gave a hesitant nod, but the lump in my throat prevented me from uttering a single word. This letter marked a pivot in momentum. It was my first 'Returned to Writer,' and I was wise enough to know what that meant. Each of my thirty soldiers was near and dear to my heart, but Bob had become more than a pen pal, he had become my dear friend. I braced myself before reading which soldier of mine would not be seeing his parents ever again. As I glanced down at the envelope, a rush of relief that it was not Bob was met by the same intensity of guilt that I had secretly prayed that be the case. Although a fallen soldier during this mission was inevitable, I failed to prepare for the loss. Nor did I prepare for the emptiness of not knowing what ultimately happened to my brave young friends. Watering eyes fixated on the name... *Eddie Z...Oh, Eddie, I pray a Welcome Home is in order. If not, I am so sorry. May you rest in peace and may God comfort your loved ones,* I prayed. With reverence, I pulled out his folder containing a dozen letters over the four months we corresponded. I reread each one of them, his last one perhaps hinting at his fate."

An Khe
May 18, 1966

Dear Joan & Paul,

Well, just a few lines as I can't sleep tonight. In fact, no one can because we are on alert. It seems like the VC broke through and are currently about five miles from here. We are told there are about 1,500 of them. They might try to hit the 1st Cav tonight or tomorrow morning. Tomorrow is Ho Chi Minh's birthday, and that means the VC will want to give him something special for his birthday. They will want to hit the 1st Cavalry because we are the only outfit that combats them with unbeatable force because of our choppers.

~ He continued for two pages about his children and wife and then closed with a touching goodbye.

You and Paul are both close to me, and I think of you both as more than just friends. Maybe someday we will all see each other when this war is over. Goodnight, and say hi to everyone.

Your friend,
Eddie Z

***

Mama resumed, "For the first time, I wondered what he looked like or how his voice sounded. I looked up at my map hanging on the den wall and thought, *should I have a designation for this? What IS this exactly?* Shuddering at the thought.

"Returning to that guilt from a few minutes ago, I thought about Bob. Grateful that the 'Returned to Writer' was not his, but anxious about the genuine possibility that one day it might be. Is this how I am to be notified? Somehow, it didn't seem right, yet the reality was, I was not family despite feeling otherwise at times. The emptiness was not something I had factored into this Operation Morale Booster, and it caused me to reflect on the longevity of what I had started. I put my heart and soul into personally nurturing over thirty 'sons' with attentiveness, thoughtfulness, and daily prayers. This new element to my mission monopolized my mind for the better part of two weeks back then. Am I setting myself up for emotional distress as I may lose one after another? Am I allowing myself to get

120

too close to each of these soldiers, caring about them like I would family? Should I distance myself and keep my letters a little less personal? Is this going to take an emotional toll on me at the detriment of the family? Was this a pie in the sky venture that was not well thought out? Thoughts raced through my head, gaining momentum, spiking with the thought of aborting the mission."

The "Returned to Writer," clearly blindsided Mama, and she was deeply affected. This munificent heart of hers may have been too big to handle the full reality of this wartime mission.

For the next couple of weeks, she chose not to write; but instead, she sat and reread all her letters, reading through Bob's twice. She particularly paid closer attention to the most recent ones he had written after recovering from months in the hospital with malaria.

June 21/66

Hi Joan and Paul:

Well, here I am back to work again, and I mean work. I got back last Friday, and on Sunday morning, I went up to join my platoon. They were on the green line (alert status), and last night we kicked off the beginning of what might be the biggest operation of the war; The Monsoon Offensives. The 101st Airborne, jumped off yesterday, the Marines are coming in from the coast, and we will be backing Air assault today. There is supposed to be a Ho Chi Minh crack shot field army at a place called CON-TOUN. We are going to try and box them up. If we succeed in destroying them, this will knock the hell out of his plans. (excuse the expression)

It seems as though I had gotten back in just the right time, meaning in more ways than one. Upon receiving orders for my return to the States, my unit had preemptively shipped my personal belongings before physically returning from the hospital. When I walked into the orderly room and got my new orders for involvement in the Monsoon Offensive, they had to get me a new issue, which I needed badly. When I left for the hospital, I only had two pairs of socks, one pair of boots, one set of fatigues; I was in dire need.

Well, I hear choppers coming in now. So, we will be leaving soon. As soon as I get a chance to write, I will.

Well, until the next time,
Bob

***

"HA! As I read the closing line of the choppers coming in, Mama, all I can think of is the opening scene to M*A*S*H, with the choppers descending on the field hospital, which I picture is much like the 85th that Bob was treated in after Operation Masher."

July 3/66

Hi Paul and Joan:

Well, today was a day full of rest and happiness for me. This morning at 0730, we had a short patrol of only 4,000 meters (most of the time, they are 10,000 to 20,000 meters). When we returned, we went to the river for baths and washed our uniforms, which we had not done in thirteen days. It felt so good to have clean clothes to wear. The rest of my day was devoted to sleep, rest, and writing letters. Then, I got your message and that beautiful picture of the kids; it topped the day. I hate to say this, but I must… you must be crazy (smile) to have sent that picture. There is no way that I would have parted with it. Kids have always been my weak spot. Every time I see a kid over here, I get mad knowing they have no chance in life whatsoever. I know this has been their way of life since the beginning of time, and they are content and happy, but I feel it is wrong to involve kids in wars. Fighting this war is hell as it is, but when you see children suffering, too, because of a group of people's ignorance and greed for power, this hurts me most.

Last winter on Operation Masher, I threw a hand grenade into a house where we spotted VC firing a machine gun. After it went off, I went in to find three VC soldiers, three kids, and an old lady; all dead. I felt sick at the sight of the kids. Last week, we hit a Viet Cong village where we only saw young women and kids. We were ordered to burn the hooches and destroy all the food because it was the Viet Cong Headquarters. This is war, and it is dirty rotten. I exist in a state of conflict between good and expected evil, and it eats away at me every day.

Well, it is true that I have several more days of battle under my belt, and I have also been put in for my second award for the Bronze Star. Operation Hawthorne ended last month; Operation Nathan Hale ends on the 5th; however, it looks as if I will be starting another mission shortly after that. I can't tell you too much about it due to security reasons, but I can say this. It is a job no one wanted because it involves operating behind or deep into Viet Cong territory with only seven or eight other men. I guess you probably think I am nuts to volunteer for such a job. Everyone tells me that I am begging for the CMH (Casket with Metal Handles), but I say when it is time for me to go, it does not matter where I am or what I am doing. I don't believe man has a choice to pick the date and time of death. The Lord giveth and the Lord taketh away!

As for your new pen pal of the 101st, he just may be dead now. They took a pretty bad beating. Sadly, this is the truth. Their casualties were quite heavy. You see, Joan, most of our infantry division, got chopped up a lot more than what is being reported at home. The only reason that the 1st Cavalry does not take a beating is because of how we are organized. We are the sole division intact at all times. This is why we are called Airmobile. We have two brigades of infantry and one brigade of paratroopers. Our division camp is almost impregnable. The Viet Cong actually fear us. Every time we get into a battle with them, they try to avoid fighting because of our firepower and support.

No, I have not received anything from the White House, and I don't expect to. I don't want medals or promotions, nothing like that. All I want is to fight this war until its completion for the good of mankind and freedom. My 1st Sergeant told me this afternoon to stay in one place so that they can promote me. I told him that I did not want a promotion. I am happy as a corporal even though I have the same job and do the same work as a staff sergeant. My platoon leader keeps telling me that Hitler, Napoleon, and myself all have something in common... they, too, were corporals. (smile) Some people just can't realize that if a man wants to be a bum, let him be a bum if he is happy being a bum.

Two weeks ago, this platoon ran into a VC machine gun. We lost four men. We had to pull back under fire. I was the last one to leave the hill. When I retreated, I was still firing my weapon. The machine gun stopped firing. Everyone thought that I had knocked out the machine gun like I was a one-man army. Two days later, I had my squad on a forward patrol of the platoon, which was about 100 meters behind me. I left my team at the bottom of a hill. One other man and I went up the hill to check a trail out. We had just come out of the jungle and into a clearing, at the same time, four VC stepped into the clearing. I opened up on them, killing three, wounding one. It was them or me. War is awful, but a necessary evil in the face of the spread of communism, but it is awful nonetheless.

I can't remember whether I told you or not, but I took the big step and extended my tour for another six months. However, by continuing, I am granted a thirty-day leave, which I will be taking in November. Well, I have to close now, it is getting too dark to write.

So, until... With affection,
Bob

***

Mama reflected on these last few letters as we reread them, marveling at how quickly his demeanor bounced back, exuding vitality immediately upon returning to combat. Dad had been right again; he simply needed to get out of the hospital and back to the front lines to feel a sense of purpose. Both of us were in awe at the idea Bob would volunteer to go behind enemy lines of these guerilla warriors, although he did seem to come alive in the face of death.

Before reaching for the next letter in the pile, she held onto this one for a bit. "It's so strange... as we were just reading where Bob wrote of the new pen-pal of the 101st probably being dead, it

124

brought back the chills I felt when I read it fifty years ago. I was so disturbed by it because the 'Returned to Writer' I had received was not from that particular soldier of the 101st. I remember thinking, is another notice going to arrive in the coming days? Is this going to be a regular occurrence now that he had claimed they were initiating the biggest offensive in the war?"

She rifled through the letters we had just read and pulled out Eddie's sealed "Returned to Writer" envelope, held it with reverence, gazing at the dozen crossed-out dates and locations it had been delivered to in its journey to reach him. She felt the emptiness once again. Mama's eyes were saddened. She recalled this moment being her first major crossroad in her mission, questioning if her heart was going to be able to endure the pain this mission will inevitably bring? Recognizing that she had just gone over this with me just minutes before, I was reminded of her dementia, which at times over the past six hours, she had given me every reason to believe it was a thing of the past.

That was all she had in her for the day; she couldn't go on anymore. We agreed to leave all the letters on the table and revisit them the following day. The day, inclusive of her total recall, had been a massive win in my book. I regretted having it end on a somber note, but I also didn't want to press her further. I was tempted to read ahead to see if indeed she was about to receive an onslaught of "Returned to Writers."

Chapter 21

Have You Forgotten

Sweet melodic chirping from the birds who made their way back early from winter's vacation or those who never left, as we have both in Tennessee, greeted me the following morning. I was rearing to dive back into the letters and the minds of both Mama and our conflicted soldier, so I prepared Mama's breakfast of choice to have ready when she woke. I knew I had to keep to her morning routine for her sake, but that didn't mean I couldn't peek into the letters while I waited for her to wake, so I did. A little anxious as to whether she was going to remember reading the letters the day before, I braced myself for the worst. This low expectation bar had come to be my defense mechanism for her degenerative condition. As Dad always preached, "hope for the best, prepare for the worst," one of the many mottos I lived by, intangible and everlasting gifts from Dad, may he continue to rest in peace.

Not more than fifteen minutes into reading ahead into the letters, Mama woke and made her theatrical entrance into the kitchen, always looking to shock her audience with some crazy dance move. "Ta Da!" she sang with one hand stretched in front, and the other equally extended behind. "Good morning, Susu!" as she endearingly referred to me. "Looks like I have another day to enjoy."

"Good morning, Mama! It looks like we both do!" I placed her cereal and her medicine in front of her and queued Ol' Blue Eyes. She immediately expressed an interest in playing a game of Scrabble. Usually, a welcomed diversion, but not today. Admittedly, I was itching to get back to the letters. Her desire to keep to our morning routine led me to believe she didn't remember the previous day's events. Not surprised, but it left me wondering if her recall was going to be as detailed as it was yesterday. Staying true to her routine, we played Scrabble, went for a short walk, and then returned to the kitchen table to work on some drawings. I grabbed this as my window of opportunity to deviate from the norm and revisit the letters.

"How about we look at some more of the letters from Operation Morale Booster?" I suggested.

"Operation Morale Booster? Where did you find these? These were written a lifetime ago." Mama asked, shocked and confused. Clearly, she didn't remember reading them the day before, but on the bright side, at least she remembered they existed, and further, she wasn't still saddened by the "Returned to Writer" turning point.

Taking advantage of my reading ahead that morning, I chose to skip ahead to what appeared to be the tipping point for her forging ahead with her mission, hardening her heart to endure the inevitable void. We began by rereading Bob's letter dated July 4th. In this letter, he reminded her once again about the significance of what she had set out to do. A handful of lines, in particular, seemed to jump off the page when I read it to her.

"We started today with a short patrol and ended with a hot coke and a can of beer (hot but wonderful). We celebrated Independence Day by having our artillery fire a fifty-gun salute to the United States of America, one shell per state. But you know Joan, I can't help but think of how many people at home think of this day only as a day from work, a day to rest, and a day to party... how many? Think of all the American soldiers serving here and other parts of the world, trying to preserve this great Day of Independence and maybe help others achieve similar freedoms. I look forward to the day these people can also enjoy a day designated to enjoy and celebrate their independence. Too many Americans take this day for granted, never realizing the price we had to pay for it; all the work and militias fighting the Brits leading up to the American Revolutionary War and countless other battles and wars fought after it. If I had half a cent for each American throughout history who gave their life for this day, I would be a wealthy man."

***

Couldn't help but be saddened by the reality that all the things he said in this letter fifty years ago would still be relevant today, perhaps even at a more extreme level of ungratefulness. It was easy for me to see that if that wasn't powerful enough to tip Mama's decision in favor of continuing the writing campaign regardless of the heartache she will endure, his next letter was.

"I got your homemade dessert yesterday. It was delicious. As a matter of fact, some of the guys said that you should be the battalion cook. You have become very popular within the platoon. I hope that Paul doesn't become offended by what I am about to say, well, here goes. Joan, I am actually in love with you in a matter of speaking. I mean a woman who devotes herself to her country as you are doing. Do you realize what you have done with your Operation Morale Booster?

"When you sent me those prayers, I read them many times hoping for them to move me, but regretfully, they no longer had meaning. This war has changed me. There is no thrill in killing nor seeing a man killed, but the sanctity of life itself has escaped me."

***

Mama immediately commented, "Oh, yes, I remember this. Bob was down in the dumps for a while. I knew I needed to be there for him even more so, but that summer, there was an airline strike that nearly stagnated the flow of communication," Mama recalled with great clarity. She continued to tell me how this mid-summer strike caused by the bargaining impasses between the International Association of Machinists (IAM) and the five major airlines, proved to be a quagmire in her logistics. Her baked goods took over a month, as opposed to a week, to get to her soldiers, and further, their delayed responses had the young Cub Scouts waning in their enthusiasm to engage. Dad's high school students were a bit less bothered by the delays because, as teenage boys, they had plenty of other areas of their lives to focus on, namely sports and girls.

Over the next few months, she did her best to keep the pace but the strike, coupled with the exciting reality that Mama was pregnant with child number four… ME!, made it quite tricky. Simultaneously, Bob's letters were slightly less frequent, which indicated he was busy running missions. His letters were shorter but always included articles from the Stars and Stripes newspaper, documenting his units' operations. Bob didn't like to complain or paint a sorry picture, so it was easier to let the journalists speak for him, allowing him to keep his letters brimming with positivity. Dad found the articles extremely interesting.

One such article was quite descriptive and eye-opening to me since I had never read anything from this war before these letters. This article detailed a typical reconnaissance mission to seek, observe, and if necessary, destroy enemy strength and position. Delta Company, 2nd Battalion, 7th Cavalry Division of the 1st Air Cavalry Division, commenced with a firm order from Platoon Sergeant, Bill Dansby, "Saddle Up!" The search for Charlie began through the swamps, dense jungle and mountainous terrain. The unbearable vapor from the released gas from the rotting marsh vegetation paled in comparison to navigating through twelve-foot elephant grass known for its razor-sharp edges, living up to its reputation of slashing faces and fatigues when not carefully shielded. The vines below entangled their feet, depriving them of the ability to command the terrain. This ground cover also served as camouflage for poison-tipped punji sticks lying just below the surface. These hidden traps, along with their ghostlike behaviors, were a hallmark of their guerilla warfare enemy. The twenty-six-man team strategically and slowly infiltrated enemy lines, reconnoitering enemy position and serving as ground support to the US aerial dominance. The article continued to illustrate how, step by step, the team scanned every inch of the vast jungle without making a sound. Well aware behind every leafy limb and under every patch of grass, there could be a deadly booby-trap or an ambush waiting to be launched. Hidden tunnels also posed a threat of a surprise attack, but if identified early, they were deemed a source for tunnel warfare resulting in high Viet Cong KIA numbers. Sadly, "numbers" were always the goal as they tirelessly fought to attain the "crossover point" that General Westmoreland had touted was within reach. This metric was the point believed to be when US and the allied troops of South Vietnam, Australia, Philippines, South Korea, and Thailand were killing more enemy troops than the enemy could replace. The fatigued soldiers, were ordered to take a break in the shade to combat the intense heat but to refrain from quenching their thirst with their canteens' contents. Soldiers quickly learned to factor for slightly longer than the expected missions when rationing their supplies. Platoon Sergeant Dansby utilized the break to reflect on the prior three weeks of battles. Calculating 461 enemies KIA, he determined it a success and decided his men needed to return home to the LZ for a few days' rest. Closing on the end of this brief rest from the sun, the men checked to ensure no leeches had made their way into their clothes before moving onward. The trek back to LZ was as skillful as the journey out, returning without further incident.

Each letter and article made me more keenly aware of the awful conditions our dauntless soldiers were subjected to on a daily basis. The diseases, the foot rot, the parasites, snakes and insects, the intolerable weather conditions, the gruesome deaths of their comrades via barbaric booby traps, etc.; it was as close to hell on Earth as I could ever have imagined. The bravery of these men never ceased to amaze me, making the "welcome home" they never received beyond reproachable in my mind.

How did our media miss the mark on this? Sentencing an entire population to a life of shame and isolation when they should have come back as heroes like those from every other war, for the mere fact they walked through hell on behalf of the decisions made by our politicians. How did we continue to hail the politicians while we spat on these soldiers? If only the American people possessed the heart and understanding toward our soldiers as Bob did toward his Viet Cong enemy.

Before Mama got up this morning, I had read a letter in which Bob wrote of a prisoner of war he had interrogated. The enemy soldier had been in his fourth year at the College of Beijing, studying Chemistry. He was visited at college by those from the Communist North Vietnam Army, demanding he leave his education and take up arms against the South Vietnam Army, or they'd kill his entire family: aunts, uncles, cousins included. He had no choice. This is how communism functions; making demands, threats and then invoking violence on those who don't comply.

Despite being his enemy by circumstance, hearing the plight of this soldier agitated Bob. He channeled his emotions of anger and sadness by drafting a poem. He sent one copy to Mama and buried the other in the Vietnam soil.

"The VC. Point of View"

I came, I saw and I conquered, but what have I conquered?
The land that can only bare wild fruit.
My brother who can only offer me a bowl of rice and bitter tea.
What have I seen? A land that has not changed since its beginning
of creation?
I gave and I shall give my life for this?
Why did I come to take from my brother?
who appeared to have so much and yet had far less than I?
The road to my destiny seemed so clear and short,
only to find it dark and long, and eternity in its place,
which is death for me.

***

Indulging in my moment of reflection, I was so impressed that even in his darkest periods, Bob never seemed to lose respect for his enemy and instead kept his perspective as fellow humans. I noticed how Bob, at worst, referred to the Viet Cong, short for Vietnamese Communist, as "Charlie," derived from the phonetic alphabet nickname, Victor Charlie (VC). I thought back to a psychology class I took in college that addressed the emotional survival techniques used in war. I envisioned my professor, Mr. Rose, pacing the front of the room with periodic dramatic pauses to ensure all his 8 am students were paying attention. He spoke of war in general, as it was the only time killing was not only justified; it was expected. In a resounding voice, he enlightened us, "As war demands, it all becomes impersonal. The number of 'killed' is what is touted in operational reports; the higher the number, the more praise they receive. These soldiers fight their internal battle to salvage their sanity. Verbally dehumanizing the enemy by referring to them with contemptuous terms such as 'zips' and 'gooks' are methods used to shield them from the egregious reality of what was expected of them. Likewise, avoiding the harshness of the word 'killed' is achieved by choosing terminology such as 'wasted,' 'smoked,' and 'greased' instead. Many soldiers become intoxicated with the vision of defeating the enemy, not necessarily the idea of killing. Still, the reality is," as he offered another dramatic pause to scan the auditorium, "winning typically requires a lot of killing. Dehumanizing the enemy through name-calling is acceptable in war," Mr. Rose looked up into the sea of students and held his stare, "but dehumanizing them through torture is never acceptable, even in war." The emphatic professor took position dead center at the front of the auditorium and gazed down at the floor for what seemed to be an extraordinarily long time before looking back up at us, delivering a final thought. "Unfortunately, during the Vietnam War, some men did not uphold this tenet; many were simply not fit to be in a war but were drafted nonetheless simply because they were the right age and gender. These men and their actions, amplified by the insatiable media, have tainted that entire population of brave soldiers. America's politicians learned from this. We haven't had a draft since, making our military, strictly fortified by those who have chosen a career in the service."

I returned from my brief reminiscent visit to college days. I got up from the table to get us both a refreshing glass of sweet tea. I randomly spouted off with visible disgust, "So, while the politicians were deliberating as to the best course of action for our country's position in this war, more and more soldiers, both enemy and American, were losing their lives and losing their sanity."

"Yes, Susan, it was awful. It seemed like we were damned if we stayed and damned if we left. Presidents from both sides of the aisle, and there were five of them, were involved in this debacle. What's worse is that some of those Presidents allowed political pressure and re-election strategies to determine their decision making."

Mama was able to tap into the portal of her long-term memory again, bringing me back to 1966. She proceeded to tell me about how the September moon brought with it an uptick in protests in the States, now to include anti-communist protests pushing back George Lincoln Rockwell's American Nazi and anti-Semitic agendas. Battles in Vietnam were escalating at a similar pace. It seemed Bob wasn't back from one operation for more than forty-eight hours before he was back out on another. His letters covered a lot of ground, but what stopped us in our tracks was his brief note where he nonchalantly wrote about his near-death experience from two weeks prior.

Chapter 22

Bad Moon Rising

I t was stunning to me how many different ways Bob almost lost his life while in Vietnam. One would expect a life to be taken in combat or by an enemy booby trap, or specifically to Vietnam, malaria, but rarely did we hear of soldiers losing their lives for other reasons like the way he described in his letter. "To begin with, I almost met my maker five days ago. I was crossing over a footbridge when it broke. I fell into a river with an under-current of fifty miles per hour. I'd like to think it was my Ranger training that paid off, but honestly, I think it was more that God saved me because the current swooshed me into a sweet spot of no current amidst fifty-mile-an-hour rapids surrounding me. I am a strong believer in two things…1. Whatever happens to me, deemed good or bad, it is all part of God's master plan. I am not going to die until He wants me to. Heaven is a figure of speech and a part of Christian belief. Hell is living. 2. When a man lives in the animal kingdom, he must act or play the part of an animal to survive."

Bob rifled out a bunch of letters over the next few weeks, shorter in length but always possessing his quintessential anecdotes and insights. The effects of the continued IAM strike wreaked havoc on the sequencing of the arriving letters, often out of chronological order, so content was harder to follow. Mama and I had a difficult time trying to piece them together news-wise. His letters, however, got increasingly more upbeat. There was little talk of the interracial issues that had previously weighed heavy on his heart. He seemed to let it go, for now anyway. Other matters took center stage, like whether to sign on for another tour or return to the States.

"Eight years ago, at this time, I wondered if I had made a big mistake by joining the Army, now I am wondering if I will be making a big mistake by getting out! (smile) If I stay in, I can finish my education, but then I won't have much opportunity to practice what I would have learned. A man can be a bum or a millionaire, but which of these two will bring him contentment, happiness, and peace? I had a job offered to me last week that was a good deal, safe anyway; I would not have been getting shot at... I turned it down. I am not one who can sit back and take the safe or easy way out. Satisfaction for me comes from doing, and I like to sleep at night, knowing I have done my part or made every attempt to do so.

"We did manage to get a three-day break somewhere between operations where we were able to enjoy the beach, a cold beer, and a coke. I wish I had a camera to show you this beautiful area—high blue-green mountains reaching the clouds on the west. On the east, you have the wide blue sea. In between, there is a fifty-five-mile long valley. There is no jungle down here like there is in the Central Highlands. This place makes me wonder. Much of God's image of beauty has been planted here, yet so much death will reside."

***

"For the past three days, recon platoon has done nothing but sit around and wait. This is the first operation where no part of the Cavalry has taken any casualties due to hostile fire. Reports are coming in from the line companies; the VCs are steadily retreating, leaving everything behind. So far, the battalion has killed a little more than 300 VC in the past four days. We captured a VC barracks, which included a hospital, medical supplies, and eighteen tons of rice. Based on interrogations with our POWs, they have received orders to run instead of fight any element of the 1st Cavalry. Everyone has been expecting the VC to make a big offensive during the rainy season, but they have not. Perhaps Ho is changing his mind about winning this war. 'Sorry about that!'

"Well, once again, that day of rejoicing is coming near for me; seven days R&R in Bangkok. If it is ok with you, I'd like to pick you up some kind of a souvenir. Also, I will call you again if you don't mind. Ok? I want to ask you something important."

***

"Did he call you again?"
"He sure did!"

Chapter 23

Letters from Home

Mama got lost in thought for a bit and grabbed the top of my hand to lead me down memory lane. The New England days got shorter and the nights longer. The air grew crisp as the summer months rolled out, allowing the fall to take center stage. Seasons were changing like clockwork, indicative by the glorious transformation of colors on the trees lining the street. With school back in session, Billy was now a fulltime student joining his siblings at Wampatuck Elementary School. Mama was home alone all day and managed to fill her time welcoming another handful of soldiers to Operation Morale Booster roster. She was as happy as she could be preparing for my arrival, corresponding with her soldiers and having a little extra time for herself now that all three children were in school.

Much like the ever-changing New England weather, this feeling of bliss was about to take a turn. In one week, Mr. Baker made four marches up to the door in a similar fashion as he did that fateful August day. Stamped envelopes "Returned to Writer," "Returned to Writer," "Returned to Writer," "Returned to Writer," all quickly solidified their status as unwelcomed guests in the Hunter household, so much so, she chose not even to mention their arrival to the children. It did not deter her from her mission as it had tempted to do so a couple of months ago, but it sure did affect the tone of her week. She yearned to hear from Bob. It had been a while since she had heard from him, but she knew the mailing logistics were still working its way back to normalcy after the forty-three-day strike.

As Mama described it, it was a Sunday; shortly after the family returned from church, the kids were changing into their play clothes while Dad was already out weeding the flower beds in the front yard. The phone rang, which was a bit unusual for a Sunday morning. Mama answered the phone in her typical singsong voice, "Good Morning, this is the Hunter residence."

"Good Morning, Joan, it's Bob." Her expression went stone-cold as if she heard from a ghost.

"Bob! Oh, thank God you are ok!"

"Of course, I'm ok. What made you think I wasn't?"

"I don't know. I haven't heard from you in so long... and...and... I don't know; I have received so many of my letters returned from my soldiers... I...I guess I was fearing..."

Bob interrupted her, "I am fine, Joan, I will always be fine. But thank you for caring," as he let out a faint chuckle. "I am on R&R right now, and I wrote that I was going to call you. I guess you haven't received that letter yet."

"No, no, I haven't. This strike has made a mess, hasn't it?" She paused. "How are you, ol' bean?"

"I am good... really good. I think the war might be coming to an end by the looks of things." Bob paused. "I wanted to talk to you further about the interracial marriage concept. I am still really torn about it all, and I look to you and Paul for sound advice. I am struggling with the idea I may be bringing a child into the world to only offer him or her a rough life."

"Are you in love with a woman of another race right now?" Mama tenuously asked, slightly fearing his response.

"No."

"Well, then just don't go looking for love outside your race then." Mama cringed as that rolled off her tongue. There was a long pause. No doubt, they both didn't like the sound of that advice.

"Joan, I just don't think that is the answer."

Dead silence.

"No, no, neither do I, Bob," she conceded. "I am just not as brave or as strong as you. I could never trailblaze such a path." Again, there was silence. Mama cleared her throat as if to clear away previous beliefs. "Bob, I think you should marry whoever you truly fall in love with. If God brings you together with a woman who sincerely loves you, who happens to be of another race, then He will also give you the strength and wisdom to raise and protect any and all children you may be blessed with. Know the road will be tough, but you are the one choosing it. I can see the type of man you are already. You are a man of honor and commitment. You are a pioneer, Bob, and for that, I admire you immensely. Generations from now, miscegenation will be commonplace because of people like you. And maybe, just maybe, we will finally all live as one human race."

"You really think so, Joan?"

"Yeah, I do. Bob, I don't know how all of this is going to turn out, but I have to hold on to the belief that what God leads us into, He leads us through. You have already escaped death a few times in the short time we have been writing, so clearly, He has a plan for you. Live your life and make your decisions as if you are making them in front of God. Always strive to be your own best version. The Jesuits have a motto we live by, *Ad Majorem Dei Gloriam*, (For the Greater Glory of God.) Everything we do, we do it to please our God. If you keep this tenet, I feel confident He will bless you with abundance."

"Thank you, Joan. I needed to hear that. I have to go now, but please give my best to Paul and the kids."

Mama wanted to share the news of her pregnancy ahead of the letter she had sent since he was on the line, but before she could utter another word, the line went dead. She was left holding the handset to a dead line. Lifting the corner of her mouth, and letting out an audible sigh, she thought, *Oh well, I hope I gave him the right advice. It felt right anyway.*

A couple of weeks after he called, this letter arrived:

Sgt. Robert E. Johnson
Sept. 22/66

To My Dear Friends:

As you can see, I am a sergeant now!

I received both letters from you today as I am just returning from R&R. Congratulations to both of you on the expectancy of a new addition to the Hunter family! I know you must be thrilled. I guess Mr. Hunter must be overjoyed with the idea of a baby boy. I say boy because we need more men in this world like Mr. Hunter, so it has to be a boy! If it's a girl… 'Sorry About That,' maybe next time. But now, I really must come and see you before you get too busy with the new baby. Here is a little poem inspired by your joyous news:

"A Child is Born"

A child is born and a man dies.
To give one, I must take one,
Just like the days,
for today shall be tomorrow and today was yesterday,
for a tear must fall, and fog shall rise.
A house must be built, a home must be created.
A wife must produce and a husband must provide,
so it all shall be life, a home, a blessing and a conquest.
For the child shall be born un-to the Hunters.

My tentative rotation date now is the 15th of October, so I should reach the USA on the 16th, and be at your home no later than the 17th.

This war must be coming to an end. The fighting has been limited to small action, nothing like it was a few months ago. As a matter of fact, the only resistance we seem to be meeting now is wounded VC snipers who have been left behind by their retreating comrades. To give you an idea, we have been on Operation Byrd since the 26th of August, and to date, we have only had one man killed, and none wounded throughout the entire battalion. All the while, we have captured more than a hundred VC, killed fifty, seized ten weapons, fifty tons of rice, two field hospitals, one field headquarters, and three trucks. So, this indicates one of two things... either we are getting exceptionally good at guerilla warfare, or the Viet Cong are tired of fighting.

I guess America is unbeatable. There is so much we have that other countries don't. ~ Love for freedom, Love of democracy, Love of our fellow man, and Love of Our God!! They say we have the best equipment and fighting men of the world, but we also have the best people in the world backing us; people like the Hunters.

With Love,

Bobby

***

Not more than three days later, Bob had scribed another letter with an unexpected turn of events.

"The way the things are now with Ho Chi Minh and the 1st Cavalry, I may be spending my thirty-day leave right here. The war has now become a personal fight between North Vietnamese troops and the 1st Cavalry. North Vietnamese have placed a bounty on the heads of the 1st Cavalry~ 5000 won (equivalent to $50) for a dead GI, 1000 ($10) for a wounded GI and 500 ($5) for a captured alive GI, which no GI intends to be captured alive. (Sorry about that, Charlie!). In response to the new initiative, our battalion commander put out a similar order... a three-day pass for every capture. So, you see how I can't leave when this has become a personal vendetta against my battalion.

"As a result of the 1st Cavalry having the air power that we do, we are the biggest threat to the North Vietnam Army. At present, we are fighting on three fronts: Bong Son, the Central Highlands, and here, where the 7th Cavalry is located now. When I extended my tour, I had the opportunity to go to another outfit, completely pulled out of combat, but I feel as long as there is a war raging, I must remain here... a part of the first team, the 1st Airmobile Cavalry. I have included some clippings of the Cavalry and the history summarized in a poem."

***

"Did he come home for his thirty-day leave?"

"Well, yes and no." Mama smiled with pressed lips and explained. "Strongly encouraged by his commanding officer, Bob did take his military granted, stateside thirty-day leave. Shortly after landing in Philadelphia, however, he fell victim to a 102-degree fever. His family rushed him to the hospital with the concern of malaria, and he spent the first two weeks in the States lying in a hospital bed. Released from the hospital on day sixteen of being in the States, he decided to visit with his mom for a few days and then returned to Vietnam ahead of schedule. Evidently, he simply couldn't stand the thought of his comrades fighting and dying while he was laughing with family, sleeping in comfortable beds, and living carefree in the States, even if it was only for a well-deserved rejuvenating break. So, he forfeited his intended visit to meet us and flew straight to Vietnam to rejoin his platoon.

"Upon returning to Vietnam, he shot off a letter to us, asking for forgiveness for not fulfilling his commitment to visit. He explained what happened, offering a sincere apology. Coupled with his devotion to his platoon that we know he has, we completely understood, and there were no hard feelings. The last paragraph of his letter brought tears to my eyes." Mama handed it to me to read.

"I had this plaque made up before leaving Vietnam in hopes of being able to present it to you in person. Since I was not able to do that, I've decided to mail it to you. I hope you will accept it. Hoping it will remind you of all the gratitude we feel for all you do to make us happy. I wish I could show you how much appreciation there is for you here.

So, Until... June Perhaps,
Bobby"

The plaque read: **Forever in our hearts, because of your heart. Joan Hunter, you have succeeded in your mission of boosting our morale. ~Gary Owen**

Chapter 24

Proud Mary

As the holidays of 1966 were fast approaching, Mama made a concerted effort to energize her groups, encouraging them to send some Christmas cheer to the boys on the frontlines. Whether young enlistees or seasoned soldiers, she imagined being away from loved ones during Thanksgiving and Christmas must-have tugged at-the-heart a little more than any other day. She had only heard from Bob once since his return to Vietnam. She was concerned that perhaps he was not in a healthy emotional state after being sick and visiting with family, which may have been a motivating factor in returning to Vietnam earlier than originally intended. She shot off a couple of letters and a package and waited anxiously for a reply. It seemed like forever since she had heard from him, but she remained optimistic. Much to her surprise, she received a letter from Bob he had composed on Thanksgiving Day and subsequent messages he must have rifled off in the following four weeks, all exuding high spirits.

"I hope this finds you well and enjoying all the splendors the holidays offer. As for me, I am doing just fine. I received your letter today. Of all days, Thanksgiving! Believe it or not, but I think this day has been my best day in a long time. Only ten minutes after being decorated with the Air Medal, I received your letter. We had a Thanksgiving dinner with turkey, wine, and cranberry sauce. Perhaps, I am a little drunk today, but I can still write. (smile) I have included a copy of my citation, and I apologize for the wax on it. My candle was dripping.

"One thing I want you to know, I honestly did want to see you. It pained me to not be able to see you and the family. You said I don't owe you an apology, well, if not to you, then to the family. I don't know why God is so good to me. He has saved me from death many times, and He gave me you and Paul. I don't deserve you two as friends.

"As for my family, I was glad to see them. I felt like a man returning from the dead. I don't regret one moment I spent with them, but they did help me make one big decision in my life, although they don't know this yet. I have decided to remain in the service. I know now that I could never be satisfied outside the Army. I guess this is my kind of life, being what I call a drifter in uniform.

"You asked if I have seen Eddie Z., I haven't seen him in 9 months. I don't know where or how he is? Don't worry if you haven't heard from him, maybe he has returned to the States and back with his family."

***

Not sure if he had written that purely for Mama's benefit or not, but she was willing to adopt this thinking going forward. Admittedly, she confided that she had hoped her pen pals would have sent her a letter upon their safe return to the States offering her closure. She then reiterated that she didn't start this writing campaign for her benefit so much as for theirs; closure was not a requirement or guarantee. Additionally, thinking they were safely back home in the States felt much better on her heart than the current assumption that they had perished or worse... were missing in action.

She put the letter aside and picked up the official citation, which did indeed have some dripped candle wax, adding character to the important military document of honor. It read:

CITATION
BY DIRECTION OF THE PRESIDENT
THE AIR MEDAL
IS PRESENTED TO

**CORPORAL E4   ROBERT E. JOHNSON
RA136382238**

UNITED STATES ARMY

For distinguishing himself by meritorious achievement while participating in sustained aerial flight in support of combat ground forces in the Republic of Vietnam during the period:

17 December 1965 to 1 June 1966

During this time, actively participating in twenty-five aerial missions over hostile territory in support of counterinsurgency operations. During all of these missions, he displayed the highest air discipline order and acted in accordance with the best traditions of the service. By his determination to accomplish his mission despite the hazards inherent in repeated aerial flights over hostile territory and his outstanding degree of professionalism and devotion to duty, he has brought credit upon himself, his organization and the military service.

***

"Mama, this is so cool! I have never seen a Military Citation before. It's sweet how he wanted you to see it." She smiled; I paused. "You are family to him," I declared, emphasizing the "are." She smiled again. Her eyes twinkled just a bit brighter than the northern star. "Aww, Mama, you are such an amazing woman. I can't believe you did all this while raising four small children. You were so devoted to these men...to Bob." I selfishly let her relish in the accolades because I thoroughly enjoyed observing the life coming back into her eyes. Before long, she defaulted to her behind-the-scenes shyness, not comfortable with this spotlight, she reached for the next letter and began to read.

Dec. 1st/1966

My Dear Friends:

While sitting here behind my bunker taking advantage of the very little free time we have, I thought that I would write this letter. Between patrols and night ambushes, we have very little time to do anything. Just about every night we go on a night ambush and come

145

back to camp at daylight at 0700 to 1200. We are on a 30-minute stand-by alert for downed helicopters. At 1300, it is back on patrol, how far and how long we stay, depends on what kinds of signals we pick up concerning the Viet Cong. Yesterday, we went out at 0900 and didn't come back in until late in the afternoon. So, you see, we don't have too much free time.

As far as the war is going, all indications have us believing North Vietnam must be getting tired of fighting. All over Vietnam, things have been pretty quiet except for small scale patrol action. As a matter of fact, I was reading in the paper that Hanoi asked the US for a truce over Christmas Holidays. Last Christmas, when we made a truce, the North Vietnamese violated it and attacked us on Christmas Eve. So, you see Joan; even an agreed-upon truce is not sacred in war. I am hoping this is the final Christmas I will have to spend overseas. This year will mark my ninth one away from home (meaning the USA). It is just about the worst part of being away. Christmas is not Christmas unless it is spent with the ones you love.

I think this year, I will hang my stocking outside my bunker. Maybe Oh Charlie will fill them up, probably with hand grenades (smile). Which reminds me...

"Ho, Ho, Ho Chi Minh"

It was the night before Christmas and all through the jungle,
not a creature was stirring, not even a mouse.
All GIs were nestled in their beds
while visions of home and their loved ones,
flashing in their heads.
Suddenly there was such a clatter,
I sprinted to the bunker window to see what was the matter.
My eyes fell on a group of Congs dressed in black,
the muzzle of their weapons,
were flashing like lights on a Christmas tree,
but he was not trying to decorate no tree,
he was surely trying to kill me.
Greetings from Ho Chi Minh,
Peace on Earth and good will to men.

This is the greeting that we got last year from Hanoi. Perhaps this year he will think differently now that he has lost the war, although he has not yet fully realized it.

So, until,
Bob

***

"It's so sad to read his letters where he is so certain the end of the war is near knowing what we know now, which couldn't have been further from the truth. We are still in the year 1966 reading his letters; we have another six years to go before he returns to the states and the war continued! Why did we allow ourselves, as a country, to be so weak and ineffective? Please... please tell me it wasn't because of politics?" Following a momentary stare into my eyes, Mama left this unanswered. Another unwritten rule, never discuss politics in your home; it is simply too evocative for a peaceful home, even if all are of the same mindset. Instead, she grabbed another letter.

December 15/66

Dear Paul and Joan:

Well, it seems as if you came through again like champs for me. I received your letter and package today. Thank you very much! I needed this pick me up.

I have just returned from a three day/night patrol in the mountains to come back and learn I have no job as of tomorrow. The Battalion is making a change in concept and making recon into an infantry platoon. If you don't hear from me in quite a while, please do not worry. I will probably be transferring to another unit. This infantry bit is not for me as I am an adventurous man. A guy adapts himself to a particular pattern in life, and he is not satisfied unless he is doing just that. Adding to my fatigue from the patrol, being made aware of this change upon returning had gotten me depressed. I tell you this, so you believe my sincerity when I say receiving your package picked my morale up a lot.

I never dreamed of having a checkerboard and a dartboard, thank you. I enjoyed playing checkers quite a bit before coming to Vietnam. My platoon sergeant and I played six games this evening using 45 caliber bullets as checkers. They worked well. (smile)

I received a package from Mrs. Turner~ Den 8, Pack 69. My squad and I really enjoyed it. I sent her a thank you note. I have not received the other package that you sent me as of yet. The mail gets a little fouled up during this time of the year. As a matter of fact, it took thirteen days for this package to get to me. Pretty soon, we will have to start using rocket mail instead of airmail. (smile)

This holiday season, my company is planning on introducing Christmas to some of the local kids. We will take a few from each small village and let them live at basecamp with us for a week. This gesture of pacification also brings to mind what Task Force Byrd is all about. Three and a half months ago when we first came here, everything had been destroyed by the Viet Cong. So far, the 2nd Battalion 7th Cavalry has liberated 275 miles of country and has freed over 1 million Vietnamese living in the area. We have turned all of this over to the control of the South Vietnamese government. We gave the countless tons of rice that we recently captured from the Viet Cong to the local people. So, we struck a hard blow to the Viet Cong again. Task Force Byrd is scheduled to end sometime around the first of the year. Then probably back to hardcore fighting again. All I can say about "Oh Charlie" is "Sorry about that."

Well, Joan, have a very Merry Christmas and allow the New Year to bring you all the happiness you two wonderful people deserve. Every time I write a letter to you, it is like writing to my own family, akin to my big brother and sister. (smile)

With Love,
Bob

***

Not more than three days later, Bob was promoted to platoon sergeant status, which was two grades up in rank. He had been chosen among three other Non-Coms, all of whom outranked him, so he was honored and quite proud. In fact, out of character for Bob, he wrote about his military accomplishments. "Perhaps this may sound that I am bragging a little on myself, well, if it does... I am. (smile) Right now, I am the most decorated man in the Company and Battalion. I am the youngest Platoon Sergeant in the Battalion; my records consist of two Bronze Stars, the Army Commendation Ribbon, the Purple Heart, the Air Medal, and a letter of recommendation for battlefield promotion to 2nd Lieutenant. So, I have nothing to be ashamed of and much to be proud of."

Mama and I chuckled at this 180 from his usual humble, "I am just like everyone else" posture; but we were happy to see it. "He should be proud," I declared. "Honestly, it pains me to know he was always trying to earn his worth. It sounds like deep-seated sentiments, and it makes me want to find him and hug him." Squinting my just over-fifty eyes as if trying to see the ideas racing through my mind a bit clearer, I uttered, "I wonder if he is still alive.

Chapter 25

Guide My Feet

We took a break from reading and decided to get some fresh air with a short walk around the neighborhood. Mama's steps were shorter in stride than even those of two months ago when she first arrived in Nashville. Her requests to stop and gaze at a sitting bird or admire the early spring buds were becoming more frequent. Mama's decline provided quite a dichotomy against the backdrop of our time spent with her, just minutes before, as a young mom. Motivated to keep her mind engaged with the letters, I continued the conversation inquiring about what the relationship looked like after returning from Vietnam and her thoughts on his probable whereabouts.

Just as we were turning onto the driveway, Mama summed it up, "Well, Susan, we exchanged Christmas cards for many years; perhaps a good ten or fifteen years after his return from Vietnam. Then, I think life just got in the way, and we stopped connecting."

We walked up the driveway in somewhat somber silence. Mama's head was hanging slightly lower, and her lips pierced just a bit. Her own audible of "life getting in the way" had struck a broken chord of the relationship sealed with the same fate. Bellies were grumbling at this point, and the idea of changing gears was making an entrance, so we indulged in some fruit salad, sandwich, and a tall glass of sweet tea before returning to our mission.

I separated all of her typed letters and changed things up. Going forward, we agreed I would read Bob's letters, while she would read her own, mimicking a stage play or script reading session. It was such a treat to have her responses attached to Bob's letters because it allowed me to share in their full dialogue as opposed to just reading one side of the conversation. In one of her letters, she had asked him about a man from Scituate who she had heard was serving in the same cavalry. She admitted she didn't know how big a cavalry was but took a shot in the dark. He was gracious in his response laying out the structure for her better understanding.

"Ok, here is a broad brush run down, solely meant to give you an idea of the enormity of logistics. A division is typically made up of three brigades (a couple thousand men). Each brigade is made up of three battalions. A battalion has a handful of companies. Each company has three platoons and each platoon has three squads (roughly ten men per squad).

"You asked if I knew of a commanding officer by the name of Colonel Casey. No, I don't, he is in the 2nd Brigade, and I am in the 3rd Brigade. The three brigades in the division, are assigned a sector of Vietnam. Although we are all stationed at An Khe (1st Cavalry Base Camp), we don't operate together. At present, the 3rd Brigade has been on Task Force Byrd since August. We are 396 miles from An Khe, right on the coast of the South China Sea. As a matter of fact, we are only 500 meters from the beach. Unfortunately, we don't get a chance to meet too many other guys outside our brigade."

January 1/ 67

Dear Joan,

I thought that I would take this opportunity to write to you to wish you a Happy New Year. I hope this finds you and the family doing well and welcoming in another big year for you with the baby soon to arrive. As for me, I am doing just fine.

Christmas this year was a little more than I expected it to be considering the circumstances. To begin with, Christmas morning was spent repelling out of a helicopter; after that, we spent the rest of the morning building bunkers. We set up a basecamp about six miles away from the Battalion, out in the middle of nowhere, so we had to fortify our position. Anyway, that afternoon, the entire battalion was treated to a special Christmas surprise by the Army. So, you can see what a morale booster this was, especially for the younger men who spent their first Christmas away from home.

This year will bring a lot of big decisions for me. The most important of them is whether I should re-enlist or not. I am torn because I believe my desire to re-enlist is out of fear for what lies for me at home in the States. If I do re-enlist, I will want to sign on for another tour here in Vietnam. I know myself well enough to know that I could not serve anywhere else if this war continues. That may sound crazy, but that is the way I feel.

Tell me, Paul and Joan, I know you really don't know me too well, but perhaps you can help me. Should I stay, or should I get out? I ask you this because I consider you both as being my most stable minded friends. I have three months to make this decision. I can get out June 8th, but since they send you back to the States eighty-nine days prior for discharge, I would make it back in March.

Here are some clippings of the fighting that the Cavalry was involved in last year, including Operation Masher, which I will never forget.

Until next time,
Bob

***

"I wonder what the treat was that made it so special," I audibly pondered in between letters.

Mama answered, "It was quite a diversion in many ways. I remember him telling me about it the next time he called, about a week before you were born." She collected her thoughts and then launched into a detailed recount of the call.

"The phone rang on a Sunday afternoon, and Dad picked up. On the other end was a gravely but cheerful voice, 'Good afternoon Paul, this is Bob, Bob Johnson.'

" 'Bob! How great to hear from you! Where are you calling from?... Let me get Joan to pick up the other line.' He hollered over to me, 'Joan, grab the other line; it's Bob.'

"I darted to the living room and picked up the receiver, 'Hi Bob! Where are you?'

" 'I am in the hospital again, but I am okay. I was playing chicken with a bullet and lost,' he chuckled, always downplaying his bravery. 'I know you two are about a week away from your baby's arrival and will be super busy. I have to make my decision about re-enlisting in the next few days, so I wanted to reach out one last time to hear your thoughts. I am so glad to have you both on the phone.'

"Dad immediately responded in that voice-of-reason tone and content, 'Well, first of all, we are glad to know you are okay. And yes, we are a little less than a week away; however, we will always have time for you, so never feel like you can't call us.' Dad paused to allow me to interject my sentiments.

" 'I second that, Bob. Paul and I will always make time for you. But you might want to stop playing chicken with bullets and stick to playing checkers with the bullets.' They laughed, perhaps more at my attempt to be funny than the joke itself.

"Dad inquired in an imperative tone, 'Well, Bob, the decision is ultimately yours to make, so can you share your thinking thus far with us?'

" 'Yes, of course. I toggle back and forth with this. When I am feeling good about my efforts here and my decision to return to the States, something moves me, and I wonder if they are nudges from God guiding me to stay. For instance, I was so sure this was going to be my last Christmas away from home. I had earned my worthiness in my mind and was ready to start my life back at home, but then on Christmas Day, hot chow was brought out to us in heated containers: turkey, pie, mashed potatoes, vegetables, even including ice cream; I felt so appreciated. Then the chaplain had a chorale of Vietnamese kids flown in by helicopter to sing us Christmas songs.' He paused, and with a crack in his voice, he muttered, 'I was blindsided with emotion as I could feel a rush of warmth run through my body. I felt so much love in my heart for these kids. Their hearts are pure, their eyes filled with gratitude and hope. They hunger to spend time with us. They are eager to learn and stay by our side to help when we rebuild their villages. I don't think I can leave them. I think it would haunt me every night while I lie in bed and think of them a world away with one less person to help protect them; one less person to fight for their freedom. I don't think I would be right with myself.'

"A long silence followed his narrative. Dad pressed further, 'Okay, what would be your driving reason to return to the States?'

" 'That's just it... I don't really have one,' Bob admitted in a dejected voice.

" 'What about your dreams of an education and starting a family?' I chimed in.

" 'I still want them both, but thinkin' putting them off a year or two really won't make much of a difference. Plus, the States don't seem safe these days for a person with my color skin; I almost fear coming back home. Ironically, I feel safer here.'

" 'Bob, it sounds to me like you have already made your decision. We had read in many of the letters of your emotional dips when you were safe in the hospitals, feeling powerless against the cause. Your last line about not feeling right with yourself stood out for me. What do you think, Joan?'

" 'I think you should follow your gut. I have always believed it to be God's way of helping us make decision,' I suggested. 'Sounds like your Christmas was a beautiful experience. When something makes you feel that deeply, it is hard to walk away from it.'

" 'So, tell us… where did you get a shot? Dad questioned.

"With a little bravado chuckle, 'Well, as the saying goes, 'March came in like a lion' alright… with a hail of bullets, and I was in the middle of it playing John Wayne. I was hit in the thigh. Miraculously, the round made a clean pass through, which will probably keep me laid up a few weeks and then back to duty again. I guess all is fair in love and war,' he jested. 'I sent a letter to you about it two days ago, when I first arrived at the hospital so in a week or so, you will have a full account of what happened when that letter arrives. I do have to get off the phone now, though. I appreciate your listening and your advice. I feel a huge weight lifted off my shoulders, knowing you both feel that I should follow my gut, thank you. Good luck with the baby; I am hoping for a baby boy because we need more men like you, Paul.'

"Dad let out a gracious laugh, 'Thank you, Bob. I am hoping for a girl, though, so it will balance off the family perfectly with two boys and two girls,' he laughed again.

"I rushed in a quick good-bye and plea to stay away from any more bullets."

Recognizing it had to have been a tough conversation for all three of them, and I inquired if she remembered how she had felt after having given him the advice to follow his gut.

"Yes, I do. I actually felt liberated. Hearing the crack in his voice as he recounted his Christmas experience told me where his heart resided. Additionally, hearing the relief in his voice after we gave our thoughts left no question."

"That makes sense. And of course, knowing he made it out of that war pretty much confirms it was the right decision for him. So, what was the story behind the bullet this time?"

"Oh, Susan, it was awful. Truly a pivotal event in his entire time in Vietnam. Do you remember the kid he called Missouri?"

"Yeah, sure do," I nodded.

"Well, it involved him."

Chapter 26

American Soldier

Mama tried her best to recall the events of this fateful day. Her heart sank, and the tears began to seep out and roll down her empathetic face as told the story of the most horrific scene imaginable. "Although all was quiet on the frontlines, newspapers reported that Ho Chi Minh said he would make this war last another two, five, or ten years if needed. Bob's cavalry set out on a dangerous reconnaissance mission to assess their forces' strength to back-up, or invalidate his statements. Navigating the dense hills, seeking evidence of Charlie, Bob led the cadre with his young protégé, Missouri, next in tow. Peril was in the air but adrenaline-filled their hearts. Astutely avoiding the Viet Cong booby-traps, step by step, and without a sound, the men scanned the landscape and took note of every sound of nature. Three hours in, Bob could see that his men were tiring, so he called for a ten minute 'at your position' break to hydrate, while he continued ahead to get a look at what was over the crest of the hill. The men halted in their positions and grabbed for their canteens. A few remained standing while others sat in the pathway. Bob adroitly traversed the remainder of the climb to peak over the hill and down into the valley. A quick scan spotted a well dug in Viet Cong encampment, so he turned to head back down the hill to rejoin his squad.

"As he approached, the men started to shore up their canteens in preparation to continue the reconnoitering efforts. Just twenty-five feet away from the group, and seemingly in slow motion, he watched the sitting Missouri roll onto his left side to get up and into position. This moment forever seared into memory and mind. A blinding fiery flash and an unforgettable blast from a buried bomb exploded beneath Missouri, fragmenting the young comrade's body right before their eyes. Without hesitation, Bob ran toward the explosion while stripping himself of his shirt. Upon reaching the engulfed young soldier, Bob extinguished the fire with the use of his shirt and nearby dirt.

"Fraught with fright like never seen before in the eyes of this consummate soldier, Bob grabbed the body parts of his young charge and threw him over his shoulder to run him back to the APC (Armored Personnel Carrier) about 2 miles away. This explosion signaled the nearby Viet Cong, exposing the US position. Enemy snipers surfaced from under camouflaged terrain and from distant tree limbs showering a fusillade of shots into the retreating US forces. A couple of his men tried to provide some form of cover to allow him to escape with his young comrade limp over his shoulder, but they were only partially successful.

"Bob received a bullet through his thigh as he was in mid-stride, but continued running to the waiting APC to get Missouri air-lifted to a nearby field hospital as quickly as possible. It wasn't until he reached the APC that he noticed that he also needed medical attention. It was clear to all except Bob that Missouri didn't make it. Bob kept screaming at the medic to give attention to his young friend instead of him. The medic grabbed Bob by both shoulders and steadied his demeanor. He looked him in the eye and said with a stern but compassionate tone, 'He didn't make it, sir. I am sorry, we lost another good one.'

"Bob fell to his knees and banged the ground with both fists screaming, 'No! No! Why?... I hate this place!' Like a flip of a switch, he stood up, shook his head slightly but with intensity and whispered, 'We lost a great one. And now there is one more fatherless boy out there.' He turned away to face the hill from which he had just come and projected in a calm but eerie voice, 'And the worst part... It's all my fault. I ordered the 'at your position break.' If only I had allowed the men to break a few minutes earlier, he would not have been in that spot.'

"The medic, trained at identifying survivor's guilt, looked Bob in the eyes again and offered, 'This is war, sir. Regardless of the decisions made, men are going to die here. If it wasn't your man here, it might have been another one of your soldiers stepping on the buried explosive. Charlie has mastered the art of camouflaged warfare.' The medic grabbed some gauze from the metal box and tended to Bob's thigh. Bandaged him up and informed the driver that they needed to make dust-off at the LZ to get him to a hospital. Bob took one last look over at Missouri and, in an uncharacteristic moment, cradled his face in his hands and started weeping uncontrollably."

Tears welled in Mama's and my eyes as she concluded the story with a recap of Bob's pain in losing Missouri and feeling responsible for his tragic death. Survivor's guilt was a common psychological disorder to which many returning soldiers fell victim.

I felt this was a good time for a break since we were both pretty emotional, so I suggested she take her afternoon nap while I read ahead a bit to see if the next handful of letters were of a happier tone. As it turned out, I loved what I had to learn.

January 5/1967

My Dear Friends:

After returning from a three-day long-Range Patrol, I thought that I would take this opportunity to write to you since it will probably be quite some time before I get the chance to write again. Rumors are going around saying the Battalion will be going to Mekong Delta to seal off the Cambodian border pass. If this is true, the Cavalry will be in for some more hard fighting again this year. The Mekong Delta has five million people living in it, and most are reported to be Viet Cong or Viet Cong sympathizers. So, you can imagine what we will be getting into if we go in there.

To tell you a little bit about our three-day patrol. To begin with, it was very successful. We captured some thirty tons of rice, which is enough rice to feed a Viet Cong field army for a week. We covered something like twenty-seven miles on foot, so you can see a lot of walking was involved, which is something I love to do.

I wish that you and Paul could see this country. You can't begin to imagine how scenic the landscape is here. Many of the building structures you see are of French and Chinese design, which set it off. For miles you may be beating your way through the dense entangled jungle, then before you know it, you're right in the middle of desert plains, overlooking the South China Sea. You climb a mountain top and you look down into the valley floors to follow its stream beds, or take in the sight of a vibrant green jungle meeting the white sandy beach; both are stunning to see. I actually would like to come back after the war and see the country when it is settled and healed from all this destruction. Truthfully speaking, this is just about the most beautiful country that I have ever known.

What is truly striking, though, is the people. Their culture has not changed in the past 200 years despite having two countries ruling here: China in the 1400s and France for the last 100 years with, Japan patrolling their borders for whatever reason in the 40s. I would like to get to know the people better back in An Khe, which is 400 miles away from where we are currently operating. There are three Vietnamese orphaned girls between the ages of fourteen and seventeen who sold Coke to earn a living. Anyway, we got to be pretty close friends, and I tried to learn their language. I felt their plight, so I bought them a laundry shop, with two additional rooms they use as living quarters. So, now these orphan girls have a place to live and a pretty steady income washing the GIs clothing. They make a decent living. It cost me 8000 won ($80), which is not bad. I felt it was a good investment in mankind. (smile) Also, at Christmastime, my platoon gave the kids in the local village twenty pounds of candy, which we get once a week. The guys go in for this in a big way when it is for the local kids.

Do you remember me telling you of Operation Task Force Byrd? Well, here is a clipping. The recon platoon that is written about is ours before they disbanded it. Well, my friends, I have to close once again.

So, until,
Bobby

***

The clipping detailed the impactful work of the 1st Cavalry Division's 2nd Battalion, 7th Cavalry, giving specific credit to the Gary Owen troops in Operation Byrd. In response to an enemy attack on a Regional Force company, killing fifty-one government troops, Gary Owen was called-on to travel 476 miles to liberate the fertile land of jade green paddies from Viet Cong control. The article states that this local guerilla force was a second-generation fighting unit, sons of the Viet Minh, who battled the French in 1954. Their vast knowledge of the landscape made it tougher for the US troops to extricate the enemy and identify those who were still living within the villages as civilians during the day and then taking up arms at night.

The soldiers had to exercise discernment in areas not typical in a war setting. They had to make peace and earn the local Vietnamese's trust while simultaneously detecting, and rooting out, the enemies shrouded by similar culture and appearance. Striking that balance of inviting the locals onto basecamp as a gesture of hospitality, and protecting the camp from being scouted for a future attack, was often a point of contention between soldiers. This war had two objectives; eliminate the enemy, being the North Vietnamese Army and the Viet Cong, representing communism, and bringing pacification to South Vietnam who were trying to hold onto democracy and individual freedoms. Some soldiers were more hardwired toward the pacification aspect and others toward the elimination. Bob was somewhere in the middle, a peacemaker at the core but a fierce and courageous protector of freedom nonetheless.

To physically survive a tour in Vietnam, one needed to be a bit heavier on the gutsy and ruthless fighter side because there was plenty of hand-to-hand combat in this guerilla warfare. However, to survive it emotionally, a healthy dose of peaceful interaction with the friendly villagers through the act of pacification had to be experienced. The slant of their respective experiences while in Vietnam were likely indicative of the scars marking them for their post-war life. If one could find love in a battlefield, that too, might give them a leg up on making it out of this war, but how likely is it that a soldier could find love amidst such an ugly war.

Chapter 26

You Make Me So Very Happy

Mama's January letters primarily focused on her emotional and physical preparations for my arrival. Accommodating their small Cape style home to welcome the sixth member of the household proved to be a little bit of a challenge. In this small three-bedroom house, it became increasingly clear to both my parents that they would have to find a bigger abode to make it more comfortable for their growing family. They agreed to start searching for a new home after they got settled into life with baby #4; however, leaving Scituate was non-negotiable.

"Is he okay, is Bob okay!" Mama shouted from her bedroom. I ran to see her just as she woke from her nap, not even sure if she had woken herself up with her holler or if her concern for him was the first thing on her mind upon waking.

"Mama, everyone is fine. Were you dreaming?"

"Oh yes, Susan, it was awful, Bob Johnson, the soldier I wrote to during the Vietnam War, was running toward our house and a car came barreling around the corner and…"

"Bob is fine, nothing happened to him, you just had a nightmare," I interrupted. "Let me get you some water. Funny you should mention Bob; I was just reading letters he wrote to you. Want to read some with me?"

"Letters from Operation Morale Booster?"

"Yes, I found them and have been reading them while you were napping." I signaled her to join me as I got her a glass of cold water.

Fortunately, I had left off my reading of the letters at a good starting point to reconvene, and so we did. Bob's letters arrived more frequently, and each reserved a line or two dedicated to the anticipation of my arrival. He always kidded about hoping that I was going to be a boy and even suggested that if a girl arrived, to just send her back and start over because girls were too hard to raise. He further illustrated the demise of women:

"Marriage… Yes, I have become a firm believer in staying a bachelor. Did you ever think back over the history of marriage? The woman tries to make the man believe (and she almost succeeds) that there is a woman behind every successful man in life. Perhaps so, but this is only a theory and not a proven fact. What is a proven fact, women have been the reason for man's downfall. Here are seven examples from the history of the defeat of great men.

"1. Adam and Eve: Life was good on Earth for Adam and Eve. Adam had become very successful in life. He owned a significant portion of the Earth. He had everything that a man could want in life to include a lovely wife. There was only one thing that God forbid Adam to do: eat of the forbidden fruit… but Eve, being of sound mind of women, persuaded him to eat of the forbidden fruit, which led Adam to his downfall in life, and you know the rest of the story.

"2. Julius Caesar's downfall was because of a woman, wine, and song. (A Roman playboy before his time)

"3. Sampson and Delilah: His defeat came when Delilah clipped his hair (Again, a man before his time as he wore a Beatle hairstyle before the Beatles were even born)

"4. The Great Napoleon of France and Josephine: Napoleon had risen in the ranks of France from corporal to emperor of France. He conquered two-thirds of the world. Everything was going well for the little general until Josephine began nagging him about a new Russian fur coat that she wanted for the coming winter. He could take no more, so in the dead of winter, he took off with his army and marched to Waterloo, searching for a white Russian fur for his love.

"5. Our President Abraham Lincoln: one of the greatest Presidents in our history. If Mary, his wife, had not persuaded him to go to the opera, he would have never met his assassin's bullet, compliments of John Wilkes Booth.

"6. Jesse James, the famous bank and train robber. For years following the civil war, he had been successful in robbing banks and trains and stagecoaches, but what happened to him? A lovely lady seduced him, and they got married. He gave up his rewarding career, changed his name, and settled down. He was shot in the back while hanging a picture.

"7. Here in Vietnam... one of the enormous fighting forces on Earth's face is assembled; the fighting might of America and its allies. Nowhere in the history of warfare has there been any military force like it; the power, the striking force, the mobility, speaking on behalf of the mighty 1st Cavalry Airmobile Division, of course. Do you know what claimed two-thirds of our casualties? MALARIA. Infected by a mosquito, a female mosquito! So, you see, it is a female that hurts us more than anything else.

"Despite all the hardships and bitterness that man must endure because of women, they are irreplaceable, for without them... what other reason could we blame our downfalls? I sure hope you have a baby boy! (Smile)"

***

"It's funny, Susan, he always made such a big deal about having a boy as if that was the end-all, yet, God is clever. You will see what I mean as we get through these letters. Sometimes He answers our prayers by presenting us with opportunities that inspire us to broaden our minds instead of just granting us what we think we need."

"What? Did he eventually have a girl?"

"You will have to wait and see," Mama toyed with my need to know.

"Oh, c'mon, tell me!" I pleaded.

"Hmmm, I think this will be an opportunity for YOU to enhance your patience," she bantered.

"Fine..." shaking my head and rolling my eyes, secretly committing to get through the letters today whether Mama could or not.

"All joking aside, he was swamped with work and responsibility but thoroughly enjoying his role as sergeant of what he touted to be the best Division in the Army; the 1st Cavalry Division Airmobile. Look at this letter dated January 22, 1967; it is on official 1st Cavalry stationery." Mama handed me the letter.

It sure was impressive stationery, donning the US Army 1st Cavalry insignia in the upper left corner. A distinctive bright-yellow Norman knight's shield with a right to left ascending diagonal black stripe and the silhouette of a horse's head to its right. Originally designed bright yellow and blue, colors long associated with the cavalry, the blue was changed to black for better visibility and illustrating the transition to iron and armor. The diagonal strip was emblematic of the enemy castle walls scaled in the early years and later, to represent the mountains climbed and conquered. The horse's head remained constant as a tribute to the Division's original differentiating element. To the right of this insignia, in a robust and bold font, was "1st Cavalry Division" and below that in light script was "U.S. Armed Forces- Vietnam." A light-blue watermarked map of the region was at the bottom left corner of the stationery. The writing paper, itself, exuded his pride for his unit, far more formal than the lined paper he typically used.

"I must admit Paul and Joan, you sure know what a GI needs here in Vietnam. Every item that you sent... we need. I hope you don't mind that I am sharing your gifts. The cough medicine that you sent me helped a good friend of mine. This guy is an old Master Sergeant with twenty years of service already. He had a pretty bad cold, so I gave him the Formula 44, and it really knocked it out of him. He had been given some APC (All Purpose Cough) that did not help any. That is the trouble with the army doctor... if you hurt from the waist up, you get APC, from the waist down, it's foot powder. (smile) Once a week, we get what is called Sunday rations, which are generally the same items you included in the package you sent to me. So, you see, you do know what we need over here.

"On the 12th, I went on a three-day pass to Vung Tau, an in-country R&R center. The short rest was wonderful. However, I did make up for it the day I got back. One of our outposts had been attacked, so we spent the subsequent five days in the mountains looking for them. When we finally caught up with them, we had a pretty good battle on our hands, killing forty-eight, wounding six."

***

February 6/1967

To Dear Friends:

I received your letter today. I was more than anxious to hear from you considering the big event that is about to take place within weeks in the Hunter household. I did not expect to hear from you too often until after baby #4 arrived.

As for life with me, I have been quite busy chasing our friendly farmers (Viet Cong). This month is a big month for them as it is their New Year's; they must have a significant victory to start their year off right. They are rapidly losing face and backing from the Vietnamese population in this area, so they must do something big to regain their support.

General Westmoreland was here last week, giving a big speech to rally the troops. While he was here, he also pinned my Army Commendation Medal on me (second award). I will never forget this day. During this speech, he informed us the 1st Cavalry Division (Airmobile) was now classified as the most crack shot division in Vietnam. He also said how good the Gary Owen battalion was. This declaration may seem untrue, but it is the truth. According to the POWs, Hanoi has put out the order to their troops here in South Vietnam, to break all contact with any elements of the 1st Cavalry Division due to our strong fighting capabilities.

***

Bob continued his letter with an explanation of the origin of the Gary Owen nickname dating back to Custer's days. He included a rough drawing of the regiment crest. The depiction showed an upright horseshoe of blue, embellished with the name "Gary Owen" in gold. Resting inside the horseshoe is a white battle glove holding a golden saber. He described a scene of the men in his unit authoritatively humming the Gary Owen tune as they walked from a battlefield, ending with a crescendo battle cry of "Gary Owen is here, sorry about that Charlie."

After hearing of Mama's suggestive plea for him to satisfy his sense of duty of staying in the Army by serving his next tour stateside, Bob responded with a mathematical equation presenting why it was not a financially wise option.

"Since I am a non-com with over four years' service of active duty, I have to re-enlist for my present duty assignment (infantry), no choice of schooling. If I decide not to re-enlist, I will be forced out for ninety-three days, and then if I do decide to go back in, I have to return at one pay grade less (corporal again), plus I lose my re-enlistment bonus.

"I am making now:

$330 base pay
30 pro pay
16 overseas pay
65 combat pay
$431/ month (if I was married, an additional $133)

"We also are eligible to receive 'Jump' pay. ($55/jump) This opportunity would not be more than once a month.

"So, you see Joan, a sergeant with over eight years of service, cannot afford to get out, financially speaking. Also, one is only guaranteed ninety days of stateside duty before I become eligible to be sent back overseas."

***

Mama's letters were filled with trivial news of Dad's sports teams' successes and losses. Keeping him engaged with another male from home, who he greatly admired, was her way to keep stoking his fire of hope and endurance. Bob loved hearing all things, "Paul." There was a sincere brotherhood between the two. A natural thought leader, Bob found every vignette as an opportunity to showcase an element of virtue or a concept to ponder.

"Regarding Paul's basketball team: I am glad that he does not get upset when his team does not win a game. There are many more ways to 'win' a game. The main thing is how well one accepts defeat. If one can lose with goodwill toward the winner, he truly is the winner and the model sportsman.

"You know, speaking of winning... here I am fighting an enemy that is poorly equipped, untrained in the art of conventional warfare, and led by a bunch of less-educated leaders, yet withstanding the mightiest military force on the planet; the USA and her allies. For two years, our enemy has been fighting and holding on. One lone sniper, having nothing but a rifle and a few bullets, about 7 cents each, can cost the US a half a million dollars every time a helicopter is shot down. Sure, he is losing the war, but look at what it costs us to win. For the purpose we are here, it is worth it, but only if we succeed in stopping the spread of communism. But one can argue that Ho Chi Minh is also winning because he is proving that it does not take great wealth and giant machines to engage in a war or deliver a costly blow to mighty forces.

"Well, we just got our Coke and beer rations, including ice. We are given this once every three days. It is thoroughly appreciated, too. The platoon has been released to the beach for central R&R. It is only a mile away, so whenever we get the chance, we run there to spend some time near the sea. The weather is about 120 degrees on most days. Heat exhaustion is a real challenge for my men. Think of it, when we go out on a mission, there is only so much weight a soldier can carry; water and ammunition are ancillaries to survive, but both add great weight. Choosing the right balance can mean the difference between life and death. One thing I do like about the extreme heat in Vietnam... it paints an environment of no racial feelings because, after about six months of being here, everyone looks the same, everyone is dark-skinned. (smile)"

***

Bob was about to receive the best and the worst news yet since landing in Vietnam.

Chapter 27

We Gotta Get Out of This Place

Dear Friends:

I received your letter today, and I am thrilled to hear that you and the little princess, Susan, are doing just fine. Congratulations! Especially being a healthy 8 pounds, 2 ounces. Not too many come into this world that size! I admit, I am disappointed that you did not have a boy. You women already outnumber us two to one. Pretty soon, we will be electing a female President because you will have us outvoted. Oh boy! What would our country look like then? (smile)

As for myself, I am doing just fine, although a little aggravated. I am no longer pulling combat duty. Yes, my fighting days are over. At present, I am acting 1st Sergeant of the rear detachment here at base camp, and it is really driving me nuts.

When I got out of the hospital, I reported back to my company, who was just returning from a two-day patrol. The first thing they said was, "Congratulations on making Staff Sergeant, you are granted a five-day R&R in Hong Kong." And an hour later, I was ordered to get on the next chopper to An Khe for permanent duty in the rear. Seventeen months was enough to combat in their minds, and I had already had my share, so here I am, sitting behind a desk and going crazy. I am already regretting my decision to stay in Vietnam as a result of this new assignment. I'm thinking now I'd be better off at home, furthering my life at home if I cannot help in the field. This desk job will be a slow death for me. I'd rather die in action than rot here behind a desk. I can't earn my worth from behind a desk.

I am, however, coming home for my thirty-day stateside leave, scheduled to be leaving Vietnam around the 19th of June, which will put me in San Francisco on the 20th or 21st. I plan on spending a few days in California and then heading to Missouri to visit the kid's parents. He was the best soldier I had in my long-range patrol, a mighty fine trooper. His death has been the hardest thing I have had to deal with so far in this ugly war. I don't even know how to tell his parents how he died; it was so awful. My mind still replays that whole event every night when I lay my head down to sleep. My nightmares have gotten so disruptive; I wonder if I have been put on desk duty because of the nightmares. Honestly, it's gotten to the point where dying doesn't scare me; living does. I never used to drink when I was leading a squad because I always wanted to make sure I was alert since things can change in an instant, but this desk duty... it is driving me to drink.

My friends, I have to close for now. It is chowtime and time to go to the club for a couple of cold ones. What else is there to do? (smile)

As Always,
Bobby

***

May 18/67

Dear Friends:

I received your letter yesterday evening after returning from Bangkok, Thailand. I was shocked to hear from you to tell you the truth since it had been so long. I was beginning to think that maybe I had said something in my last letter that might have displeased you or Paul, maybe about the idea of women becoming President or merely hoping for a boy. Then, I thought that perhaps the demands of the new baby were keeping you from being able to write as often.

You can see that I am a staff sergeant now, and still killing time behind the scene, as you say. Being in the rear is sickening. There are NCOs (non-commissioned officers) and privates back here who have never fired a shot or seen any combat since being in Vietnam, yet they wear CIBs (Combat Infantryman Badges). They are also collecting the $65/month combat pay. I think this is so wrong. As fighting reports come in from the field of a company or battalion, it hurts me because I am safe behind a desk while men are out there dying or having their legs blown off.

Last week, I visited my company commander and my old squad. The guys told me how they have been praying that I come back and take over the team again. Two of them even said that they did not believe they would make it out of Vietnam alive if I am not there to lead them. So, you know how I feel. The next twenty-two-days I have left here will feel like twenty-two-years. I have done more drinking here in the last month than I have done in the past two years. I need to get out of this place.

Now my sights are on '68. I am trying to think about what my future will look like when I reach the good ol' USA next year. That sounds good, doesn't it? I envision going to school for commercial arts and drafting. As much as I hate to admit it, Paul even inspires me to give up my bachelorhood and instead follow in his footsteps, settling down to marriage and developing a model family, such as the Hunters. From everything that you have told me about him, I envy him. You must be the proudest wife in your neighborhood, having such a fine husband. I have told many of my comrades about you and him. Perhaps, when I get home next month, I will be able to visit you, and you two can help me plan out my future. The only problem is I don't know where to start. To tell you the truth, you and Paul are the only ones that I can call real friends.

Well, I have to close for now and get some work done.
See you soon,
Bobby

***

Days, weeks, months, go by with no word from Bob. Summer months were comfortable living in Scituate, with the beaches teeming with recreation and the harbor bustling with boaters, fishermen, and shoppers alike. In this small town, it was business as usual, carrying no evidence of wartime-mentality. People went about their day enjoying coastal activities. Dad did some local house painting during the summer months to supplement his teacher's income. Simultaneously, this afforded him a little more time to spend with the family than he usually had during the school year when he was teaching, coaching and refereeing. Days looked like this: Mama would walk us to the beach in the mornings with the routine of returning to the house for lunch. Going back to the house would give us a break from the hot sun and allow for Maryellen, Mike, and Billy to meet Mr. Baker at the curb to receive the mail. Meeting him at the curb was her way of willing away Mr. Baker's ability to make the melancholy trip to the door and hearing his dreaded knock. We would return to the beach mid to late afternoon joined by Dad by 4:30 pm. The older kids would enjoy building sandcastles with Dad while Mama would walk me back home and start dinner preparations. He would take each of my siblings, one at a time, out into the water, over their heads, and give them a fifteen-minute swim lesson. The one-on-one time was precious for all of us and a priority for Dad. By 6 pm, Dad and the kids made their way back to the house and washed up for dinner. Evenings were simple. Showers, pajamas, dinner, and then board games until bedtime.

Mama was exhausted by the end of the days with the summer months being so active and, of course, me requiring so much additional attention and energy. Her letter-writing suffered as a result. She appeared to have lost a little something inside, and an element of "going through the motions" became more prevalent. Not hearing from Bob for quite some time exacerbated this feeling and made a gaping hole in her heart. It was so perplexing because, as of his last letter, he was scheduled to leave Vietnam in June, returning to the States, meeting with her and Dad to set up a life for himself.

The agitation was revealed in the tension blanketing her face. It had been over three months since she last heard from him, and this was completely uncharacteristic. Mama had worried long enough without taking any action… so, she sat at her IBM and set off to get some answers.

August 2, 1967

Department of Defense
Pentagon Building
Washington, D.C.

Dear Sir:

I would like to know if you could give me any news about the fate of one of your soldiers in the 1st Air Cavalry. I have been a "pen pal" of this man for over a year and a half, and suddenly, since May 18th, he stopped writing. He had been planning on visiting my husband and our family when he returned to the States sometime in June. Since we are not related, I naturally would not have been informed if anything happened to him. His address is as follows:

S/Sgt. Robert E. Johnson
RA 13 638 238 Co. D
2/7th Cav. 1st Cav. (AM)
APO 96490, San Francisco, Calif.

Please write to me if you have any news of him. I would greatly appreciate knowing. Thank you.

Sincerely,
Mrs. Paul J. Hunter

***

Months followed, still no word from Bob, and no word from the Department of Defense. Mama was simply left to wonder. Although she continued her correspondence with the dozens of soldiers, there wasn't a day that she didn't think about Bob. Seven months in total had passed since his last letter. Preparing for the coming of a new year, she decided to take Bob's pictures down from the kitchen and tuck them away in a manila envelope along with the Life's February 11, 1966 issue, highlighting a story with images from Operation Masher. The cover photo of this issue was of the 'bandaged medic in the foxhole,' the loyal medic, Bob had written about. This image earned fame and significance beyond the Hunter household by being named Life's Picture of the Year. Accompanying the inside story of Operation Masher, were a handful of pictures, one of them being of Bob and his comrades resting in a foxhole.

Mama took one last long look at these images, her throat swelled, and her eyes watered and then tucked them away in a dresser drawer. She kept his Operation Morale Booster index card in the active section despite holding onto little hope of ever hearing from him again. For her, the photograph was all she had; for now, anyway.

Chapter 28

Fortunate Son

Out of the blue, roughly eight months since she last heard from Bob, a letter arrived. Almost in disbelief, Mama explained how she held it in her two hands and scrutinized the entire envelope before grabbing for her letter opener. Checking the postal stamp's date, secretly hoping it was dated many months earlier, proving it had simply been lost in the mail. She was immediately deflated and admittedly a little hurt when she noticed it was sent recently as the week before. As immediate as the hurt surfaced, she once again re-centered herself as to her role in this mission. This time, she had to dig a little deeper to do so, however.

January 17/68

Dear Friends:

It has been some time since my last communication. I am sorry for that. I thought that I would take this opportunity to drop you a few lines to let you know that I am doing fine, and likewise, I hope the entire family is enjoying all the many splendors that life may have to offer.

I am without a reasonable explanation as to why you haven't heard from me; please forgive me. I arrived at the 1st Cavalry's basecamp four days ago and managed to get my old job back; the same company and platoon. No more desk job for me, that was honestly killing me. The only difference is that two of my best friends were killed in a battle a couple of months ago on Thanksgiving Day, none in total from my company.

Some of the guys were surprised to see me back in action, but I told them that I came back because I know the guy who shot me and I intend to get him this time. (smile),

The entire division is making a big move north tomorrow morning, rumored to be heading to the DMZ. I'm glad they waited for me to return (smile) before heading out on this mission because I have been looking forward to this for a long time. By the way, I am acting as a platoon sergeant now. I am becoming a big wheel around here. (real joke)

Things are better here than they appear to be at home, though. I honestly couldn't take anymore of Rap H. Brown's "Black power" rhetoric when I was home this past summer. He is a disservice to our race and nothing but a loudmouth. He should be ashamed of himself. I would like to see him shoot off his mouth over here. Let him experience the Viet Cong for himself and see what real oppression looks like. Although I am not from the south, and the only time I spent in the south was with the Army, my experience made me feel that it is not the White man who is preventing my race from advancing; instead, it is ourselves. Leaders like Rap Brown, who focus on sorrow and pity, and calling for a change in such a radical way as he is, is wrong to do so and will not bring about the change needed. Violence should never be aligned with my race.

Martin Luther King, Jr. himself holds this tenet as paramount. His march on Washington a few years ago proved this. Change through peaceful protest and dialogue. His efforts are making great strides for the Black community because he shows the country, we are equal, respectful, and God-loving people. His stance is not for Black Power or White Power, but rather, God Power. Did you know, Joan, that Martin Luther King Jr.'s father was actually named Michael King, a pastor as well, of course? Yes, this is true. He changed his name to Martin Luther King as a result of becoming so aligned with the belief system of the German theologian, Martin Luther, and his stand against certain aspects of the Catholic Church in the 1500s. He broke away from the church in a radical movement to become a seminal figure in the Protestant Reformation. The very pillar of Luther's foundation was to preach and practice non-violent protesting. This separation was a gigantic move in the sixteenth century when there was no distinction between church and state. Standing up for one's rights is admirable, and I am proud to be earning respect from all colors by serving in the Army, just as all colors are earning my respect. Rioting in the streets as Rap Brown is igniting tarnishes my race and will inevitably set us back in our movement toward the ideals of our country's founding documents.

Well, I need to ready my squad for the hard slog toward the DMZ. I will leave you with a poem I recently wrote called Yesterday.

"Yesterday"

It seemed as if it was only yesterday that I was racing around the
block of my neighborhood,
on my skates, or bike, and later my car.
And today, I am in Vietnam, fighting a war.
Oh, how those days of yesterday seem so far.
Remember those days when it cost only a dime for the movies?
Now, the kids all gather around to watch TV.
Oh, what I would pay to relive yesterday.
Flash Gordon and Buck Rogers were my favorites on the screen,
that was fiction then.
But now Buck and Flash are the ideals of men.
I could hardly wait to become a man. To be able to visit far-away
lands.
Now, I have seen them and home is far away. Oh, how I long for
yesterday.

***

His letter, following seven months of silence, was received with mixed emotions. There was so much implied but not mentioned in his letters; she needed to sort them out, allow time to ruminate, and then decide how she was to respond.

"What were you thinking, Mama? Honestly, I would have been a little crushed myself."

"Well, yeah, I was a little crushed. I also felt a little disrespected, yet he had never given me any indication of being a disrespectful person. I remember wracking my brains and talking it over with Dad. Was it the stateside racial tensions running rampant that drove him back to Vietnam with no visit? Was there someone at home who said something about us that convinced him not to visit? Then, there was the whole unknown as to why he never reached out to us the entire seven months he had been back in Vietnam." She could not deny that an element of hurt accompanied these questions. Not exactly sure what was going to spill out onto the paper, Mama returned to the typewriter, she took a deep breath, sending up a petition for words, and started her keycap symphony once again.

"Here I am back at the ole typewriter again; it has been some time indeed. I hope you enjoyed your time back in the states with family and friends. It has been busy with little Susan, a pure delight as she completes our family, but she is a lot of work and the occupier of any free time. I have found it more difficult to write letters at the pace I became accustomed to, but I am doing my best to continue to be there for all my pen pals in whatever capacity they need."

***

She continued her response absent of any visible hurt or disappointment, not even mentioning the letter she had sent to the Department of Defense, choosing to focus on the blessing that he was okay. Summarizing the family's summer activities and reporting on Dad's football season monopolized the content. The words came through her and landed onto the paper, further emphasizing her supportive role in this Operation Morale Booster. She was at peace with this realization and even liberated by it, taking on a whole new level of selflessness.

"Mama, this is beautiful! Pastor Joshua just spoke about this concept last week at church. He told the story from the Bible when Joseph was reunited with his brothers long after they had sold him into slavery. While Joseph was in slavery, he did not grow bitter toward his brothers or God. In fact, his devotion to God grew deeper. As a result, God raised him out of slavery to rule over Egypt, under Pharaoh. When he, now in a position of power, reunited with his remorseful brothers, he did not seek revenge for he knew he had a higher purpose, directly called on by God." Pride beamed across my face, "Albeit not nearly the gravity, but this is in a similar vein Mama, of what you extended to Bob by focusing on the good news that he was ok and forging ahead with your relationship and purpose."

February 3/68

To My Dear Friends:

I hope this letter finds you well and enjoying all the splendors life has to offer. As for me, I am doing just fine. It feels good to be back on the ol' pen pal relationship again. Things have been pretty quiet for us. In the last few days, most of the division has moved north to the DMZ, while my battalion is… guess where? Sitting right here in the area where that unforgettable battle I wrote about; Operation Masher. After Operation Masher (Jan & Feb '66), the area was pretty well secured, although there were still a few of my "friends" running around; those who failed to realize that they had been beaten. But it is frustrating; we come in, conquer, hand it over to the local authorities and then move onto the next offensive only to return months later to retake it. You know Joan, I think the Viet Cong have reincarnation going for them. We are killing them by the hundreds, but they keep coming back. As a matter of fact, I think I have killed the same man twice already. (smile) I don't know if we will ever get to General Westmoreland's crossover point.

The men, however, are better fighters and supplies are more plentiful and varied. We are also getting a batch of young ROTC officers. They are really green yet run around here like little generals. We have a platoon leader who would get lost in an empty footlocker, even if supplied with a diagram showing him how to get out. (smile) The guys call him Lt. Fuzz from Beetle Bailey.

***

A few days later, another letter from the hospital arrives.

Dear Joan and Paul:

I hope this letter finds you well and enjoying all the splendors of life. For me, I am doing just fine. Please don't be alarmed by the envelope. I am in the hospital again, but not due to a bullet or malaria. You know how I told you that I think I am protected for some reason because God has allowed me to escape death so many times? Well, wait until you read this. A comrade and I were burning brush to clear a field for a landing zone. The area had been overgrown and sectioned off with old concertina wire circling the perimeter. We were pouring gasoline to enhance the fire when the gas can exploded, trapping us in the middle of a raging blaze. While trying to escape, I got entangled in the barbwire enshrouded by the fire. I thought it was over for me, but somehow, by God's grace, I got out, slightly burnt and cut up from the wire, but nonetheless, I got out. I am a little sore and have burns up my entire arm to my ear, but I got out. But here is the jaw-dropping part... Hours after I was evacuated to a hospital for the burns, my company fell under a mortar attack. Many of our men were wounded, but fortunately, none were killed. But had I been there, maybe things would have ended differently for me. So, you see Joan; God must have been looking out for me. He must have something specific He wants me to accomplish, so I am glad I re-enlisted. Maybe your letters are some sort of talisman for me, so please keep on writing.

Joan, as I have told you before, I highly admire Paul for his dedication to teaching, studying, and coaching; an admirable set of tasks for any man to take on. BC High must be grooming a sea of outstanding young men. If he is molding the boys after himself, then America's future leaders will surely be great. But I also admire you for your dedication to family and community. I guess I best stay with the war and this army life; it's a lot simpler. (smile)

I went before the division promotion board two days before being evacuated to the hospital; for PSG rating (Platoon Sergeant, which is the same as Master Sergeant). I came out number three on the list. This ranking makes me think I might be making it in two to three months, which is pretty good as most guys usually have fifteen or more years before they make it. Or perhaps it is a sign that we are losing a lot of our leadership. Well, all of this may change now that I am laid up in a hospital again. I guess I will have time once again to write and work on my sketches to pass the time. Also, this hospital in Japan offers educational opportunities sponsored by the University of Maryland, so I will probably take advantage of this.

Joan, you know how I feel about integration...well, I am fully integrated now. These burns have me part pink, part brown, and a little white. (smile)"

***

The weeks turned into months, and the reality of Bob returning to the front lines was becoming less and less likely. A soldier to the core, steeped in patriotic duty, the idle time required for a full recovery was ironically killing him. Honing in on his artistic skills and writing to Mama soon found value as an outlet to keep his sanity amidst losing his "purpose." Utilizing black ink on white silk, Bob sketched out four different depictions that had become familiar to him from his time in Vietnam.

The first is titled, "Paying Last Respects to Fallen Comrade." Four soldiers are the center of the scene; an abstract of the fallen GI and three others watching over him, paying their last respects. A blindfolded, shirtless prisoner, down on his knees, hands tied behind his back was off to the scene's side.

The second image is titled Singing Around Bunker at Basecamp. A recreational scene of four soldiers, one of whom was sitting with his back up against wall made of sandbags, strumming a guitar, and appearing to be singing. Two others crouching down, facing the guitarist, and the fourth soldier standing, also facing the entertainment with his hands in his pockets.

The third sketch captures the moment of "dust-off." A Huey, just touching down with the medic standing at the entrance, ready to grab ahold of the incoming wounded soldier who was being assisted to the chopper. A fourth soldier was standing guard, back toward the helicopter and rifle-ready. His presence was inferring a quick in and out of a hotbed.

The fourth in the series depicts a Vietnamese village being attacked by two choppers, coming in hard just above the treetops and a couple of hooches billowing thick black smoke.

These drawings, along with his poetry, served as priceless gifts to our family. The artwork arrived well preserved as Bob had the wherewithal to cover them with white tissue paper before folding them into the manila envelope. Mama recognized that expressions of art are often conduits to healing, so she kept him well supplied with art materials to help them pass the time while recovering in the hospital.

Although he was trying to keep busy crafting artwork of varying types, Mama could sense his morale was dipping, and once again, she thought back to Dad's theory that Bob was the type who needed to be where the action was in order to feel purposeful.

184

~Fortunately, his subsequent letters revealed a sea change.

Chapter 29

If You Leave Me Now

To My Dear Friends:

I hope this finds you well and enjoying all that life has to offer. For me, I am doing fine. As far as the war in Vietnam is concerned, it looks as though it has already ended for me. My doctor said that I definitely would not be going back. All the hospitals in the Philippines are filled as they are here in Japan. Our guys are taking a beating. There is no doubt we are winning this war but at a helluva price.

I have read in the papers that people in the States oppose General Westmoreland's strong actions in Vietnam. Perhaps this is not my right to say, but if the US weaken and pull him out of Vietnam, we will lose everything we have been fighting for these past three years. I feel that we should invade North Vietnam by bombing Hanoi. The Viet Cong haven't thought twice about killing innocent people in Saigon and other places in South Vietnam.

A lot of guys are dying because of some of the clean rules that only we are forced to fight and die by. But see here, those same men who make these rules don't have to bear the pain that a dying soldier does, nor do they have to weep with the mother, father, wife, or children of that soldier. President Johnson said, "We stand firm in Vietnam." Well, what does that mean, Mr. President? I have covered the same ground, taken it in long hours of combat, and yet have had to go back and retake it, mainly because we cannot go where the heart of the enemy is... Hanoi.

We (GIs) don't believe the war will last much more than six months. The communists are making one last-ditch stand, hoping that the US, will crack, but that will never happen, "Sorry About That, Ho." The enemy is now coming out in the open and fighting our kind of war, that of conventional tactics. They showed that when they brought their tanks in two weeks ago and that didn't go too well for them.

Most of us are afraid of Korea jumping on South Korea again, which will probably happen while we are still fighting in Vietnam. This act of aggression will compel us to split our forces more evenly in both countries. At present, we only have two infantry divisions in Korea and eight in Vietnam, so you can see what this will mean. I am hoping that this won't happen, and the war in Vietnam will end soon.

You would think that twenty-one months of fighting would be enough, but this is the way I feel. If I could, I would go back today. I would surely go and earn my 5th Purple Heart. Overall, I think that our guys are doing a great job, and the Marines are standing their own.

And as far as little Billy wanting to write to me…tell him that the fact he wants to write to me is just as good as him writing, perhaps even better. Often, it is not what one writes that holds the significance so much as his desire to write that matters. Tell all the kids that I surely appreciate their love for me. I better change my name to Hunter because I feel like I am truly a part of the family. Perhaps a long-lost uncle, ok?

So, until,
Bob

***

February/68

To My Dear Friends:

I hope this finds you well and enjoying all the splendors of life. For me… well, I thought I would get this last letter out before I ship out of Japan on Friday. I am being sent to Korea, the one place that I did not want to be sent. I think the US is trying to build its forces back up in Korea since they have been cut below the halfway mark since we entered Vietnam. All indications coming in from Korea show communist troops are pouring across the DMZ through infiltration. This aggression hints at the strong possibility of an escalation of aggressive activity, so it may very well be that I am jumping out of the frying pan and into the fire. Like, "Sorry about that, GI" Everybody wants to pick a fight with the United States or is it the United States who wants to fight with everyone else? Either way, leaving us poor citizens in the middle.

As for the war in Vietnam, everything has been concentrated along the DMZ and Khe Sanh. At Khe Sanh alone, there are 20,000 North Vietnam soldiers dug in around the fort. Elements of the 1st Cavalry have been moved up to help the marines. I have heard that my unit is one of them, but I am not sure. I am sure, however, that I wish I were there with the guys. Khe Sanh is the gateway for the commies to the South, so if we don't stop them, hell only knows what may happen. This strategic move is how the French were defeated at Dien Bien Phu, and the commies are trying to do the same to us. But we have a surprise for ol' Charlie... We will teach him a lesson that he won't forget, as the Indians say, for many moons.

As far as duty in Korea, it is the worst kind for an infantryman. Actually, in so many ways, it is the worst for anyone. In the winter, it is often thirty below, and in the summer, as high as 120 degrees. Monsoons follow the summer. I guess the Army could have picked a worse place to send me... like Hanoi... by myself. (smile) It's dreadful; it is going to be hard for me to find something good to write about, so I apologize in advance.

Well, let me stop complaining. Most of my burns are healing nicely. However, my arm will take a bit longer to recover fully, before I can use it to its fullest extent. I will only be here for ten months and then a tour of duty at home, that is if I am ready to return home. My mother thinks that I should return to the States and find myself a wife and settle down like the rest of the family. But who needs a wife? The Army cooks for me, gives me clothes to wear, and even washes them for me, so I don't need a wife. Seriously, I doubt there are any more wonderful women around like the one I know who is married to a guy named Paul Hunter.

Well, Always a friend,
Bobby

***

"Wait! Was he just flirting with you?" I teased. Mama rolled her eyes and shook her head as if to say; I am not even going to flatter that comment with a response.

Mama received the news of his departure to Korea with mixed emotions on many levels. Feeling deeply for the burned-out soldiers' overall wellbeing, she wondered about the tipping point for the already thinning US forces due to the expansion of the theatre. Additionally, she was unsettled with the fact the military believed there was even a need to build up the troops in Korea, while still very much in the throes of the repudiated war in Vietnam. Regarding Bob specifically, Mama was concerned that he was deemed not well enough for combat yet was assigned to an area of the world where military tensions were increasing, fearing imminent conflict. Korea was an area of the world that also carried a stain on US history due to the Korean War, claiming the lives of over 30,000 US soldiers. The antiwar fervor was heating up in the States and around the world, as the student activists became more prevalent and far more violent. It seemed like things were spiraling out of control for our nation with elevating political pressures rising to a historical height. Bob certainly had some harsh thoughts on Korea in a few of his letters over the last two years, undoubtedly garnered from his experiences in Korea in 1961 and 1962. Still, there was something telling him that this time could be different.

Chapter 30

Turn, Turn, Turn

March 15, 1968

Ecclesiastes 3
1.   There is a time for everything, and a season for every activity under   heaven:
2.   a time to be born and a time to die, a time to plant and a time to uproot,
3.   a time to kill and a time to heal, a time to tear down and time to build,
4.   a time to weep and a time to laugh, a time to mourn and a time to dance,
5.   a time to scatter stones and a time to gather them, a time to embrace and a time to refrain,
6.   a time to search and a time to give up, a time to keep and a time to throw away,
7.   a time to tear and I time to mend, a time to be silent and a time to speak,
8.   a time to love and a time to hate, a time for war and a time for peace.

Dear Bob,

I hope this serves as a rock to get you through the tough times and, conversely, allows you to celebrate the good times even if others are knee deep in a rough patch. Everything happens in His time. I can't deny that we are in for some rough days ahead based on the tensions building here in the States, so I can only pray that I can accept God's will as just that, His will, and, therefore, how things must be. I pray you find the positives in your new assignment in Korea because there will be positives, there always are. Perhaps in areas not familiar to you, tangibly and intangibly. Just be open to goodness coming to you.

In the meantime, keep yourself safe and write when you can. We will mark Korea on our map, so know that we are still thinking about you and praying for you.

Susan is already one. She is a delight, and the kids spoil her with attention. We have started our search for a new home in Scituate. This house is just too small for a family of six. We plan to move this summer, so it does not interrupt the kids' schooling if we have to change school districts, nor will it be disruptive to Paul's athletic seasons. There are many houses on the market right now in Scituate, so I am sure we will be able to find our dream home soon.

Well, ole bean, we are anxious to hear about your new role in Korea, and we pray for your safety and health all the time. May God continue to bless you, Bob.

Always,
Joan and Paul

***

Crossed in the mail, Joan received a quick note from Bob, hinting at the wave of good fortune this year is about to bring.

March 17/68

To My Dear Friends:

…Here I am, an instructor; this is a position in which I have always desired. To add to my good fortune, the division education center is only 100 meters from my quarters, so that long-desired education I wanted and greatly need, is now at my fingertips. So, it looks as though I am going to have a good year over here, even though I hate this country, and nothing could change my thoughts on that. (smile)

***

April 14/68

To My Dear Friends:

I received your letter with the news of Dr. Martin Luther King's death. I had heard the news on the radio the morning he was shot. At first, I thought that I had listened to the news wrong, then later, when the death was broadcasted again, sadly, I knew that I had gotten it right. It was almost unbelievable.

The death of Dr. King is a significant loss to the American people, both White and Black. I do believe; however, our country will achieve great things as a tribute to his life of vision and love.

To begin with…

1. The whole world seems to suddenly recognize the struggle we are having at home and abroad for "equal socialty" (not just rights). Being accepted by the mere fact that we are human beings, regardless of skin color, or perhaps our financial status in life.

2. I believe that God has put each man on this earth with a sole purpose in life and perhaps Dr. King's purpose in life, God's chosen purpose, was for him to open the eyes of mankind, to remind us of the fact that all men were created equal in His image.
   (A) Jesus died on the cross (a violent death) to open the eyes of mankind.
   (B) President Lincoln died a violent death. Although he was the architect of the Emancipation Proclamation, it wasn't until after his death that the people worldwide searched their souls and opened their eyes to realize that all men were created equal.
   (C) President Kennedy died a violent death who was also searching for human relationships.

Now we have the death of another God-honoring man, Dr. Martin Luther King, Jr. Perhaps if he had just passed away from an illness, news of his death may not have rocked the world like it did. This unjust taking of his life brings into focus, what he did with it, and how all of mankind has been robbed by this assassination. No, I do not think that Dr. King's death will be in vain. God has a purpose for all of us and Dr. King faithfully served his.

On another note, as I once told you I hated Korea and the Korean people with a purple passion, but in the past month and the beginning of this tour of duty, I formed a different opinion. These people over here are no different than me, or any other race in this world. Perhaps their living conditions and ways of life are quite different, but what remains... they are human beings, seeking the same things we do.

I spent the last few weekends in my "house-boy's" village. He is a wonderful man with a lovely family of five kids and has taught me some Korean customs and language. Through him, I met his daughter, a very nice Korean girl of my age.

I am very intrigued by her. She feels and thinks strongly of humanity. As you once said that I have a unique way of expressing myself; well, this girl does as well. Her name is Pok Son Song. She has a strong affection for orphans and other kids in the village. To give you an example, last week we were talking about marriage and kids. During this conversation, she told me that if she ever got the opportunity to get married and go to the States, she would like to adopt two orphans: a girl and a boy, and take them to the States to offer them a decent chance in life. There are very few of these kids that ever get a break in life. I see these kids in all parts of the world and empathize with her feelings and desires.

In a way, this goes in line with the works of Dr. King. Not only must we prepare the way for our race, but we must also conceive and achieve it for the entire human race.

I can remember back several years ago, before I came into the Army, back in 1953, when my mother and father separated. Times were hard for mom and the seven of us kids. Often, I went to school with only a cup of tea and toast to eat. Well, to make a long story short, one morning, my mother went to take the trash out, and in a vacant lot next door to us, a White lady and three half-starved kids were sitting in an old beat-up car. They were undernourished, cold, dirty, and ragged; their eyes filled with despair. My mother brought them into the house, fed them what we had, and cleaned the baby and kids. The lady's husband was out looking for work. They had driven from Texas with virtually nothing. These people stayed with us for two days sleeping on the floor. The point is, we had so little, yet my mother was ready to share the little we had.

With people like my mother, you and Paul... why do we have so much greed and civil unrest at home?

In the twenty-two months, I was in Vietnam; I ate and slept with White and Colored guys from all parts of the states. We shared the same razors, toothbrushes, and wore each other's pants and underwear. Why must only in war and hard times we unite? Why can't this happen in good times, too? I have shed my blood with the White man; it is the same. A White man has given his life for me as I would have gladly done for him, so there is no difference in our feelings or blood, so why should there be any conflict at home between people due to our skin color?

Remember when we first began writing to each other, Operation Morale Booster? That was two years and two months ago. Well, I also started writing to a girl from Mississippi at that time. I wrote to her, just as often as I wrote to you, and like you, she answered every letter. Then in one letter, I told her that I was Black, as I told you, well, she stopped writing. I can't honestly say why she stopped, but it certainly makes me wonder if it was because of my skin color. And if so, how can a person feel this way? Especially since her brother was also fighting in Vietnam, so I am in a sense fighting alongside her brother.

When the enemy fires his weapon, each bullet is marked, TWMC (To Whom It May Concern). Sure, I was one of the lucky ones who's alive to show off my ribbons. To this day, I am not sure why God has spared me so many times. But four Purple Hearts will tell anyone that I have earned the right to be proud and grateful, not because of my skin color, but because I have served this country. I am fighting for the same thing that the White man is fighting for; freedom, family and faith. I believe our founding fathers spoke for the whole world when they declared that ALL MEN WERE CREATED EQUAL, and as such, we should all be given the right to pursue happiness, even those in foreign countries.

I say all these things, and you know I am sincere because of my actions, so you must also see why it is hard for me to comprehend the racial tensions. Why can't I come home and be treated as any other American and enjoy the freedoms I have given so much to ensure? I don't want to hear, "Negro, you can't come here or go there." Nor do I want to hear, "Whitie, you are not wanted around here." No, I don't want to come back to this.

The President is trying to stop the war in Vietnam, what for? How many people in the States are dying right now because of racial violence? How many soldiers and National Guardsmen are committed to combating in our streets? And whom are we to blame? The Whites? The Blacks? The guilt is placed on both sides; it takes two to start an argument. The American people, even over leadership and the media, control our society, for now anyway. We have to get right with God, like really right with God, and then it will be easier to get right with each other. I only hope and pray that Americans soon learn to live by the laws of humanity we preach and by which our country was established.

At present, I am so confused, it is not funny, and it bothers me more than the war in Vietnam itself. I keep telling myself that I am only imagining what is happening at home. Every time I receive a letter from you, I am reminded that there are some good people at home and that life is still worth living in the States. Life is a small price to pay to ensure Dr. King's death will not be in vain, and to that end, I will not stop; I, too, have a dream.

As for the President asking the Hanoi government to the peace table, along with Kennedy, well, I feel that this action is akin to us getting on our knees, which the United States has never done before. Sure, we all want the war to end, but not this way. If we don't inflict the maximum pressure on the commies, we will only be back there fighting another day. End it now and forever. If we have to fight Red China and Russia, let's do it. Complete victory or no victory at all. In total defeat, a man can still walk with his head high in triumph, but only in shame in surrender.

Well, I am going to have to close for now. I sincerely hope that I have not offended anyone by expressing all these feelings. If I have, please forgive me. I am sending you a painting. It's called God's Light Will Show the Way.

Everlasting Friendship and Love for the Hunter Family,
Bob

P.S. Don't be surprised if I return to the USA a married man!

***

"HA! Well, I didn't see that coming. This, from the man sworn to bachelorhood while serving in the Army? And in Korea, no less, the place he dreaded even going." Jaw dropped a bit and hanging in shock, I shook my head in disbelief, "This is like something you only see in the movies!

Chapter 31

Sounds of Silence

Over the next few weeks, Bob kept himself busy with his new roles as both a tactical instructor for the young conscripts and a student at the academy. After completing preparations for the divisional arsenal inspection, he set aside some time, on the eve of his twenty-seventh birthday, to pen Mama a note.

He wrote of his continued relationship with Pok Son. He is learning a little Korean, and she is working on learning English. As the days grew longer, their feelings grew more profound, and they soon were talking about marrying. Bob put in the paperwork for the marriage license, but it was met with uncharacteristic silence, lacking a response, even after several attempts. He persisted with increasing desire to marry Pok Son; however, he experienced roadblocks at every juncture. He wondered if these were deliberate efforts made by the non-commissioned officers to block the mixed marriage. Although this weighed heavy on his heart, it only made him more determined to do so. Something about being told he couldn't do something always ignited a fire in his soul. He was now motivated by love and anger, two of the most intense feelings.

Conversely, he admitted he was happy to be reading of less rioting in the streets at home in the wake of Dr. Martin Luther King, Jr.'s death. "So perhaps people at home are beginning to wake up, although it took the death of a good man. I hope the calm continues, and we can get back to progressing our race to the ideals America has promised us."

"Sadly, God's law has become a pastime for some and a scapegoat for others, and personal accountability has been tossed aside. I know there are many people at home, in the States, who can't take care of themselves, and these people should be helped, but there are too many who can but choose not to because they are lazy. The Bible makes it clear that being habitually lazy (or slothful) is equivalent to being sinful. God calls on us to help our brothers and sisters, this is true, but I am pretty sure he means the brothers and sisters who truly can't help themselves. If those who truly can take care of themselves, do, those who can't would not have to succumb to a life of begging. There would be plenty of food and services available to help them live in dignity. The problem arises when too many people claim to be poverty-stricken. If people at home had the opportunity to see how some people over here live, they would stop feeling sorry for themselves. To give you an example, the average man over here makes 4,000 won a month (equivalent to $4), and it takes much more than that to live because they even have to pay for the water they drink. At present, there has been little rain, so the rice crops and supplies have suffered much. This drought drives the price of rice sky high, yet the people still live in harmony and work together improvising for the shortfall.

"If I ever have to depend on begging to survive, then I deem my life is not worth living. I will already have lost my pride and self-respect. A country as great as ours, there should be no one having to beg. Delineating the line between those who need help and those who are just lazy is our problem.

"I hope someday I will be a voice for those who need help, but also a voice to inspire others to better themselves. I do this now as a tactical instructor, but I mean for humanitarian efforts."

***

"I wonder if he ever did go on to become a thought leader of some sort. He has so much insight and clarity, all founded on authentic love for God. We could certainly benefit from hearing his thoughts these days, that's for sure." I paused. "Do you know what he ended up doing after the war? Or is this something I will have to wait to find out as well?" raising an eyebrow and leaning in close to Mama.

"Hmmm, yeah, you're going to have to wait on this one too," she chirped back with a victorious grin.

Two months pass with no word from Bob. Mama was busy with me, now an energetic toddler, who required and received a tremendous amount of attention. The busyness of the summer months was compounded with the selling of their sweet little Cape on the corner of Tilden and Fay, and moving into a bigger Cape style home at the corner of Acorn and Spring. The summer days seemed to fly by for the family, and although Mama wondered about his well-being, she was not going to fret about it like she had the previous summer. His latest letter had mentioned the initiation of the marriage license, so it was safe to assume he was preoccupied with his new life, which was new territory for this confirmed bachelor. This understanding gave her enormous comfort and allowed for a little more attention to be directed toward some of her other soldiers.

Late August, a letter arrived from Bob, bringing news of two developments. As hoped, Bob and Pok Son married in a quiet ceremony on August 10th. Despite all being invited, only one non-commissioned officer showed up for the formalities. The sound of silence reverberated so loudly in his head that the next day he put in a request to be transferred out of Korea and back to Vietnam for another tour.

He expounded on this, revealing the ugliness existing in humanity and courageously admitted that he was not exempt from this ugliness at times.

"What animals we are, the human race. Few of our fellow men take the time to look up to and build up one another, but so much time we spend looking down upon each other. This belief is not just how I felt due to the lack of representation of non-coms at my wedding; I am embarrassed to admit that I felt a little strange and ashamed of myself when I first went to fill out the paperwork for Pok Son and me to marry. As I stood in line, I thought about what the people might say behind my back, and some to my face, about me marrying a Korean. Then I made myself realize that if I had let this stop me, then I would not be much of a man, myself. I would be a part of the problem instead of the solution. Koreans are no different from any of us, and I love her for the very person she is. Her heart is extraordinary. We need humans to experience humans. Experience teaches what books can't.

"Before going back to Vietnam, I have to take a two-week course 'to learn' about combat in Vietnam. The officers' reasoning was that you can always learn more. Although I agree about continually seizing opportunities to learn more, I told them that I thought it was crazy that I had to do this. I reminded them that I learned all I needed to know about combat in Vietnam through my experience in Ia Drang and Bong Son in '65 and '66, and no book or classroom would be able to teach me more than what I had already experienced.

"Joan, you mentioned in one of your letters that television is dedicating five hours a week to 'educating' white folks about the Black race. This development is encouraging, but how many years of suffering did it take to get us to this point? Why is it, the death of a good man, or the suffering of a child, has to happen for people to work toward reform? You and Paul knew very little about the hardship of a Vietnam War GI, so you took it upon yourselves to find out and experience what we are going through via your Operation Morale Booster. Man learns what he wants to learn when he wants to learn; simple as that. When I was here, in Korea, fifteen months ago, I learned but two solid words, but now that I am interested in learning the Korean language to communicate with my wife, I have learned to speak it pretty well. Maybe the television exposure to my race will spark a desire to learn more by connecting with us and getting to know us personally and not from afar.

See you soon,
Bob

P.S. My second love… The Hunters

***

A month later, just as Dad was walking through the front door on a Wednesday afternoon after football practice, the phone rang. Shooting a welcome home smile before directing her attention to the phone on the wall, Mama answered the call with a silvery voice, "Good afternoon, this is the Hunter residence." The response from a somewhat unfamiliar voice on the other end caused her to look back up at Dad in disbelief; her sea-blue eyes remained fixated on Dad's as she acknowledged in a gentle but somewhat guarded tone, "Yes, this is Joan."

Chapter 32

Green, Green Grass of Home

"Hi Joan, it's Bob! He blurted out.

"Well, hi, Bob! It's so good to hear from you. You sound different, where are you?"

"I'm in Pennsylvania, visiting with family."

"How wonderful. Is Pok Son with you?" Mama inquired, beaming up at Dad.

"No, we could not get a passport for her in time for my granted stateside leave, so she is still in Korea with her family. I am in the States for another six days, and I was hoping I could come and visit with you and the family at some point before returning to Korea. Would that be possible?"

"Of course!" jumped out of her mouth in pace with her bouncing in place. "What days are you thinking?"

"How about Friday?"

"Sounds great! Paul will be at work, and the three older ones will be in school until 2:30 pm, but Susan and I can show you around the area during the day, and then Paul will join us at dinner time."

"That sounds wonderful, Joan, thank you!"

"Will you spend the night so Paul can spend some time with you on Saturday? He has practice Saturday morning, and I know he'd love to bring you to meet his players; a couple of these boys you've received letters from over these last two years."

"Oh, I don't know about that, Joan. That is too much of an imposition, but thank you for offering." Mama hands the phone to Dad, who was standing within earshot, listening intently to the conversation.

In a modulated voice, he petitioned, "Hey Bob, it's Paul. So good to hear that we are finally going to meet you. Please consider staying the night. We have plenty of room now that we are in our new home and we have so much to discuss. Plus, Joan is right; my players would benefit from meeting you. We'd love to have you stay with us."

"Hi, Mr. Hunter..."

"Please, it's Paul." Dad interrupted.

"Okay, Paul. Thank you for your kind invitation. If you think the boys will enjoy meeting me, sure I can stay the night, thank you."

"Great! Well, then I will see you on Friday night! I am going to put Joan back on the phone. Good to hear from you, Bob. I look forward to meeting you on Friday. Have a good night." Dad handed the phone back to Mama and gave her a big smile and a playful 'thumbs up.'

Mama continued the conversation covering the logistics of the visit and providing him driving directions. She closed the conversation with, "Well, Bob, I know you don't like a lot of attention and fanfare, but you know this family has been excited to meet you for a long time now. I hope you truly come this time. We really want to meet you in person."

"Yes, Joan, I understand. And yes, nothing is going to stop me from coming this time. I will see you on Friday at 11 am."

"Okay, Bob, we will see you then, looking forward to it."

My parents decided not to tell any of us of their anticipated guest in case he was not able to visit again, but they prepared a room for him nonetheless. Friday morning was busy in the Hunter household as Mama wanted to make sure the house showed no signs of the hectic morning tidying up my toys and getting my siblings off to school. Figuring a deployed soldier would always welcome a home-cooked meal; she had the table set for a hearty lunch inclusive of a colorful array of fruit, potato salad, and an assortment of bread and cold cuts. After lunch, since it was a one-car family, Mama had arranged for her beautiful Swedish neighbor, Margaretha, to drive the three of us to the harbor. Together, we could walk around the picturesque marina for an hour before returning to greet the kids at the close of the school day.

Dad was at work, my siblings were at school, and I had been down for a nap; the house was quiet, too quiet. Mama turned on the radio to the new station of WRKO, Boston, and dialed it down just to serve as background music. She had made a sign to welcome Bob but displayed it inside the house, not to scare him away with unwelcomed fanfare. A simple "Welcome to Our Home" with an American flag hanging from the door jamb leading into the kitchen.

Ready for his arrival, she sat herself in a rocking chair facing the window with a book in hand. The excitement of finally seeing him overwhelmed any ability to squeeze in a chapter or two as she found herself periodically looking up from the book, and down Spring Lane to capture the earliest glimpse of Bob driving his borrowed blue sedan around the corner.

Where is he, she thought. *He is already a three-quarters-of-an-hour late. That is not like someone in the military.* Of course, there were no cell phones for communication in those days, so they were at the mercy of trust and fate. *I wonder if we are going to be stood up again. Why would he do that? How long am I going to sit here and wait before concluding he is not coming? This time I don't think I will be so understanding.*

Chapter 33

God Bless the USA

Bob arrived an hour late, on the dot of noon. He pulled into the driveway, exited the car grabbing a bouquet and a bag with wrapped gifts peeking out the top. He turned to the front door, and there was Mama, relieved they had not been stood-up again, already with the door opened, walking out to greet him on this crisp sunny October day. They met halfway on the walkway to the house. Bob placed his bag on the ground to salute her. She smiled, perhaps even blushed at the strong gesture of respect, and extended her arms, signaling for a hug. "I'm a hugger, Bob. It is so good to meet you finally." She reached up and threw her arms around him and gave him the warmest of hugs. It was clear Bob needed that hug, and he held onto it as long as he could without making it awkward. As they broke away, smiles remained on their faces; there was a sparkle in their eyes. It was a sparkle that couldn't easily be described, as it was not the sparkle of new love that most are fortunate to feel in their lifetime. It was something that originated from a deep connection of pure human desire to serve others, spiritual soulmates perhaps. This commonality was fertile ground to this least likely pair, a type of love many go through life without ever experiencing.

"Joan," he said with reverence, "I cannot tell you how honored I am to be here. You are a hero to me. I will never be able to thank you enough for all you have done for me." Compelled to reach out for another hug, she was happy to oblige.

"Ok, enough of this lovefest, let's take this mutual admiration club inside. I have a nice lunch prepared for you, Sergeant." Mama quipped.

Bob chuckled, "Don't you dare call me Sergeant!" as he picked up his bag of gifts, and enjoyed a lasting gaze at "the Hunters' home" following her up the walkway and into the house. After finding a proper vase for the flowers, Mama quickly gave him a tour of the "command center" for Operation Morale Booster, explicitly pointing out his red dots on the maps and his stapled index cards filled with her notes over the past thirty-four months. The smile never left his face.

She welcomed him to take a seat at the kitchen table and poured him a cold glass of ginger ale. Just as they were about to dig into the meal fit for a king, the sounds of me waking in my crib diverted their attention, and they both let out a chuckle. Mama excused herself and came to get me, the now inquisitive eighteen-month old toddler. As she turned the corner with babe in arms, Bob let out in an uncharacteristically high-pitched voice, "Ahhh, look who we have here! It's Princess Susan! The baby of the Hunter clan!" I just smiled and giggled at his animation. I was content sitting on Mama's lap as they continued to serve themselves some lunch. They thoroughly enjoyed the benefits of face-to-face conversation, such as body language, facial expressions, and impromptu questions and comments, all enhancing the depth of the exchange. Not more than thirty minutes since I had woken from my nap, I reached out for him to hold me. Bob looked at Mama for approval at the very moment she was handing me over to him. Bob had a look on his face of Heaven on Earth. She joked, "Not a boy like you had hoped, but she'll do, huh?" Bob looked up at her with the brightest smile revealing a piece of his heart had just been touched. This was the first time he had ever held a baby girl. Bob looked into my eyes and held that smile as if to say, I want a baby girl of my own someday and then he let out the most contented sigh. This lunch proved to be such a treat, the planned visit to the harbor paled in comparison, and had been totally forgotten about as a result.

At 2:30 pm on the dot, the dismissal bell from Cushing Elementary School sounded. The signal indicating the end of the school day was the first time the two had checked the time. Both were shocked to see that their conversation had taken such flight yet never left the kitchen table. The school abutted the backyard, so it would be minutes before the kids would be barreling through the back door, surprised to see Bob in the kitchen. Like clockwork, Maryellen, Michael, and Billy with lunch boxes in hand, came bustling through the back door, stopping midstride as they turned the corner and entered the kitchen. There was Bob, standing at attention, holding their baby sister. If the respectful stance wasn't enough, Bob's military fatigues were, giving assurance to my startled siblings that he was not be feared as an intruder. Instantly, eight-and-a-half-year-old Maryellen ran to him for a hug exclaiming, "Sergeant Johnson! Sergeant Johnson! I can't believe you are here!" The boys followed suit but in a less animated manner. The warm welcome from the kids visibly affected Bob. He got down on one knee to gently let me down while positioning himself on eye level to the boys. They came over to him, Michael slightly ahead of Billy. Michael gave him a high five followed by a hug and then dutiful, Billy, stood at attention and offered a firm and respectful salute. Billy didn't have much to say that afternoon, but there was no doubt he took in every word evidenced by his eye contact and attentiveness hinting he was keenly observing it all.

Bob and the kids made their way to the front yard to toss the ball a bit while I stayed in with Mama and cleared the kitchen from the leisurely lunch, and then set it for dinner. When she finished, we all walked the beaten path, behind the house, through the woods to Cushing Elementary School. Bob made it an adventure by pointing out things the kids had never noticed before, like moss growing on one side of the trees, indicating the north side. Keeping it playful but drawing from his tactical training, he offered advice on what to look for when seeking great places to hide for the game hide-and-seek. Bob's lesson on the advantage of using the natural camouflage of leaves, sticks, and rocks in a game of hide-and-seek may have gone over the heads of the kids but was utterly transparent to Mama. He was subtly teaching them how to be an infantry soldier in guerilla warfare. Breaching the top of the hill where they could see the basketball courts in the foreground and the entrance to the school in the distance, in an exaggerated voice and full animation, Bob gasped, "WOW, this is YOUR school? You get to go to classes here? And this is YOUR playground? You are all so lucky! I bet your teachers are so nice, and I bet you learn a lot here." For a man who had to leave schooling in the ninth grade to help provide for his family, he had an innate passion for education and educating others. Beaming with pride, looking up at him, the kids smiled and, in unison, blurted out affirmatively.

"Yes, and my teacher, Mrs. Deacon, is the best in the whole school!" Maryellen boasted, jumping up and down as if she had just won the Olympic Gold Medal.

Not to be outdone, Michael chimed in, "That's my classroom over there," pointing to the large window on the corner of the building. "My teacher, Mr. Flaherty and our classroom won Most Spirited this month!"

Billy remained quiet but engaged. Since I was already in his arms, which had already become my spot of choice, Maryellen grabbed hold of his hand, "Oh Sergeant Johnson, this is only our little playground, come, let me show you our never-ending playground." She led him around the back, and the group followed. Rounding the corner of the school building, a sight to behold...there was the never-ending playground.

"WOW, this IS a never-ending playground!" Bob exclaimed with full animation. As far as the eye could see, there were playgrounds of all sorts; some with slides, jungle gyms, swings, and obstacle courses, while others had basketball hoops and markings for four square and hopscotch, and still others with ballfields inclusive of pitcher's mounds and bases for kickball and the like. The vast recreational area spilled down the hill at the far end, emptying into the high school campus, which held claim to an even more impressive array of fields and facilities. Growing up in the city, Bob indeed had never seen anything like this. That look from earlier in the day permeated his face once again. There was a burning desire to have what the Hunters had.

The afternoon flew by, and it was nearing time for us to return home. Dad would be arriving home soon, so we made our way back through the woods to get washed up for dinner. Bob got to experience our routine of running to the window to see who could spot Dad coming around the corner first. The delight in their screams the moment his car was spotted through the thinning trees was the most magnificent sound he had ever heard, visibly filling his eyes with emotion. Bob's exhilaration about meeting Dad had just been trumped by our eagerness to see "Daddy". After all, this was the man he had come to admire more than any other man in his life. More than ever, he realized how genuinely admirable Dad was for having all that was important in life. In some ways, Bob was more nervous to finally meet Dad than he was being dropped into a hotbed of fighting in the combat zone of Vietnam. He was the one man he wanted to emulate. The gravity of it all did not escape him.

Bob excused himself and headed to the driveway to meet Dad privately before our ambush took center stage. Bob descended the walkway with purposeful steps. His eyes met Dad's as he exited the car with a briefcase in hand. Offering each other an immediate salute, Bob held his slightly longer than Dad. Meeting at the edge of the driveway, Dad placed his briefcase down momentarily. The men shook hands while giving a manly hug with their free arm. "It is so good to meet you, Paul. I cannot thank you enough for allowing me to befriend your family. You have welcomed me into your home in a way I have never experienced. I am truly humbled."

"Ah, we are the ones who are humbled to have a brave soldier as our guest. Thank you for making the long trip here from Philadelphia." Dad acknowledged.

"Well, you have a lovely home and perfectly located close to the schools. The kids brought me there this afternoon to show me their 'never-ending' playground."

"Yes, that was one of the selling points for us. We looked at a lot of houses in Scituate and decided this was our dream home where we could build a nice life for our family. Now, the rest is up to us."

"Well, you have everything a man could ever want, and I am happy for you. You inspire me to work to build a similar life." Bob admitted.

"Yes, congratulations! You are a married man now! Finding the right woman is the most important step in the whole process, so congratulations!" Patting him on the back, he suggested, "Let's go in and join the rest of the family." The two men continue talking as they made their way back to the house. Bob respectfully opened the door for Dad, but Dad signaled for him to enter first. These gestures of mutual respect and admiration went back and forth for the balance of his visit. After a delicious dinner, we all retreated to the family room where the kids pulled out some games while the adults continued their conversations. Genuinely grateful for how this friendship had flourished into such a meaningful relationship, and before it got too late into the night, Bob pulled out the bag of gifts he had brought from Vietnam. The kids put their games aside and gathered around.

"First, I'd like to say thank you for all the cards and packages you all have sent me over the last two and a half years. I cannot tell you how much it all meant to me, and in some cases, to my comrades.

You are the All-American family, and I am honored to call you friends." Michael, always seizing opportunities to liven things up a bit, jumped up and started to high-five everyone in the family to heighten the night's festivities. "First I would like to give you, Maryellen, a little something that I picked up in Japan." Bob handed Maryellen a collector's Japanese doll donning perfectly coiffed jet-black hair with a coordinated color fan protruding from the back of her hairdo, dressed in a traditional silk red floral kimono.

"Thank you, Sergeant Johnson, thank you!" she leaped toward him to hug him.

"Now, for the boys in the family, I brought you these." Pulling out two wrapped shirt boxes from the bag, he hands one to each of the boys.

"Thank you, Sergeant Johnson," the boys said in unison. "Thank you!"

"Well, wait a minute, you haven't even opened the box yet. Who knows, you may not even like the gift," he joked. The boys ripped off the wrapping paper and removed the top of their boxes to reveal thick canvas rugged jackets typically worn by Vietnamese boys. Michael immediately jumped up to put the coat on, and Billy soon followed his lead. As boys often do when excited, they started running around the room, mimicking a soldier's moves in the woods, ducking behind end tables and rolling across the floor. I had been sitting on Dad's lap during this time and enjoying all the excitement, but now it was my turn to receive a gift. Bob got down on one knee and looked into my eyes, "And for you, Princess Susan, I have something very special," as he placed a small wrapped gift in my hands. Dad helped me tear the wrapping paper off to see what was hidden inside. Much to my delight, it was a soft fabric angel doll; light brown hair made of thin velvet strips, a white cotton dress with a light blue collar, a black stitched smile and round blue felt eyes, no more than ten inches long. Perfect size for my little hands, and it was soft enough to bring to bed. She was perfect; I immediately named her "T," which was a product of my limited vocabulary at eighteen months. I held "T" to my chest with one arm and wrapped my other around Bob's neck. He grabbed me and plopped me up on his lap as he sat back on the couch. He finished the night by teaching us a sweet children's song Pok Son would sing to the kids at the orphanage. We each gave him a goodnight hug, and then Mama led us up the stairs to our bedrooms.

My parents and Bob stayed up for a bit after we were in bed, talking more about the current state of the world. The conversation was more in-depth in gravity but remained conceptual. As a history teacher, Dad was intrigued tracking the ebbs and flows of Bob's feelings towards the justification of US involvement in the war, having far less to do with the actual victories and defeats in Vietnam, and more to do with the media's coverage of the season of activism at home. Reading the anti-war vehemence in the States appeared to be breaking his spirit more than having to go back and retake land that had already been conquered. The time between letters often made it hard to accurately monitor his feelings in direct correlation to what he was reading from home at the time. Having the luxury of interjecting questions, comments, and sidebar stories was tremendous in thoroughly understanding his experience. Like most luxuries when enjoyed and then lost, this would undoubtedly leave a void to their depth of conversation when they resumed their epistolary relationship.

The chemistry between the three was so benevolent it was as if they had known each other their entire lifetime. The night culminated with a review of the following day's intended agenda. Dad wanted Bob to join him for morning football practice at Boston College High School in Dorchester, which was about thirty-five minutes away. Then, Mama wanted to tour him around Scituate to coincide with the literary tour she had taken him on years before in one of her initial letters. She was also hoping to take the liberty and bring this history buff to Plimouth Plantation, home of the historic first Thanksgiving Dinner. The two were still on a high from finally having met, not in the vein of a romantic desire, but rather a physical human connection to complement the already established emotional connection. The night passed as quickly as the morning arrived.

Bob woke to the chill of the crisp New England fall air, and the sun was cascading through the open window. He couldn't remember ever feeling so alive and full of inspiration. Jumping out of bed and into his fatigues, the aromatic trail of the freshly brewed coffee and sizzling bacon seeped into his room and lured him out within seconds of opening his eyes. After eating like kings, the two men dashed off to football practice while Mama got us up and ready for the day.

Bob thoroughly enjoyed the interaction with the boys on the field and was even given the opportunity to say a few words to them after practice. "You boys are individually striving to become a man in the most real sense of the word. Well, let me offer you one bit of advice. First, put the time and effort necessary into becoming a man of God." Indulging in a dramatic pause, "Once you have done that... the rest will come easier. Times change, but morals don't. If you are firm in your conviction, making decisions will be much easier. Keeping this tenet will not always be simple, but it will be worth it."

One player respectfully raised his hand, signaling he had a question. Coach Hunter gave an affirmative nod, and the boy proceeded to ask, "How can we be men of God and yet be forced to kill in war?"

"That is a great question and one I struggle with at times myself. There are two ports of safety I come back to every time I have this question ricocheting around in my head. One is found in the Bible itself; check out Ecclesiastes 3: There is a time for every activity under the sun, including hate and love, and war and peace. Look it up and see for yourself. The other thought I always circle back to is that I firmly believe God knows my heart. I did not ask for this war, nor did I do anything to provoke it. I don't fight for the love of fighting. I fight for the love of a free mankind. Do the ends justify the means? I don't know, but I have to believe He, being omniscient, recognizes this conundrum I am in and understands my heart." He paused for a moment and then continued with some further elaboration of this response. "The desire from which we do things is paramount to the action itself. Even on a lighter note, if we do a good deed for the sole purpose of being recognized for the good deed and having our ego stroked, it is not good. God wants our hearts to be pure and solely devoted to Him. Like your school's adopted motto, Ad Majorem Dei Gloriam... For the Greater Glory of God~ this is what should motivate us to do good. Once we are solely devoted to Him, by default, our actions are done for the right reasons." Bob released a gentle smile and asked, "Does this make sense to you?" The players collectively nod in agreement. "Mr. Hunter and his wife, Joan, have said they think I should become a minister when I get out of the Army," he chortled, "I guess you all can see why they say that." The team chuckled. Bob felt fulfilled, having had his moment to teach a little something to the young men, perhaps even the next sea of conscripts. He was full of gratitude to Paul for bringing him along.

On the way home from practice, Dad purposely drove Route 3A, which hugged the South Shore's coastline. The long stretches of Wollaston Beach were teeming with walkers, joggers and kids flying kites. This idyllic sight was one Bob had never experienced before having grown up in a landlocked state. The winding cliffs of Cohasset's Jericho Road, inclusive of the affluence these homes revealed, could also tout the breathtaking views of the deep blue sea raging up against the dark, jagged rocks below. Not to steal Mama's thunder on her tour around town, he diverted from the scenic route as soon as he approached the Scituate border.

The men arrived home just before lunch, and as expected, Mama had the table set and sandwiches prepared alongside fruit, chips, and ginger ale. Following an enjoyable lunch, we all went for a walk around the neighborhood and up to Cushing School's playground. Dad stayed with the older kids for another hour or so while Mama and Bob, with me in arms, walked back to the house through the wooded path to begin their tour around town.

Bob thoroughly enjoyed riding around Scituate, which was reminiscent of the ones he had virtually taken so many times before while lying out under the Vietnam stars. Some of the sights were just as she described while others were enormously more striking to see in person, specifically, the spectacular views from First and Second Cliffs. Ironically, driving over the bridge at the junction where harbor meets marshland, it was exactly as she described. There were two young boys with lines hanging in the harbor water below and an artist set up with canvas and a palette of watercolor paints. The October marsh grass was light brown and swayed ever so slightly in the cool zephyr.

Saturdays brought about family outings, adding to the idyllic charm of this New England coastal town. As they crept closer to winter, every park was crawling with the northeasterners' taking advantage of every fleeting last day of friendly temperatures. Mama drove to the Old Oaken Bucket home to tantalize Bob's passion for history, and then as she promised, they headed south to Plimouth Plantation and the famous Plymouth Rock.

From the crest of the hill, truly breathtaking for any historian, the view of the Plymouth harbor below proudly showcased the Mayflower II, a seaworthy replica of the original 17th century Mayflower. The original ship touted for bringing the pilgrims to the New World in 1620, boasted three masts and six sails to power the 106-foot vessel across the Atlantic Ocean. The replica, a collaborative effort by entities in the United States and the United Kingdom, had only been home to the Plymouth Harbor for the past decade, after making its maiden voyage from the United Kingdom.

With me in Bob's arms once again, the three of us navigated the ship and ducked in and out of the 17th century homes along the Plantation's dirt paths. If Bob's dark black complexion and Army fatigues weren't enough to grab the attention of those passing by, the fact he was walking with Mama and carrying me, surely was. Not escaping glances from many, and raised eyebrows from some, neither Mama nor Bob seemed to care or even notice. It wasn't until she stepped up to the ticket booth to purchase tickets for the Plimouth Plantation that it was brought to their attention that they were a sight to be seen.

"Two tickets for the guided tour, please." Mama bubbly requested as she opened her purse and propped it up on the counter. No reaction. "Excuse me... I'd like to purchase two tickets for the guided tour." No reaction again. Mama looked up at Bob with utter confusion in her eyes, indicating she has never experienced this type of rudeness before. In a louder, slightly less cheerful tone, "Hello... excuse me... I would like to purchase two tickets for the guided tour, please." The woman remained with her back to them and continued about her business of flipping through papers. Bob got agitated witnessing Mama being disrespected and signaled her with a nod to move a bit to the side to let him move in closer to the counter.

In a deep throaty voice commanding attention, "Excuse me Ma'am, how much are the tickets for the guided tour?" She turned around and looked directly at Mama.

"Ma'am, you and your family have complimentary passes to the Plantation since your husband..." shooting a snarky glance over to Bob, "is a serviceman."

Mama looked at Bob, letting out a stunted chuckle and then returned her attention to the woman, "Oh no, he is not my husband; this is my friend, Sergeant Johnson."

216

"Oh, pardon me, I assumed he was your husband because he was carrying your child," emphasizing "child." "Please forgive me, ma'am."

Mama half-smiled still perplexed as to why she didn't acknowledge her beforehand. "No apologies necessary, I can understand why you thought that."

The woman offered a half-smile back and proceeded to ring up a ticket for Mama. Then she had a moment of pause, almost visibly seeing her reflect a bit, and looked back up at Mama. Holding a cool but friendly stare, she waved them all through as guests. As Bob passed by, she looked up at him with a forced smile and mumbled, "For your sake and ours, I hope this war ends real soon."

"Yes, ma'am, I do, too," Bob replied with an appreciative nod. He strolled through the gate alongside Mama and, with me in his arms, held his head high and took in a deep breath and exhaled with the most prominent, brightest smile like a person having just passed the bar exam.

"Well, what was all that about?" Mama naively questioned.

"I don't know, Joan, but I'm guessing that woman felt it was her duty to judge us, me… or the war."

Connecting with a guided tour already in progress, Bob was in his glory, listening to the guide speak of the Plantation steeped in history. The Wampanoag homesites were of particular interest to Bob. He loved the self-sufficiency of the Wampanoags and how they built homes large enough to house three or four families in each. These larger bark-covered homes, called *nush wetus*, require three fireplaces for both cooking and warmth in the colder months, and their proximity to the river allowed for plentiful fishing and successful harvesting. Bob was fascinated to be walking the paths of our nation's infancy years; truly in wonder of how far we, as a nation, have come since the first foreign settlers.

There was so much to learn and much more to see, but being only eighteen months at the time, I was getting fidgety, so Bob led us ahead of the guided tour and back to the harbor. We concluded our day of tourism by stopping at the renowned Plymouth Rock. The rock was believed to be the disembarkation spot of all the pilgrims arriving at the New World in 1620 and '21. This proved to be quite the anticlimactic ending to the day. It was just a large rock separated from all others and placed twelve feet below the viewing area. Mama and Bob looked up from the pit and at each other and let out a jovial belly laugh. "This is it?" shaking his head with utter disappointment.

"I'm afraid so," Mama laughed. "It very well may be the silliest tourist trap. Good thing, there is no charge for this part of the attraction, huh?" They both laughed as they turned to walk back to the car.

The twenty-five-minute ride back was dominated by the conversation surrounding all they had just learned. Bob peppered in questions of wonderment of how the early settlers conjured the courage to leave their families behind to plant new roots in the New World, adopting a whole new way of life. Of course, Mama brought it to current relevance by pointing out that they were courageous pioneers. Men and women who were willing to endure hundreds of years of struggle to gift future generations with the independence we enjoy today. This concept was not lost on Bob as he knew she was subtly tipping her hat to him for his dream of full acceptance of miscegenation.

Arriving back at home, they were pleasantly surprised to see that Dad had the kids in line, prepared dinner, and set the table. He was grilling hamburgers and hot dogs for us kids and steaks for the adults, all the while; my siblings were putting the finishing touches on the salad. I was understandably overtired but was noticeably rallying to stay awake, not wanting to miss a single minute with "our soldier," my new best friend. During dinner, we all convinced Bob to stay one more night so he could attend church with us in the morning before heading back to Philadelphia.

"I am not Catholic," Bob warned. "I don't want lightning to strike while I am in the church." Of course, I didn't get the joke, and my sibs looked momentarily concerned but then quickly joined in the laughter led by my parents.

Chapter 34

If I Don't Make it Back

"If I don't make it back…" were Bob's parting words to Mama before she shushed him mid-sentence.

"Don't even put that thought in your head," she ordered. "Next time we see you at our front door, you better be standing there with Pok Son, your beautiful bride."

"I will surely do my best to oblige. And yes, she sure is beautiful." He turned to open his car door but stops mid turn. "Wait, I almost forgot to give you something." He rustles through his rucksack and pulls out an 8x10 envelope and hands it to Mama.

"What's this? A picture of you?"

"Even better. Go ahead and open it," he encouraged.

She carefully unsealed the envelope and pulled out the picture, letting out a gasp as she did. "Oh Bob, this is stunning…she is stunning! And you both look so happy." Mama marveled over Pok Son's wedding gown and his sharp uniform donning colored tangibles of bravery. "Thank you for this! I will frame it and hang it in our home." She gave Bob a hug, and like their first hug, this, too, lasted unusually long. Both were reluctant to let go as they were well aware it may be their last time seeing each other.

Bob headed to Korea to spend a couple of weeks with his bride, Pok Son, and her family before returning to Vietnam. While in Korea, apprehension filled his heart about returning for his third tour in Vietnam. The President's decision to halt all bombing concerned the troops greatly. North Vietnam offered no gestures of deescalating the war on their end, before or after the President's decision.

While in Korea with Pok Son's family, Bob wrote:

"Ho Chi Minh took full advantage of the President's decision to halt all bombing by stepping up the action. He has been pushing more and more supplies into South Vietnam via the Ho Chi Minh Trail, encouraging his troops to fight harder. Ho even described this as 'North Vietnam scoring a great military and political victory over the United States,' and it was." He further frustrated, "We had North Vietnam on the defensive. Now, it looks as if the tides have turned. It looks as though, I, along with thousands of other GIs earned Purple Hearts for nothing. But then again, who am I to say? I am only a small fish in the sea. If we lose this war in Vietnam, I truly hope I am killed soon before it happens." He closed the letter with, "In every life, a little rain must fall. Well, they are having a helluva flood right now in Washington, yet we are the only ones drowning. ~ With love from, Bob and Pok Son"

***

Bob returned to Vietnam alone, leaving Pok Son to spend what they planned to be their first year as newly-weds, apart from each other. Initially, this was a financial decision, allowing them to save more money if she stayed in Korea. However, it was also preferred now that he was not sure he'd survive much longer under the new strategies. He did not want to uproot her from her family and then make her a widow. He returned to Vietnam beset with apprehension, so he transferred to the 1st Infantry Division to change things up on this third tour. The separation from his new wife played heavy on his heart, undoubtedly exacerbated by the dichotomy of having just experienced his pastoral visit with the Hunters. Minutes seemed like days, days like weeks, and weeks like years. He wrote:

"I think I made a mistake by getting married before coming back to Vietnam. Now, I constantly think about my wife, which can prove to be fatal over here. Meaning, when I should be thinking about the Viet Congs, I am thinking about her. You know, Joan, women sure have a way of fouling up a man's mind. Three months ago, I was a happy bachelor. Now, I am confused, in love, and a victim of circumstance~ a married man. The worst part of it all... I don't regret it!" He continued to profess his love for Pok Son, "If my love for Pok Son and her love for me lasts, I will have found the land of endless paradise. When our first son is born, (it will be a son), I am going to name him 'Complete,' because along with Pok Son, my life will then be complete. If I am to have a girl, I will bring her back to the hospital and trade her off. I just can't picture bringing a girl into the world and having some other young man, like me, having his whole life clustered up by some beautiful woman. (smile)"

***

Bob had ten more months to go to complete this tour and head back to the States with his bride to start their life together. He dreamed of taking a bus trip across the United States to show her much of what will be, her new homeland. These hopes and dreams got him through so many rough days ahead.

Having just returned from a five-day, arduous operation, Bob attempted to beat the 110-degree heat by relaxing in his tent and writing a letter to Mama.

"My luck held out pretty good on this last operation. We lost eight men, and as you would have guessed, I was in the middle of the main firefight, a nice way to start a new tour of duty. (smile) The company is hurting so badly for officers; sergeants are currently running the company. I am the platoon sergeant and the platoon leader. The company has lost five officers in the last two months."

A week later, he wrote of another defeating blow to the company, "We returned from a four-day helluva operation. We lost fifteen men, thirteen wounded and two killed. We go out again tomorrow for a four to ten-day operation."

Showing a subtle sign of vulnerability to his fate and perhaps a little loneliness, he told Mama, "I received your Christmas card today; Mr. & Mrs. Claus and the four elves, unique. I hope you don't mind; I cut it up to fit into the picture carrier in my wallet." Ending with an unusual sign-off, "I won't be able to send you a card this year, but I send my sincerest wishes and hopes. Merry Christmas and Happy New Year. With love, thoughts, and care...Robert."

***

Although a short mutual cease-fire had been agreed upon for a few days leading up to and including Christmas, Viet Cong had violated cease-fires in years past, so Bob was only cautiously optimistic. Nevertheless, he and his battalion committed to setting up a seven-day blocking force while hoping for the enemy to honor the truce. Unfortunately, this uncertainty meant they spent Christmas Day in the field with the promise of a celebratory New Year's Eve, inclusive of more beer than eighty men could responsibly consume.

Disappointments frequent soldiers in wartime, and Christmas and New Year's proved to be no different. On the third of the month, the men got into a devastating battle, losing twenty-six men in total, four killed in action. The following day, Bravo company had three more expire in the same area. It was evident that the Viet Cong and the PAVN had fortified their forces and supplies during the extensive Presidentially ordered US cease-fire, and the US troops were suffering as a result. Bob admitted, "For the first time since Operation Masher, I was actually afraid."

A reporter, or as Bob would refer to them, a "straphanger," took a photograph of him in the field on Christmas Day, which he subsequently sent to Mama in a birthday card marking her thirty-third trip around the sun. It was accompanied by some sweet words of wisdom in the form of a poem.

"Years Passing"

Years passing are those ever-lasting.
We often think of tomorrow,
but yesterday we don't have to think about for they are days of
history.
Yesterday, years passing, now a memory.
Yesterday, I was a year younger,
Today, a year older.
Tomorrow, well, a year I have yet to borrow.
Years passing, they brought the good times and the bad times,

but most of all,
They were God given years so I can't regret.
So, we can't weep about the passing years,
we must regard them as a gift from Heaven.
Day and night, this is time,
Time measured in light making years passing,
Those wonderful years ever-lasting.

"Joan, thirty-three is a good year but not the best year. For the best is yet to come. May you see three times thirty-three. I am looking forward to two ages; thirty-six and fifty. Thirty-six, when I can retire from the army (after twenty long, hard years) and fifty because that is when my son will be graduating from college. Now, don't be wishing any bad luck on me like my first child being a girl... there won't be any of that 'Sorry About That' (smile) ~Your Everlasting Friend, Bob"

***

That was the last she heard from Bob in January. February and March came and went without a single word from her dearest pen pal. She paced in front of the TV day and night, never having been more concerned. The tensions in the States continued to rise with the confluence of the civil rights activists' groups garnering energy from each other. The country was spiraling out of control for some time now as the war had never been more repudiated. She was kicking herself for not getting Pok Son's address for times like this. Again, she found herself in an uncomfortable position, not knowing what had happened to her dear friend and having no way of finding out.

Victory in Vietnam was deemed to be out of reach. The country was pleading to the authorities to bring the troops home as this war had now besmirched American history. Mama kept her Operation Morale Booster to herself as others in the community no longer supported her efforts. The reputation of the soldiers themselves had been stained as if they were responsible for entering the war and provoking the enemy. The Vietnam War became a taboo topic for conversation. Only the brave openly championed the plight of the GI. Mama fell into a shallow depression realizing the indelible memories from her mission of the past three years were all for naught and further, now they were even shunned to be shared. As high as her hopes had been at the onset of this journey, they were crashing now. Even Dad's typical sagacious support was no match for the outpouring of disgust and abandonment the media was propagating throughout the country, inflicting shame on these young soldiers. Dialogue and voices of reason could no longer find their way to the surface above the noise.

Chapter 35

If You Have the Right to Burn
My Flag

T he conflux of the civil rights activism was broadening and now reached three arms of contention; Black rights, women's rights, and the unflagging intensity surrounding the Draft Dodgers' controversy. The anti-war fervor and the realization that America's heart was no longer with the soldiers was like a tidal wave crashing down on Mama. Additionally, world opinion against the US involvement in the war only heightened her overall consternation for the country and concern for the well-being of the soldiers. Being a peacemaker at heart, this was all too much for her to handle, yet she couldn't give up. She knew firsthand of the power of the media, so she took to her typewriter once again and wrote to the Boston Globe and every other news source in her database to quell the anger of the people. To no avail, the noise was simply too loud, and the era of dissent continued to amass.

Mr. Baker's eyes expressed increasing sadness, as he noticed Mama's air mail letters from abroad had slowed to a trickle. Most of her pen pals had stopped writing, perhaps from despair, perished, or end-of-tour with no closing note of "I'm home." She downheartedly continued the mission despite the void most of the relationships had left. Admittedly, she was just going through the motions at this point, but she was determined to see it through to the end.

Just as her letters had instantly perked Bob up over the years, receiving a message from Bob rejuvenated her spirits.

April 7/69

To My Dear Friends:

Lasting friendships don't necessarily have to be expressed in writing, for if one can truly maintain friendships within their thoughts, then it is undoubtedly in their hearts and can never be forgotten.

Well, here we are again back to the stroke of the ol' pen. I received your most wonderful card yesterday, and it found me doing well and still surviving. Before I say another word, please accept my sincere apologies for not writing for so long. There is no acceptable excuse for me not writing. As a matter of fact, the company XO (executive officer serving second in command) made me sit down and write a letter to my wife yesterday because she had written to him asking why she hadn't heard from me in two weeks.

However, in my defense, the battalion had been moving around so much and fighting on days we weren't moving, it made it difficult to write. The Battalion, and my Company have been taking more than our share of the casualties lately. We lost almost two entire platoons, a lieutenant, and a company commander in the last four months. However, I can knock on wood because I have made it through hell month(s). You might recall, every time I have been wounded, it has been in either January or February, so the fact that it is April, and I am still here is a blessing. I have six more months, and then Pok Son and I will be coming to visit the Hunters... I hope.

You know Joan, it has been a little over three years since we started writing to each other. Back then, the American heart was in this war, and the price of American life was worth the reward of giving freedom to a whole population of good people, but now, everything is so different. It is now a war of big political mouths shooting off the fat. Who could have imagined, the Paris Peace talks being stalled for two months because they could not decide whether to hold the conference over a round table or a square table, all the while guys are dying over here? It makes me wonder if our lives even matter to them. I have completely changed my mind about this war and the cause. I have lost a lot over this; brothers, sweat, blood, and spirit... and for what?

When you took me through your little town of Scituate, I thought that it was the symbol of America, and the Hunters were the best part of our history and our future. Yet I can't help but think of this war and how it is tearing apart our heritage right in the face of the rest of the world.

Last month, US troops were finally permitted to invade the Michelin Rubber Plantations. I don't understand- the rules of engagement are unlike any other war I have studied. My battalion was relieved of this area two weeks ago. The Marines are still there. I don't understand why they sent us here to fight a war and then not allow us to fight strategically. What do politicians know about fighting a war? We are sent to settle the arguments they start. Let us do what we were sent here to do. The government's duplicitous behavior is messing up our psyche, and it is wearing on me considerably.

Well, I must close for now. This rhetorical rant is not serving any purpose, and I have to get myself prepared for another day of fighting.

I will end with this thought... True friendship is like day and night; separation does not keep them from being together.

Until next time,
Bob

P.S. Please give my best to the kids. Tell them I said to work hard in school because education will allow them choices.

Chapter 36

Carry on Wayward Son

Tensions continued to rise on the streets of every American city and university campus. Conversely, the morale of the U.S. troops was equally deteriorating to a dangerous level. Bob found himself at the lowest point in his life. If the circumstances surrounding the war and civil unrest in the States weren't enough, news of a series of hospitalizations and deaths from his family in Philadelphia threw him over the edge. He needed Mama's comfort more than ever, and he penned a couple of letters but couldn't bring himself to send them to her. He was now conflicted as to her role in his life. Who was he to confide in; his wife, who he loved dearly but did not want to give reason for worry, or the friend, a world away, who got him through the war thus far? He struggled with this, which only made matters worse and amplified the fact that although he was married on paper, for all intents and purposes, he was still alone. Pok Son stayed in Korea with family waiting patiently for her husband to complete his tour of duty in Vietnam. Mama was even farther away. He was alone and in a dark place. It was about to get darker.

Shortly after morning chow and drenched from the walk back to his bedroll during the height of monsoon, Bob received a letter from Pok Son informing him that her family's village had been ravaged by devastating floods, drowning 600 of the villagers. Additionally, cholera had invaded this same village attacking the survivors. What kind of a husband am I? I am not there to protect my wife and her family. Here I am protecting people I don't know all the while; my family is suffering. Coupled with the plethora of bad news from his family in Philadelphia he received earlier in the week, Bob petitioned for a transfer of duties to Korea. He was immediately granted along with a thirty-seven-day drop due to personal hardships.

Bob found himself in a real dark place. Thoughts ran through his head at such a rapid rate; he couldn't differentiate the end of one and beginning of another. Desperate to escape to think and sort things out, he ventured outside the bivouac's perimeter to seek a place of solitude and peace; if there ever was such a place in Vietnam. This humbled servant relinquished all control. He fell down to his knees, with tears streaming down his face and hands tightly clasped together, he began his fervent prayers at sunrise, and continued long into the night. Petitioning, "Please God, free me of this pain, fill me with your light. I want to serve you to the best of my ability, but I know I have neglected the means of fortifying my soul. I have lost my ways in the darkness of this war. Please see me through this season of destruction. I am alone; I am confused; I am depleted of all strength." Incessantly weeping with his head in the palms of his hands, he smashed into rock bottom. He stayed there for hours, crying, praying, and talking to God like he was talking to a father he never really had. Lifting his head to the sky once more, he cleared the tears from his face and donning the most contrite eyes; he paused before his final query, "What is my purpose, Lord? Direct me as you see fit.

Chapter 37

Daddy's Little Girl

Although emotionally drained and exhausted from having been up late into the night, Bob woke to a new day and a new beginning. He mapped out a plan to best utilize the thirty- day leave to redirect his life out of the current pit. His first duty was to head to Korea to spend some time with his wife before commencing his new position, which would allow him to finish his tour in Korea. He most urgently wanted to make sure Pok Son and her family were ok from the recent traumatic flooding and aftermath. While waiting for transportation to the airfield, he scribbled a note to his family on some nearby lined paper, informing them he would be calling as soon as he could. Still, an emergency with Pok Son and her family compelled him to hop a flight to Korea immediately.

He packed up his rucksack and hustled over to meet the driver. Throwing his sack in the back of the truck, he hopped into the passenger side next to the driver. They made their way to the airfield in silence outside of their initial greetings. Bob was preoccupied with deep thought. Soldiers this deep into the war zone knew enough not to probe a quiet comrade. Arriving at its destination, Bob simply jumped out, grabbed his bag, and returned a respectful salute before turning toward the aircraft in the field.

The flight to Korea seemed to take twice as long as other times he had flown there. His heightened anxiety had his heart beating like a racehorse, egregiously pronouncing the veins in his neck and forehead. He utilized every minute of the flight to emotionally prepare for what he was about to see, canvassing the flood-stricken village, and what he wanted to accomplish during this trip. He knew he needed a sea change, but these were new waters for him having been a bachelor for twenty-seven years. He was very well aware, blending the varying cultures was going to be tricky.

Immediately greeted by Army personnel, Bob exited the plane and leaped into the truck without hesitation. Within a minute of landing, he was on his way through Korea's back roads to Pok Son's family's home. Time had not been a luxury afforded to Bob, allowing him to alert Pok Son of his impromptu trip, so his arrival was going to be a surprise to the family. Washed out streets and destroyed vegetation were prevalent as far as the eye could see in her village. He braced himself as he neared her road. As the military truck pulled around the corner to their humble abode, Pok Son and her father popped their heads up from the side garden. Frightful eyes pierced through the glare on the windows, desperately trying to distinguish the faces within. The presence of a military truck showing up unexpectedly often proved to be the bearer of devastating news. Pok Son and her father tempered their emotions to maintain composure for whatever developments were about to be dropped.

Pok Son never saw such a welcomed sight as this handsome dark soldier, standing five feet, ten inches tall, and donning a smile that could light up the entire street. He stepped out from within the muddied truck, dropping his sack to the ground. Pok Son shot an approval-seeking glance at her father before jumping the row of sweet potatoes to leap into his welcoming arms. Their embrace lasted longer than it took for her dad to make his way over to them. He awkwardly stood by and waited for his turn to greet Bob, his friend, and now son-in-law, with a traditional gentlemen's bow.

Together, they went inside to see the rest of the family. Formalities aside, Bob and her father perused the home and property to assess the damage from the floods. Having been his house boy when Bob was assigned to Korea a year ago, Bob and her father could communicate well. Together, they concluded that the damage was minimal and all repairable. The harvest may not be as fruitful as a result of the excessive water and washed away soil, but they remained grateful for having survived the floods virtually unscathed. While the men were surveying the property, Pok Son prepared an array of food to delight all senses. Partaking in some *sul* (Korean alcoholic beverages), Pok Sun, her father, two brothers, and Bob gathered in the main room and laughed the night away. It was hard for him to fathom just hours before, he was serving as the First Sergeant of Lai Khe Post in Vietnam, and now he was in a family room in Korea, holding hands with his wife and singing songs with her family; his family now, too. A long day of traveling but so well worth it. He had a lasting taste of what he wanted in life. Wonderfully satisfied for the moment, no one could have prepared the newlyweds for what the next day was about to bring.

The morning's soundtrack of the chirping birds sounded sweeter in Korea, or perhaps it was merely because Pok Son was lying in his arms as the sun peaked through the curtains, greeting them to the new day. Not a word was spoken between the two while they gazed deeply into each other's sleepy eyes. He was mesmerized by her beauty, and she by the protective nature he exuded in every touch. Taking his time and indulging in every minute, he reacquainted himself with her slender, curvaceous physique, gently running his fingers along her velvety skin as he caressed and kissed every curve of her body. He lovingly studied every contour as if this was the first, and last time, he was to be with a woman. Although her culture nurtured submissiveness, this was not that. They were indulging in an intimate start to the day and a start to their married life together. She wanted him to touch her, to caress her, to worship her body. He was happy to oblige. She was a woman; heart, soul, and body and no longer her *appaui eolin sonyeo*, "daddy's little girl." Empowered by this realization and thoroughly enjoying the intensity of sweet coitus sacred within the boundaries of real love, she encouraged him to linger longer with the softly spoken sounds of bedtime pleasures. "I want to kiss you the way you want to be kissed," she whispered.

"And I want to hold you as you have never been held, and protect you for all the days of your life," he lovingly responded.

The newlyweds enjoyed each other's company for well over two hours before leaving the bedroom's joys to sneak down to the overflowing river. They walked hand in hand in silence alongside the riverside until Bob abruptly turned to her and grabbed her other hand, saying, "Let's start a family." Pok Son, only slightly more shocked than Bob was himself hearing those words roll off his tongue, was visibly startled but not resistant. He continued, "When I first met you, you told me of your dream to adopt two children and bring them to the United States to give them a chance of a good life. Let's do that, Pok Son! Let's adopt two children and start a family." He looked down at her hands gently held in his and then again into her eyes, and clarified, "However, I would like to adopt two Black Korean children; these mixed children have no hope here."

Pok Son smiled with her eyes and spoke sweet words of adoration with her lips, "Bob, you are the most loving and wonderful man. Your compassion is unparalleled." Pok Son knew too well of the atrocious acceptance of the "mercy killing" of mixed-race babies prevalent in Korea. Newborns of interracial couples were often thrown into the river or left out in the mountains to be eaten by the tigers. This heinous act was accepted as merciful killings because the Korean society felt the life of a *twigi,* a mixed-baby, was worse than enduring a cruel death. His elated wife was speechless, flinging her arms around him in the most animated affirmative gesticulation. "Yes, yes!" she managed to squeak out. "Yes, let's start a family!"

That entire week, Bob and Pok Son were inseparable except for the hours Bob would go to Camp Casey Base to check on the status of his upcoming new assignment. While there, and as usual, the local children would roam onto the base to get Chicklets and candy bars from the soldiers. This particularly sweet little girl with bigger eyes than the rest warmed up to Bob and called him "Daddy" as she thanked him for the candy bars. Her large round brown eyes grabbed his attention, but her sweetness grabbed his heart. Although this angelic little girl did not appear to be an orphan, her engaging large round eyes were a tell-tale of mixed race. He returned home to Pok Son with an idea.

"Pok Son, there is a sweet little girl, I'm guessing three-years-old. She has been coming to the base this week. I think she is Black Korean. I don't believe she is orphaned as she is always neatly dressed and has been taught her manners, but she appears to be mixed. Her parents clearly love her dearly since they did not choose mercy killing at birth, but maybe they want more for her than what Korea can provide. Can you find out who her parents are? And maybe ask them to meet with us?" Pok Son agreed to go to the base the next day to meet the little girl and have the little girl bring her to her parents' home. As planned, Pok Son was able to meet with the little girl's mother and explain to her their desire to adopt two Black Korean children and raise them in the United States. She left her address with the woman and asked her to think about it and let them know if she would be interested.

Later that week, a woman approached the home and knocked on the door. Bob was the first to greet the guest with Pok Son closely behind. He opened the door, gesturing her to enter, to which she bowed respectfully and proceeded over the threshold of the home. Pok Son immediately recognized her as the little girl's mother and took over the conversation from there as Bob's Korean was not up for the sensitivity of the task. The woman looked long and hard into Bob and Pok Son's eyes as if to have a conversation with herself before uttering a word. The pause was dramatic but heartfelt, and both were sensitive enough to recognize that whatever this woman was about to say, it was clearly painful and undoubtedly monumental to her. Pok Son extended her hand to hold the woman's hand, assuring her she could say anything to them. The woman nodded as she let out the tiniest hint of a smile. Inhaling the deepest of breaths and slowly exhaling, she began to speak.

She spoke of a budding love story between a caring Korean woman and a strong, handsome Black man that began four and a half years ago. She took the two through the early stages of their interracial relationship and the struggles they were willing to accept to nurture their love. Both Bob and Pok Son could not help but relate and be thoroughly engaged. "In the most beautiful expression of divine love," she smiled, "...a beautiful baby girl was born. They named her Melody." The woman continued in her soft, silvery voice. "She was the apple of their eyes and just the perfect baby." The woman's eyes were as bright as her smile when she spoke of this baby, Melody. Then her eyes saddened. "When Melody was two years old, her father disappeared, and his wife has not seen him since." She paused and looked down into her hands, which were folded in her lap. Looking back up, she boldly stated, "I am his wife. Melody is our three-year-old baby girl." She began to weep, cradling herself. Pok Son shot a sorrowful look toward Bob while in motion to wrap her arms around the distraught woman. The woman tried to speak through her tears of despair but was inaudible. Bob and Pok Son consoled her and were sincerely heartbroken to hear that she had been raising her by herself this last year.

After a short while, the woman regained her composure and explained to them how she was genuinely fraught with distress over her sweet Melody's destiny, especially since she was raising her on her own now. "My baby is neither accepted by my people nor the Blacks because she is mixed." Sobbing and trying desperately to speak through the hyperventilating, "She is not allowed to be educated because of this!" Again, the tears streamed down her face.

Sitting in a pool of tears, she looked up one last time, and with the most woeful eyes, she blurted out, "Her only destiny is to be a 'businesswoman' enslaved to work in a brothel!"

At that moment, Bob flashed back to the conversation he had had with Mama about her concern for the first generation of children of interracial marriages and how they would suffer the most. Although his eyes were fixated on the desperate woman's face, he only saw the words from the pages of Mama's typed letters, 'suffer,' 'concern,' 'pain,' and children being dealt with hardship of society's evolution. His heart physically ached as he listened, truly feeling her plight.

She paused, clearing the tears from her face, she took a deep breath and continued. "You are the answer to my prayers for Melody's wellbeing. I have come to ask you to adopt my sweet baby girl and offer her an education and a respectful life in America." Her brave smile could not hide the evidence of pain in her heart at the idea of having to let go of her child. This level of love was something Bob had never witnessed. This woman cherished her daughter so much; she not only gave her life when many would have chosen otherwise; but now the second act of pure love, she was willing to give her away to offer her a better life than what she could provide. This selflessness shook Bob to the core, leaving him speechless and staring deep into her eyes. Pok Son extended both arms to hold the heartbroken woman, comforting her with words of support and encouragement.

Bob stood up with emotion-filled eyes and slightly parted lips that still could not utter a single word, gently placing his hand on her shoulder and offering a heartfelt nod. Using only hand gestures, he excused himself to go outside for a walk. He couldn't even bring himself to look back at Pok Son before walking out the door. He recognized this moment as the crossroads it was. He walked out to the front porch area and sat at the top of the small stairway, arms resting on bent knees. He allowed himself to sink deeply into his thoughts and prayers. "Lord, is this what you want for me?"

Fond images of holding me flashed in his mind, and he wondered if he was ready to protect a daughter of his own. His struggle was real. Dutiful by nature, he held strong beliefs that God presented opportunities to seize. Still, he wondered if the timing was right or had he acted on impulse, suggesting that they start a family so quickly after getting married. He was a soldier, and the country was still in the middle of a controversial war. Bob had hardly adjusted to married life, and now he was about to throw himself into parenthood. Additionally, his desire for a son was so paramount in all his dreams of being a father; he surprised himself that the idea of adopting a baby girl was his initiative. Then there was the cost of raising a child. *Could I even provide for a wife and child?* He questioned. *What if I am killed in action, making Pok Son a widow and Melody, fatherless once again? Then there was the question of emotional preparedness.* "Lord, am I ready to be a father... a good father? Will I have the wisdom to guide her through this rocky road that is ahead of her?"

Like a ton of bricks, the answer to his last question came back to him like a pendulum and hit him with the response; *YES.* Who better to protect and guide her through this life she has been born into than me? Mama's description of him being a "pioneer" kept replaying in his head, empowering him to recognize that things don't always happen in *our* time, rather everything happens in "His" time. *I will raise her to be strong, confident, a free thinker, and a pioneer herself. Pok Son, Melody, and I will start the fire that will lead us to a world where love is indifferent to skin color.* Overcome with relief, eyes brimming with tears, he looked up to the sky and offered a prayer of gratitude, "Thank you for delivering sweet Melody to us. We will love and protect her all the days of our lives."

With a definite purpose in his step, he made his way back into the house and took Pok Son aside. After a short discussion, the two agreed on the concept of adopting sweet Melody, but the logistics would still need to be ironed out. Bob did not want to accept responsibility for Melody until they were living as husband and wife in a home of their own, whether that be in Korea or the United States. This time would also allow Melody to gradually get to know her new parents while her mom remained nearby.

Together, they walked back into the room to confer with Melody's mother. Riddled with anticipation, she stood as they entered the room. As Bob and Pok Son held hands and began to tell the woman of their decision, Pok Son reached out to grab ahold of hers. Recognizing the gravity of the moment, Bob cleared his throat and said in a thick voice stifled at times by emotion, "We are grateful you trust us to love your Melody as our own. We do believe this to be a clear example of Divine Intervention. And as such, we promise you and God to care for Melody to the best of our ability." He cleared his throat again, "With some conditions." Her face was filled with joy, and her head was shaking in agreement before even hearing the conditions. Bob couldn't contain his smile as he witnessed hope rejuvenate her soul. "We cannot, in good conscience, accept full responsibility for Melody until we can provide a home for her where both Pok Son and I are living; this we hope to secure in the coming weeks. Additionally, we plan to go to the United States in November when my tour of duty is over; we will want her to come with us at that time, but you must realize she may never come back to Korea."

"Yes, yes, of course, I understand," she bowed. "I am so grateful, thank you. She is a beautiful little girl... and this... this is the hardest thing I will ever have to do, but I have to do it... for her sake." Tears pouring down her face, the three hugged, sharing mixed emotions, but all believed they were doing right by this sweet little girl.

Chapter 38

Break on Through to the Other Side

Not quite the sea change he was expecting when leaving Vietnam, but it all felt right, and he was excited about catching this new wind in his sails and setting course in a more fulfilling direction. He had much to share with Mama in his next letter.

November/69

To My Dear Friends:

I hope this letter finds you and the family well and enjoying all the splendors life has to offer. I thought I would take this opportunity to write to you this Sunday morning to let you know that Pok Son and I are doing just fine and like always, thinking of you.

A couple of months ago, I had some very upsetting news from my family at home in Philadelphia, and simultaneously Pok Son wrote to tell me about an awful flood in her village. With all this hardship, coupled with my impending new assignment and my multiple tours in Vietnam, the Army granted me a thirty-day drop ahead of a transfer to my new position in Korea. Yes, you read that right, I will finish my tour in Korea with my wife.

I have been in my new company and position for the past week and as funny as it may sound, after a thirty-day leave, it feels good to be back to work. Pok Son and I found a small home about ten miles from the Korean DMZ (Demilitarized Zone), which allows me to come home most nights. Ten miles may not seem like a lot, but with transportation, like it is here, it is equivalent to being a hundred miles away at home in the States. I come home every weekend and even some nights during the week. She is getting her first taste of being the wife of a soldier.

We had a memorable thirty-day leave together, spending most of it at her family's home. We have exciting news to share. We have decided to start a family. We are in the process of adopting a Black-Korean, three-year-old girl, Melody. Her mother very much loves her, but the life of a mixed-race child in Korea is bleak at best. Her mother wants her to have the opportunity to grow up in the United States so that we will raise her as our own. I will send you a picture of her as soon as I get one. She is about the same age as Susan and just the sweetest little girl. Maybe they will grow up to be friends. (smile)

How is your family? I bet the kids are excited for the first snowfall, that is if it hasn't already happened. Well, sorry I have to close this so soon. I will try to write more next time.

With all the racial troubles in the United States, I heard the Blacks have come out with a new drink. Well, you know how gin and lemon juice is known as a Tom Collins, well we decided to call gin and watermelon juice, an Uncle Tom Collins. (smile)

Always your friends,
Robert and Pok Son

***

Over the next twelve months, while waiting for his stateside assignment, Bob and Pok Son gradually assumed responsibility for Melody. Their home at Camp Casey was near both Pok Son's family and Melody's biological mother, so it allowed for the weening of visits. The transition was seamless and the least upsetting for sweet Melody. They thoroughly enjoyed their first Christmas together as a family. Bob explained in an early January 1970 letter to Mama:

"It was the best Christmas I have ever had in my entire life. Being here with Pok Son and Melody made it so special. We got Melody a life-size baby doll, but she refused to believe it was a doll from

Santa. She thinks Pok Son had another baby during the night. Melody is something else, a pure dream. I am the happiest man on Earth.

"Pok Son is doing a great job teaching her English as I have little time to spare. When I do come home during the weekday, I arrive home around six or seven at night but have to be back at the barracks by midnight, so it doesn't leave me with a lot of time with my little girl. I am not complaining, though; it is much better to see them only three times a week than to be separated from them for the entire year."

***

Parting with humor as he often did, Bob closed the letter with this riddle for Dad. "Paul, you know why it takes women longer to get ready than it takes a man? Because women have to slow down around the curves. (smile)"

***

Mama was relieved that Bob seemed to be adjusting to married and family life quite nicely, and he was zeroing in on coming back to the States for good. His letters were less frequent, but this silence didn't worry her at all. He was not in inherent danger, being in Korea as an instructor, and was understandably busy with his new life.

The day had come, it was June of 1970 when Bob received his stateside assignment.

June 17/70

To My Dear Friends:

I hope this finds you well and enjoying all the splendors life. I know that this letter may come to you as a surprise. It has been quite some time since I have last written and I apologize. No one could have prepared me for how busy I was going to be with a wife and a spirited little girl running around. Having been a bachelor for twenty-seven years, and only having to be concerned with my own needs and schedules has been challenging for me.

Well, I finally got my stateside assignment, and it looks like I am coming home for good this time. I will be stationed at Fort Benning in Georgia, as an instructor at the basic training center. I am bringing my little family with me. Pok Son already has her passport, and we intend to apply for her visa on the first of July. We are due to leave here October 28th or earlier.

I have included an article from our newspaper about the passing of Major General Casey; commander of the First Air Cavalry Division. He is the General from Scituate you had asked me about a while back. He was just killed in a helicopter crash on his final mission. He was known as a compassionate leader, so it was particularly fitting that he chose his last mission on behalf of the military to be one of visiting the wounded, sadly, flying the final mission of his life as well.

Speaking of Scituate, we intend to visit Scituate after we settle into a home. I want to visit all the states to give Pok Son, and Melody a chance to see the countryside of their new home.

In a way, I am glad to be leaving Korea. I think I have been over here a little too long. I am beginning to think and act like a Korean. (smile) At this point, because I have been away so long, returning to the States will be like a soldier going overseas to a foreign country.

How are the kids doing? I bet they are quite grown up now. I never realized how fast kids grow until I started to notice my little girl grow. It was only yesterday; Melody was no bigger than a fly. And now, she is so grown up.

I have to cut this short to go and check on my troops.

So, until the next time,
Robert and Pok Son

***

"Mama, do you remember how you felt when you heard he got his orders to return home for good?"

"Yes, I do. I felt more apprehensive than ever about his safety. It was almost like he was so close to the finish line; I was afraid he'd let his guard down at the wrong moment." She paused and looked around the room as if searching for a memory. "I think that feeling came over me because my uncle, who served in World War II, had been killed by a dissatisfied enemy after the war had been declared over. He had made it through the war but got murdered when a bomb detonated eviscerating the bus carrying US soldiers through England. So, Susan, you just never know. I won't breathe a sigh of relief until he is back on our soil."

Back in the States...

November/1970

Hi Friends:

I thought that I would take this opportunity to write to you to let you know that although it may seem like we have forgotten about you, we have not. We are still in the process of getting settled down. I never realized how much time and money it takes to settle into a home.

One good thing to report is that we have sweet Melody settled in school and is doing well. Pok Son has met about four or five Korean women who live nearby who have been here in the States for anywhere from four to eleven years, and they are helping her quite a bit. As for me, everything is still a rat race.

I started going to ITC (Instructor Training Course) today, which will be for three and a half weeks, and no sooner I finish that, I start night school. I am taking courses in English and Advance Math at the University of Maryland. I hope to be in the States for at least a year before being transferred so I can get the girls settled.

As far as my role in the Army, I have made up my mind that I want to get out. The Army has a new program called Operation Transition, a program designed to help servicemen retire from the service and revert to civilian life. It helps them with furthering their education and getting jobs. So, Joan, I plan to take advantage of this program.

Sometimes a man doesn't realize until it is too late that he needs an education to get anywhere in life. No matter if you are Black or White, you need an education. We often use our race as an excuse to hide behind when our limitations are more accurately a result of our lack of training and drive. Funny thing Joan, I think one perpetuates the other. Now if we could just figure how to start the ball rolling. It's like the man who digs a ditch for a living for a construction company…it doesn't take brains to dig a trench, but it takes brains and drive to teach someone to dig a ditch.

Well, my friends, I have to close for now. Please say hello to the kids for me. I hope to see them soon.

With love and everlasting friendship,
Bob and the family

P.S. Here is a picture of sweet Melody in her traditional Korean outfit on the day we left for the United States.

***

March 27/71

To My Dear Friends:

I hope this finds you doing well and enjoying all that life has to offer. As for us, we are doing just fine.

Please accept my apologies for not writing to you for so long. These last few months have been quite hectic for me. Most of my time is spent taking classes outside of my duties for the military. At present, I am starting the basic course here at the US Army Institute for Military Assistance, Special Forces (better known as the Green Berets).

Yes, I will be Special Forces as soon as I complete this four-week basic course. It is a new challenge for me, and it offers a wide field of education, which will help me significantly both in the military and when I return to civilian life.

As for my wife and baby, they both love it here in the states. Like you once said that you and Paul had finally bought your dream home, we have done the same. I purchased a brand new freshly built three-bedroom split-level home in North Carolina, which we hope to move into May 1st. It is in a small town, which is about half the size of Scituate. A mixed population with no racial friction, everyone seems to live in harmony. There is a tiny pond here where most of the older men spend their days fishing. We are only a five-minute drive from Fort Bragg. This home will leave me broke for the rest of my life, but I guess that is life. A wise man once said that a happy man has bread and meat on the table for his family and a roof over their head, even if that means his bank account is forever red.

Your friends,
Bob and Pok Son

***

One never knows when the final letter is to come, nor what it is to bring, but receiving this letter from Bob was as good as any closure Mama could have imagined. She had done her part in the Vietnam War efforts. Mama never took a side on the United States' involvement as she recognized that her opinion had zero significance in reality. Always trusting God was in control, as chaotic as things may have appeared, she was able to offer her unwavering countenance to the soldiers. For this, she may never know the full impact of her kindness. For her place in Bob's journey, she had a pretty good idea.

June 3/1971

To My Dearest Friends:

I hope this finds you enjoying all that life has to offer. As for me, I am doing just fine. Thank you so much for the birthday cards. Believe it or not, my birthday was spent taking a four- hour intelligence examination. One can stop eating, one can stop living, but for sure, one can never stop paying taxes and learning. (smile)

Pok Son and Sweet Melody love it here in America. Melody has completely forgotten her Korean, and Pok Son has become thoroughly Americanized. So much so, I think I may divorce her and go back to Korea and marry again, but this time, not make the mistake of bringing my new wife to the States. (smile)

I hope you and your family enjoy your upcoming X-country trip this summer. It should be gratifying, especially for the kids. I think the greatest knowledge a kid can gain is from things seen and experienced. You can read about America and look at beautiful photographs, but nothing compares to seeing with your own eyes and having experiences there. Imagine the difference of seeing a picture of a bird in flight in the Grand Canyon and then imagine seeing that same bird soaring through the canyon, gliding with the air currents with only the sounds of nature as the soundtrack... there is no comparison.

Before our lives get too busy, and I fail to reflect on time spent, I want to leave you with a couple of thoughts I hold close to my heart.

First~ The 39 months that I spent in Vietnam was not in vain, for America, the beautiful, I would spend three times that thirty-nine months to preserve her and her ideals.

Second~ We can only pray that when the boys grow up, they won't have to wear a uniform to preserve what we have, but instead, they wear a soldier's uniform because they choose to do so as a profession.

Third~ True friendship is so hard to find, but when one has friends such as the Hunters, he surely has all the riches in the world.

With Love and True Friendship,
Bob and Pok Son

***

"Mic-drop!" as I gesture dropping a microphone.

"What?" Mama crinkles her eyes and forehead. "What the heck does that mean?"

"It means you can't get any better than that." I laughed. "That has gotta make you feel good, Mama," as I turned over the last letter and placed it carefully on top of the pile. "Had you ever heard from him after this aside from Christmas cards?"

Mama reiterated how the tradition of exchanging Christmas cards that would continue for many years post-war, but how each household had allowed life to get in the way of their correspondence, not their friendship, just their communication. Fortunately, for both, their story did not end here.

Chapter 39

Please Remember Me

Mama continued to live a life centered around the five of us and the home but did indulge in a few professional endeavors along the way. In the early 1970s, her entrepreneurial spirit took flight, inspiring her to repurpose attractive bottles found at the dump, whereby creating seventies-style candlestick holders and then selling them at local bazaars for a little extra spending money. Later, but also in the seventies, ahead of the boom of staffing solution agencies, she made up some business cards calling herself "Temporary Solution" and found herself some temporary administrative jobs. When my siblings were in college, and I was the only one left at home making my way through junior high, she ventured into real estate sales for the picturesque South Shore towns, quickly earning a spot among the higher-performing agents.

Tapping into her creative talents, she created themed Christmas cards, which were always highly anticipated by friends and family, each year trying to outdo her previous year's card. In the bicentennial year of 1976, she sewed costumes for every member of the family to portray a scene where she posed as Betsy Ross stitching the first American flag. Alongside her was the rest of us donning American Revolutionary garb, including gold-trimmed tricorns for the boys, and long gowns with matching colonial bonnets for the girls. Another year, she posed us peeking around the stairway corner to see "Mommy kissing Santa Claus." The efforts she put into Christmas were some of the many ways she graced our home with her magic touch that provided my sibs and me with the gift of a wholesome childhood.

Each of us flew from the nest on Acorn Street and into a life of our own. Maryellen, Michael, and Bill, planted roots in Massachusetts while I ventured out of New England to New Jersey and then later to Nashville, Tennessee.

Mama was always the unsung backbone of the family, content living in Dad's larger than life shadow. She was indeed the wind beneath his eagle's wings, whether preparing him a "stage," or cheering for him at every turn, she was the epitome of the perfect wife and homemaker of yesteryear. Dad, a formidable pillar within the reputable Boston College High School community, led by example, inspiring countless young men. He was a teacher and coach for twenty-nine years and then switched hats to join the administration as the Vice Principal, Dean of Discipline. For many years, up until I graduated from college, Dad led a summer house painting crew made up of teachers from BC High and co-ed college students. In avant-garde fashion, in the late 1970s, Dad hired six females to the summer paint crew; me and five others. We worked as hard as any of the crew members and in doing so, broke through a gender barrier for such work despite a number of apprehensive clients putting pressure on Dad to eliminate us from the crew for their particular house. Dad wouldn't hear of it, and firmly stood by our capabilities and his reputation for quality.

An equally satisfying life after Vietnam, Bob fulfilled much of what he had dreamt about years before while staring into the star-filled Vietnam skies. He sought an education at the University of Maryland, settled in his dream home with his wife and daughter, and retired after twenty years of service with the Army. After completing four tours in Vietnam, he joined the Special Forces-Green Berets. Later he held assignments on behalf of the United States, as a retired US soldier, in Egypt and Saudi Arabia. He received individual recognition from both the Egyptian President and the Saudi King for his leadership. He proudly retired from all military and quasi-military duties with an admirable military record inclusive of Purple Hearts, a Bronze Star, Air Medal Awards, and many other awards and recognitions citations, and badges. But all of this did not come without tremendous physical and emotional cost.

Mama, too, was suffering. Twenty-five years post Operation Morale Booster, and a few years shy of retirement, Dad suffered a massive fatal heart attack while playing a pick-up game of basketball in the Boston College High School gymnasium. His passing left a void never to be filled; as he used to say, "You can always be replaced, but you can't be duplicated." While his days on Earth were arguably cut short at sixty-one by this massive heart attack, he lived a fulfilling life exemplifying the Jesuit motto, "A Man for Others." Twenty years after Dad's fatal massive heart attack, Mama remained in fabulous health "for my age" as she would tout, except for the unwelcomed signs of dementia.

As a passionate seeker of silver linings, this same beast of a disease I cursed daily, had proven itself to be the catalyst for uncovering the treasure within these letters. I am not confident I would have ever taken the time to read through all the letters as she had always billed them as "fluff" just "silly letters to pass the time" if it had not been for my desperation to engage her long-term memory. Reading the letters was only half the story. What happened next is the real jaw-dropping part of their story.

Chapter 40

Get Together

That next morning, the first words I uttered were, "Mama, we need to see if Bob is still alive!" I insisted not sure Mama would even remember reading the letters.

Much to my pleasant surprise, "You think he might be? How can we find him?" Mama wondered aloud.

"The internet!" I grabbed my laptop and quickly queried all derivatives of his name that could lead us to confirm he was still alive. The adrenaline raced through my body while Mama chuckled in the amazement of technology. Within minutes, I received probable confirmation that Bob was still living at the address he wrote on the last envelope we had from 1972. "Looks like he never moved from his dream home in that small town in North Carolina. Additionally, I have reason to believe that he and Pok Son are still married." My eyes filled with pure joy, and my heart was racing faster than a racehorse. "Mama, we have to write to him!"

Before she had a moment to respond, I was already petitioning for the words to come to me. My letter had to be carefully crafted, bearing sensitivity to the possibility of triggering post-traumatic stress disorder or a plethora of other issues. The last thing I wanted to do was present Bob with Pandora's Box. The whole sequence, enthusiasm included, seemed much like the scene when Mama was commencing Operation Morale Booster over fifty years ago, merely exchanging the 1964 IBM typewriter for a MacBook Pro. I was on a mission of my own; to reunite these two unlikely soulmates. As I typed away, erasing, adding, moving, and underlining, I stopped abruptly and looked up into Mama's eyes. "Dang, Mama, you did all that typing without any of these features!" This realization took the admiration to a whole new level. A rat-ta-tat symphony of my own and "print," and I am off and running. I dropped the letter in the mail and then waited, praying my greeting was going to be received as intended, all the while waiting anxiously for a reply.

Paralleling Mama's behaviors during her writing campaign, I would rush outside at the earliest sound of the postal truck accelerating toward my mailbox, and as the circle of life often holds, with Mama in tow. I understood the idea of being there to personally get the mail to shorten any time I had to wait for a response. Each day that passed with no word from Bob seemed like a week. Again, similar to Mama's emotional side when there was silence, I was left to wonder, fearing I had made a big mistake in reaching out. Questions of doubt and regret were creeping into my head, praying I had not been the catalyst for any heartache.

About ten days after I had estimated he would have received the letter; I woke to a life-altering email from Melody Johnson.

Dear Sweet Susan,

My name is Melody Johnson, the only child of Robert Johnson. I'm so sorry for the delayed response, but there was the time lapse between my father receiving your letter and his mailing it to me. Wow. First of all, you need to know that my father felt exalted by your words. I'm only writing now to acknowledge his receipt of your correspondence. I want to let you know because of multiple strokes and crippling arthritis; Daddy lost writing mobility in his hands and some speaking ability. Hence, no response via letter or phone call, which is what he had wished to do. My dad wants you to know how touched he was by your message - just that you remembered him, and you were only a baby.

I am emailing you now, so you know that he did receive your letter. He is so very happy for your kind words and thoughts. I will write again once I have been able to speak to him with this in mind because he'd like to "speak" to you directly. Susan, he told me just a week before he received your letter in the mail that he'd been wondering about your mother and father. With older parents, it's like this, no? They have time to reflect on their past and relish in all the joy it brought.

Before I drafted "his" letter to you, you must know that he was so very touched, as I was, by your recognition of him, his writing, and his artwork. My father always downplayed his ability to draw, but his calm and silent expressions on paper, whether through writing or sketching, was still something others recognized, but so long ago. I remember your mother and father. They never missed sending a Christmas card for many years. And now, the curiosity of where you all are is finally satisfied. His condolences for your loss of your father. He welcomes a memorable reunion. Wow, again. I am so grateful, as his daughter - whom he adopted as a four-year-old kid from Korea (yeah, that's his wonderful heart) to have you bring some joy all these years to his otherwise day-to-day life and bring a smile to his face. I will write more in a few days when Daddy can dictate all he wants to say to you.

Susan, God bless your generous heart and kindness for taking time out of your life. You have no idea of the happiness you have just brought to my father. Your mother had a good heart too, this I recall my father teaching me. We are both wishful of her good health and happiness until we all meet together so very soon.

~Melody

***

"Mama, Mama! Bob answered us! He answered us!" I bounded down the stairs. Leading with my cell phone in hand to show her. Pulling it up on the screen, I read Melody's email aloud. Mama's eyes sparkled, hearing that Bob was so grateful for the letter and further had been wondering about her and Dad as recent as a week before.

"It's crazy how the universe works, huh? Just a week before, he was wondering about us," she commented.

"Yeah, and that was about the time we were writing the letter to send him." I reached for her laptop and began my reply to Melody.

YOU MADE MY DAY, MELODY!!! Thank you for your thorough and heartfelt response. I am beyond thrilled the letter was received as intended, a reflection of mutual fondness. I am sorry to hear of his challenges as a result of the strokes, but through his letters, I know him to be a "when there's a will, there's a way" kind of person so I am thrilled to know we can continue this dialogue and even set up a reunion. There is so much in his letters that are riveting for so many reasons. What started to be just an activity for me to do with my mom to tap into her long-term memory ended up being uncovered as a real treasure. I cannot wait to share them with y'all. I have read through them all once and have them separated by year and chronological order. There are just under eighty letters, a dozen photos, a half dozen drawings, and a dozen or so newspaper articles.

Yes, I read of his joy regarding your adoption, and I have a picture of you on your last day in Korea before moving to the United States. You are in an adorable gold traditional Korean outfit, so precious. Your mom will be touched to read the letter he wrote to my mom about the day he met her. He talks of her beautiful heart and his admiration for her caring for the orphanage in Korea. At the end of the letter, he even writes, "Don't be surprised if I come back a married man..." which was a 180 from his confirmed bachelor talk of being only devoted to the Army. Your mom stole his heart from their first meeting. It's adorable, and something you think only happens in the movies.

Melody, there are so many little stories within the big story of the two of them corresponding. Your dad's insight expressed in these letters is nothing shy of extraordinary. He is incredibly humble as you say, and I see that even in his letters. Honestly... that is a good thing because a big ego often ruins a great man :), but these letters just had to become more significant than just sitting in a box in my mother's home. I have to share them with y'all if nothing else. I reached out to the Ann Curry show, 'We'll Meet Again,' hoping that they may want to be a part of the reunion if I was successful in finding your dad, etc. I have not heard back from them. Their story is epic if you think about it.

This is truly a miracle of sorts in that I could not locate any of the other soldiers my mom wrote to; your dad was the only one I was able to find perusing the internet. I would love to plan a reunion. The earlier, the better if possible. My mom's state has declined, and the more I am learning about this beast, dementia, it only declines. But on a positive note, we are so dang excited about all of this!

Thank you again and again… both of you! I look forward to seeing where all of this takes us!

All the best,
Susan

***

Heart pumping with utter exhilaration, no sooner did I hit send, I immediately started creating the spiral-bound books of all the letters to send to Bob. It was perfect timing to send these booklets as Bob's birthday was later in the month. There were so many letters between the two of them it produced two thick spiral-bound books. I added eye-catching covers to each titling them "Operation Morale Booster-Letters from Vietnam; respectively Volume I and Volume II" and typed at the bottom, "Forever in our hearts… Joan and Susan Hunter."

The next morning, I overnighted the package to Bob to arrive two days before his seventy-sixth birthday. The evening the book of memories arrived at Bob's doorstep; Melody shot me a text detailing his reaction to this new-found treasure. "He was like a kid at Christmas, donning a permanent smile with each turn of the page. Daddy had forgotten about the drawings he did on the white silk, so when he saw the pictures of them, my mom said his eyes filled with tears. He can no longer draw due to his arthritis, so he was thrilled some of his art had been preserved. Susan, this is the best gift you have given him. I haven't heard of my father being this happy in years… a lot of years. Thank you so much!" She elaborated on his status quo; how hard his daily activities were due to all his physical limitations. Hearing about how happy he was and how these letters brought tears of joy to his eyes meant the world to Melody. "He is going to send them next day carrier to me so I can read them too. I should get them a day after tomorrow."

Chapter 41

I Can See Clearly Now

O verwhelmed with anticipation at the sight of the mail truck barreling around the corner, Melody ran to the curb to retrieve the arriving package. Inside the box, containing two thick volumes of the compilation of letters between her father and "Joan Hunter," the woman she had heard so much about throughout her entire life. Offering a gratuitous greeting to the driver as he extended the box out from the sliding side door, she grabbed ahold of the box with both hands and quickly made her way back into the house and to her kitchen table.

Ripping open the box and laying out each Volume in front of her, she took a deep breath and was instantly fixated on the pictures on the cover of Volume I, Letters from Vietnam, 1966. Eyes toggling back and forth between the two portraits on the front, she took note of how young her father and Mama were in these pictures. Both about twenty-five years younger than she was at the time, yet appearing to be so mature in their respective uniforms; her father's Army fatigue and Mama's TWA "stewardess" uniform. Melody immediately checked herself with a fleeting thought of what she was doing with her life at a similar age, briefly recalling her typical morning commute into work and stopping at her favorite coffee shop on the way into the office.

Mama's portrait, clearly taken at a photographer's studio with the gradient backdrop, studio lights, and climate-controlled room, showcased a perfectly coiffed headshot, inclusive of a pillbox style hat, indicative of the era. Donning the TWA embroidered fitted suit jacket, she possessed the look of a Hollywood starlet with her porcelain white skin, radiant smile, and long eyelashes rivaling those of Elizabeth Taylor. On the contrary, her father's photograph was arguably limited, given it was taken in the combat zone of one of the ugliest wars memorialized in our history books. Photographed in front of a stark white background in a room that was undoubtedly in excess of ninety degrees Fahrenheit, his inescapable sweat caught the light from the flash, creating a glaring white sheen over his dark, rugged skin and telling a story in and of itself. Melody was captivated by the catchlight in her dad's eyes. He appeared to be looking intently into the camera, almost as if knowing one day she would be looking back into his, via this diary of letters, providing her with a trip of a lifetime. His eyes seemed so innocent, kind, and approachable, yet his uniform inferred otherwise. She was paralyzed with the fascination that the reality of his Vietnam War was about to be spelled out for her, word by word.

Flipping to Volume II, Melody examined the image of the vintage Air Mail envelope, addressed to "Joan Hunter" in her dad's handwriting. His name and the military return address were written in the top left corner, again in his handwriting. Already conjuring chills thinking that these letters were written during the war and from a foxhole or bedroll.

A decorated combat soldier and a member of Special Forces, he re-enlisted for four tours of duty in Vietnam, earning multiple purple hearts and other recognitions of honor. He inevitably saw things that could not be unseen, experienced things he would not wish upon his worst enemy, and did things he did not think himself capable of doing.

Melody braced herself for what she was about to read, vowing not to think of her father any differently. She emotionally prepared herself for gruesome and horrific narratives of which she would soon not be able to shake from her memory. After moments of preparation, sitting on the edge of her kitchen chair, she grabbed Volume I and opened it, laying it in front of her on the table. She turned to the first page; a poem written by her father when he was twenty-four years old. Underneath the poem was a picture of him as a young paratrooper about to make a jump. He had a seriousness in his eyes, his uniform proudly displaying the First Cavalry Division Airmobile insignia. His helmet noted a large military identifying "N709" on one side and a more personal marking of "We Die Equal" on the other. At that moment, her heart sank, thinking of her father being identified solely by a number. She continued with both hands actively participating in reading. Her left hand cradled the top of the page, and her right lightly skimmed across each line of the poem as she read.

"Country's Call"

Soldier standing oh so tall, awaiting to answer his country's call.
He stands to serve her well, from the clouds of heaven
to the gates of hell.
Wearing a green uniform, he has served America
since the day she was born.

At Yorktown, to icy banks of the Delaware shores.
He fought without fear throughout the long year.
From Berlin, to the Philippines he was seen,
in Korea he was there too.
Yes, he stands ready to serve America and you.

Here in Viet Nam he stands to fight on another foreign land.
He serves America and NATO now but his goal is still the same.
Here he stands for freedom's name.

In La-Drang Valley and An Lo, his blood ran free,
for America and liberty.
Here he is seen in the Army green, some wearing the green beret,
others with silver wings on their chest.
The whole world knows that here stands America's best.

Here they cry and die with pain of wounds delivered by the
enemies' hand, but they know that they died
for freedom of this war-torn land
and to answer America's call.

Here he stands without any doubt,
he is determined to stomp communism out.

I am that soldier standing tall, awaiting my country's call.

Chills rushed throughout her body as she finished the poem,
rereading the last line... "I am that soldier standing tall, awaiting my
country's call." How incredibly brave and dutiful he was, she
thought. He was hardly on the other side of boyhood when he

answered his call of duty, making army life his way of life, and his comrades ~ his family. Seven years later, he volunteered to go across the world to fight another soldier's war in another soldier's land. This was a war with no clear borders, no identifiable enemies, and no definitive objectives and outcomes. It was a war that would ultimately be remembered as a stain on American history, and he fought because he believed that humankind of every color, creed, and nationality was created equal. All deserved to be free to govern themselves.

She immediately sent a text to me, *The package just arrived. I am so excited, but also a little apprehensive!*

Yay! I am so happy for you, I shot back with overflowing anticipation. *Understandable, Mel, but really, don't worry… you are about to meet your dad as a young man. Look at it as a rare opportunity to be in the head of a soldier, in real-time, as he goes through one of the darkest periods in our country's history. And then every time you feel empathy for him, or are proud of him… think… this is my dad! I know I developed a much deeper respect for my mom after reading these letters, and I know you will too! Enjoy!*

Melody poured herself a glass of red wine and allowed herself the evening to dive deeply into the treasured correspondence. She was completely floored by a few letters describing his fierce distaste for the non-combatant challenges such as snakes, leeches, sandflies, and every other insect you can name, that he had to contend with living in the jungles of Vietnam. Shaking her head in amazement that these horrendous conditions, specific to this war, were hardly ever talked about. Merely a handful of letters in, she noticed a reoccurring concept in his letters to Mama expressing his belief that "the quicker we get to fighting, the quicker we can win this war and return home," inferring an understanding of a short mission. The reel of images from Vietnam, which have made their indelible mark in history showing the horrors of that war, enveloped her mind compelling her to a breakdown of incessant tears. For the first time, she was in the head of her twenty-four-year-old father, who was about to endure a hell he could never have imagined. A period of his life he would never be able to outlive.

She abruptly closed the book and firmly placed her hand on the cover as if not allowing it to reopen. She offered a moment of pause and then grabbed for her phone. Begrudgingly, she shot-off a text my way. *Susan, I just can't do this. I am only a handful of letters in, and I am bawling. Reading the words of my father as a twenty-four-year-old, knowing he was always one minute away from death and knowing all that he is about to go through... and me?... When I was twenty-four, I was worried about what coffee I was going to order at Marylou's Coffee Shop. I just can't do this.*

I was playing scrabble with Mama at the kitchen table, but I sent back an immediate reply of encouragement. *Melody, you've got to keep reading! You will love what you are about to read. Your dad is an amazing man. Please keep reading.* There was no response.

Four hours later, my phone pings with another incoming text from Melody. An initial glance at the message, I wondered if it was a further declaration of her resistance, but seemingly pronounced from the screen, I saw the words *"salvation of sorts."* My heart skipped a beat, and I took a quick breath as I reached for the remote to pause the tv show. I read Melody's text aloud. *Susan, I cannot thank you enough for taking the time to find us, and further making these booklets of the letters for us to read through and cherish. Reading these letters has been a "salvation of sorts" as although I have always loved my father dearly, I have always held a little resentment toward him, thinking he was a part of what slaughtered my people because he hated them. Reading these letters, and his words, I can see that he didn't hate my people at all. In fact, he LOVED my people. He tried to help them in so many ways and whenever he could. I never knew any of these stories. Thank you so much! I need to go see him and make amends right away.*

I was taken aback like never before. Melody's text caused my eyes to well with tears and chills to rush through my body as my thumbs eagerly texted back, *Melody, do you know what just happened here?*

No, what?

This story doesn't end with MY mom and YOUR dad. YOU are now a part of this story! I am sure you are not the only product of this war who unwittingly holds some resentment toward their father. Your story is going to heal so many relationships, heal so many hearts, and heal so many souls.

Melody's heart raced with overwhelming emotion as she thought of how these letters had humanized her father in the best way possible. No longer did she think of him as just a dutiful and decorated soldier, void of feeling and conflict. He was a young man with a warm heart who answered the call to duty for all the right reasons. Having been able to read seven years of his thoughts, she was able to evolve with him from his bachelorhood at age twenty-four, become a family man, and complete four combat tours of Vietnam by age thirty-one. She got to read, in real-time, of his struggle trailblazing the road to the acceptance of miscegenation. Further, she felt his pain when considering the suffering she would inevitably have had to endure as a mixed child. *He was right; who better to protect me than him?* She smiled. This unique literary journey illuminated the evolution of how, where, and why things changed for him. She was able to grasp how incredibly selfless both her parents were to adopt her at a time where they were not yet on stable ground. Envisage a life for her which could not possibly have been achieved in Korea. It may not have been the right time, but she was the right child. She immediately picked up the phone, deeming this too important for a text, and called me.

"Susan, I have to book a flight to North Carolina and spend some time with my dad. I understand him so much more now, and I need him to know this. I had forgiven him a long time ago for the PTSD that he put my mom and me through, but never really understood how much of a victim he was to the horrors of that war until now. I need to go home and be with him."

"Aww, I am so glad to hear that this has been so healing for you... and will be for him as a result of this deeper understanding of yours."

"I am going to North Carolina for a couple of weeks. I need to tell him I'm sorry."

Her last two words seem to hang in the air as my eyes once again welled up with liquid joy. I was silent as the lump in my throat was too big to get around. Mel filled the silence reciting excerpts from the letters she found particularly fascinating. As she read the passages, her voice was muffled in my head like the adult characters in a Peanuts cartoon as I remained fixated on those two redemptive words, "I'm sorry" which I felt I had somehow been its conduit. I got chills thinking, *Aha! THIS was His master plan for these letters; redemption.* To help right a wrong paid to these brave veterans from the Vietnam War, dare I say, the bravest generation.

Chapter 42

Our America

Melody treated herself to a two-week visit with her parents back in her childhood home, the same "dream home" her father bought on the GI bill back in 1971. As she made her way up the walkway, she rehearsed the moment she would first see her dad with her new eyes and ask for forgiveness. Melody was extremely close to her father, and there wasn't any doubt how it would be received; however, she wanted it to be special for his sake. Grabbing the front doorknob, she felt it turn from the inside. Bob had seen the rental car pull in the driveway and made efforts to greet her at the door. Despite all the rehearsing, the second that door opened and she looked into her father's eyes, she lost it, tears streaming down her face, she fell into his strong arms just as she did as a little girl. "Daddy, I need to tell you something."

"No, you don't my little one." As he brushed away the tears rolling down her cheek.

"Yes, yes, I do. It's not enough that we put all the past PTSD behind us. Mommy and I were not the only victims. Stop carrying the world on your shoulders, Daddy. YOU, Daddy, YOU were the victim, and then YOU came home to an ungrateful country to be the scapegoat for all the bad decisions made. I know you watered-down your experiences in your letters to Joan. You did that to protect her. You are always protecting everyone. Well, I want to protect you somehow."

"There is nothing you can do to protect me, my little one. I am old now and at the sunset of my life. I am fine. Your mother and I are both fine."

"No, Daddy, I want to offer you a shield of understanding. I want that shield to be marked as you marked your helmet, 'We All Die Equal.'" That is all you ever wanted, all you ever worked for… and I cannot thank you enough. Thank you, on behalf of all who have enjoyed the friendship or the romance of a person of another color or creed, thank you. You are a pioneer like Joan kept saying, and pioneers by definition, are the first... and, therefore, alone. Thank you for taking all those brave steps and thank you for protecting me from the less open-minded, even when I didn't even realize I was being attacked."

Bob wrapped his arms around his "little one," resting his chin on top of her head. The two held the embrace until Mel could feel his tears dropping on her head. He broke away to take a good look at his Melody. Through the tears of joy, staring into her eyes, he whispered, "You are my greatest joy, Little One, I couldn't have imagined my life without you." He gestured to the couch, and the two walked arm-in-arm. Together, they read through the letters one by one, indulging in side-stories. They reminisced about some of the tougher days they had been through with his PTSD, but always circled back to the good days and the wonderful times spent together.

This abandoned war was no longer going to be a cloud over their heads. Bob, Pok Son, and Melody were a part of history. No one could fully understand the path they had walked nor the road still in front of them, but together, they hold their heads high knowing intimately, they were pioneers in making this world a better place in many ways. Among other accomplishments, they were among the unsung heroes ushering miscegenation into the United States' mainstream.

As for Mama, she too will be leaving a legacy ascending from the ashes of that war. Her footprint is one of kindness, a simple gesture of love for another human being... or an army of human beings. To just do something, regardless of how insignificant or dynamic it may appear to be on the surface. One never knows the impact a simple act of kindness may have on a person, a whole generation, or humankind. Her legacy is just to do something, no matter how small. Loving one another, even strangers, may be too much of a leap for some, but being kind to one another doesn't have to be.

~ MAY PEACE BE WITH EVERYONE ~

AFTERWORD

I hope you enjoyed their story and it touched something inside of you. If so, I would genuinely love to hear about it. Please know you are welcome to email me directly at SusanHunterAuthor@gmail.com or leave a review on Amazon. These reviews are so important to the success of independent authors' stories. If you found any part of it to be healing or inspiring, please be a part of the equation of propagating more healing by sharing this with friends, family, social media. (Please feel free to tag me if you do.) If you have contacts in the mass media, or with an influencer, please consider telling them about the book. There are so many riveting stories, even in the writing of this book, it would make for a dynamic article, podcast, TV segment, etc. in and of itself.

This journey has been incredibly rewarding with regards to the people I have met along the way; for that, I am incredibly grateful to have taken on this endeavor. Still, I will say, it has been far more work than I anticipated, and I have a whole new respect for authors as a result. I have done the heavy lifting of giving birth to this story, but now I need your help to give this story life and propagate the sincere Welcome Home for our Vietnam Veterans and the healing for our country. We do need to be "in this together", so please join me in this mission to right some wrongs.

Vietnam Veterans from all the countries involved, and on both sides of this war, may you feel God's grace, blessings, and comfort. You cannot change the past, and no one can judge you negatively because they haven't walked in your shoes. We can only thank you for serving your country and pray for your well-being. So again, thank you for serving on behalf of your country and WELCOME HOME! #BravestGeneration

Although I have been in regular contact with Bob and Melody since reading through this trove of letters, I have yet to actually meet Melody and reconnect with Bob, but I hope to as soon as we are on the other side of Covid-19. Welcoming any and all prayers for that to happen.

As for my next project... I have already begun an eye-opening dive into the MIA of the Vietnam War. Again, looking to touch upon the heart of the matter, I will document the stories from several soldiers who have been successfully repatriated as well as some of those still missing. I would love to hear your story of your loved one who was listed as an MIA. Please reach out via email.

According to the DPAA POW/MIA, since 1973, there still remains over 1,500 MIA. That's over 1,500 families never receiving closure, and simultaneously, over 1,500 soldiers never granted a proper burial. As a result of collaborative efforts by Laos, Cambodia, Vietnam, and the United States of America, 1,000 soldiers have been successfully repatriated. There are touching stories for each of these.

I would love to connect with you via my social pages:
Instagram @susanhunterauthor
Facebook Susan P. Hunter- Author
Website: www.SusanHunterBooks.com
I can also be contacted directly at SusanHunterAuthor@gmail.com

God bless you all, and may
God continue to bless The United States of America.

SHOUT-OUT TO SONGWRITERS

You may have noticed each of the chapters is titled a song title from the Vietnam War era. This was done intentionally as my subtle shout-out to all the songwriters in the world. These are the creatives whose music entertain, educate, shape, and heal us. What I didn't know until I started to research songs from the Vietnam era was the Vietnam War itself, marked that point in history when songwriters first stepped out of the confined box of writing little ditties about love and heartbreak and onto a larger stage. It was from this platform; their songs took on a more evocative tone as lyrics expressed support for and against our involvement in the war. These songwriters were also pioneering, serving as the trailblazers to the musical landscape we enjoy today.

* I feel like I need to include a disclaimer: Titles chosen were explicitly at my discretion. In no way am I inferring the respective songwriters, artists, or publishers of these titles are endorsing this book... although I would love it if they would. (smile)

ABOUT THE AUTHOR

Susan P. Hunter, a born and raised New Englander, emerged as an author in the still of the COVID-19 era. A mother of three, she was fulfilled as a stay-at-home mother and an active civic volunteer until her youngest reached high school. She was then appointed as the only civilian on the Sheriff's Office's command staff, serving as the Chief of Staff and the Public Information Officer. She enjoyed this position for three years before moving to Tennessee, where she currently resides. She is an editor and contributing writer to a local magazine.

She is inexhaustibly passionate about her Christian faith, family, and The United States of America.

*Photo by JDK Images Photography

Made in the USA
Middletown, DE
29 October 2020